- Winner of the Phi Beta Kappa Prize for Science
- An Amazon Best Science Book of 2019
- A *Science Friday* Best Science Book of 2019
- A *Kirkus Reviews* Best Nonfiction Book of 2019
- A *Science News* Best Book of 2019
- A *Nature* Top Ten Book of 2019

"A crash course in the amazing new science of space archaeology that only Sarah Parcak can give. This book will awaken the explorer in all of us."

—Chris Anderson, head of TED

"A renowned space archaeologist gives readers an insider's look at her field, which is basically Indiana Jones meets cutting-edge satellite technology. It's every bit as exciting as it sounds. . . . In this fascinating adventure memoir . . . Parcak has a lot of great stories to tell, and she tells them with clarity, enthusiasm, and humor. . . . Exciting and futuristic, this book elicits that anything-is-possible feeling—a must-read."

—*Kirkus Reviews* (starred review)

"Her writing is full of evocative anecdotes and personal insights gleaned from years of experience in dusty trenches as well as behind the computer screen, poring over satellite images. . . . Throughout the book, Parcak's love for her work and the people she studies is evident, and her enthusiasm is contagious. From Vikings in Iceland and Canada to amphitheaters in Italy and back to her first love, pharaonic Egypt, she brings both the present and the past to life."

—*Science Magazine*

"Parcak's book provides a revelatory look at an exciting new field."

—*Publishers Weekly*

"This book is so much more than the memoir of a dedicated archaeologist—it's an open invitation for all of us to become explorers. She has pioneered crowdsourced archaeology and shows how we can join her on the adventures of discovery that we've always dreamed about."

—**Peter Jackson, Academy Award–winning director**

"This is a fascinating glimpse into a young field just as its technological possibilities are exploding. . . . By panning out, we perceive what's invisible on the ground: features that relate not just to the physical landscape but to the history of humanity and our relationship with Earth."

—*Nature*

"Parcak's love for her field and her deep wonder and excitement come through on every page. . . . Clear, accessible, and fascinating, peppered with witty asides and informative photos, *Archaeology from Space* is an excellent introduction to an exciting subfield that's still flying under the (satellite) radar."

—*Shelf Awareness* (**starred review**)

"*Archaeology from Space* presents a lively and engaging narrative about not only what it's like to be an archaeologist but how archaeologists use the data they gather to understand the ancient world."

—*Forbes.com*

"Parcak is an extremely engaging writer and has done a lot of very interesting stuff. . . . Parcak shares enough of herself to entrance anyone who shares her Indiana Jones dreams, while elucidating the exciting new field of satellite archaeology. This is a thoroughly delightful and downright fascinating work of popular science."

—*Booklist*

"I once had the privilege of accompanying Sarah Parcak on an archaeological dig in Lisht, Egypt. It was an adventure straight out of the movies. In *Archaeology from Space*, Parcak takes readers on a similar adventure, at once down-to-earth and out of this world. With wit and breezy elegance, she takes you around the world, back in time, and out into space. She's a time traveler and a captivating writer."

—Bill Whitaker, *60 Minutes*

"Sarah Parcak is a scientist, a historian, and an explorer—but above all, she is a writer. Her work illuminates our past, and, in so doing, helps us to understand our future. Lively, generous, and inspiring."

—Jennifer Finney Boylan, author of *She's Not There* and *Long Black Veil*

"What can wonder do? Everything. That's what the book is about, really. It's about a kid who was inspired by her grandfather and Indiana Jones and the great women of archaeology to grow up brash and questioning, to win the TED Prize and bust glass ceilings to pioneer ways to identify unexplored archaeological sites from satellites."

—John Archibald, for AL.com

"Divining clues about what's hidden beneath the earth from satellites high above, Parcak takes the reader on a worldwide adventure through our shared and ancient past. With delightful wit, infectious wonder, and a big dose of wisdom about where we're headed, she offers anyone with a computer the chance to become a virtual Indiana Jones."

—Juli Berwald, author of
Spineless: The Science of Jellyfish and the Art of Growing a Backbone

"Warm, impassioned and funny . . . [Parcak's] passion for her work is omnipresent, leaping from every page with an enthusiasm that is undeniably infectious. . . . It's not just a smart book or a thoughtful book or an informative book. It's a FUN book. It's a book that will prove enlightening to all manner of reader, but perhaps most of all, it's a book that one could see being the catalyst that sparks a young person's passion, whether it be space archaeology or some other scientific endeavor."

—*The Maine Edge*

"Parcak's career has sent her zooming around the globe, and in *Archaeology from Space*, her many fascinating discoveries and colorful stories are rendered in lively, conversational language—though they are always backed up with painstakingly fact-checked notes and citations."

—*Bangor Daily News*

"Part memoir, part pop-history, Sarah Parcak's writing bursts with enthusiasm and illuminates her pioneering research that seems more like science fiction than the hard science it is. Reading this book makes me want to become a space archaeologist!"

—**Steve Brusatte, University of Edinburgh paleontologist and author of the** *New York Times* **bestseller** *The Rise and Fall of the Dinosaurs*

"Fun and informative, full of interesting nuggets and personal anecdotes from the brightest star in space archaeology, this is a book unlike any other. Highly recommended!"

—**Eric Cline, author of** *1177 BC*

Archaeology
from
Space

Archaeology
from
Space

**How
the Future
Shapes
Our Past**

Sarah Parcak

A Holt Paperback

Henry Holt and Company New York

Holt Paperbacks
Henry Holt and Company
Publishers since 1866
120 Broadway
New York, New York 10271
www.henryholt.com

A Holt Paperback® and ⓗ® are registered trademarks of Macmillan Publishing Group, LLC.

The Library of Congress has cataloged the hardcover edition as follows:

Names: Parcak, Sarah H., author.
Title: Archaeology from space : how the future shapes our past / Sarah Parcak.
Description: First edition. | New York : Henry Holt and Company, 2019. |
Includes bibliographical references and index.
Identifiers: LCCN 2018040565 | ISBN 9781250198280 (hardcover)
Subjects: LCSH: Archaeology—Remote sensing. | Artificial satellites in
remote sensing. | Aerial photography in archaeology. | Space photography.
Classification: LCC CC76.4 .P36 2019 | DDC 930.1—dc23
LC record available at https://lccn.loc.gov/2018040565

ISBN: 9781250231345 (trade paperback)

Our books may be purchased in bulk for promotional, educational, or business use. Please contact
your local bookseller or the Macmillan Corporate and Premium Sales Department at (800) 221-7945,
extension 5442, or by e-mail at MacmillanSpecialMarkets@macmillan.com.

Originally published in hardcover in 2019 by Henry Holt and Company

First Holt Paperbacks Edition 2020

Designed by Meryl Sussman Levavi

Printed in the United States of America

D 3 5 7 9 10 8 6 4 2

This book is dedicated to Susan Young,
our family Pensieve

Contents

Introduction   1

1. Time Capsule   8

2. Space Archaeology   26

3. The Promise of Space Archaeology   44

4. A Risky Business   67

5. Digging in the Wrong Place   87

6. A Grand Tour   104

7. Empires Fall   123

8. A Capital Discovery   145

9. The Future of the Past   165

10. The Challenge   185

11. Stolen Heritage   199

12. Space Archaeology for Everyone   216

Acknowledgments   231

Notes   237

Index   267

Note to Readers

The author will donate a portion of the author advance from this book to support the mission of GlobalXplorer, a 501(c)(3) nonprofit organization registered in Alabama. This includes fieldwork and field schools in Egypt, training foreign archaeological and cultural heritage specialists in innovative technologies, and empowering a global citizen archaeology movement. If the ideas shared in this book have moved you, I encourage you to visit www.globalxplorer.org to become a space archaeologist in training.

Introduction

My entire life is in ruins. Quite literally. No, this is not a cry-for-help book, nor a journey of self-discovery. I am an archaeologist. I've spent much of the last 20 years working on excavations in Egypt and the Middle East, exploring ruins in Central and South America, mapping sites across Europe, and even digging for the occasional Viking. You might say I am obsessed with the dirt beneath my feet and all the wonders that might be there; it doesn't necessarily glitter, but it is priceless. That dirt contains nothing less than the clues to who we are, how we got here, and how we might thrive in the future.

Most of us can look back at our lives and identify pivotal moments that influenced our journey to where we are in our career: an unexpected event, maybe, meeting a key individual, an epiphany of some kind. Something. In my case I can identify one influence rooted in fiction and another solidly founded in facts.

Pizza, Videos, and My Path to Becoming an Archaeologist

If you are a child of the 1980s like me, your Friday night routine might have included getting pizza and picking up a VHS cassette from your local movie rental place. Wow, even writing that makes me feel old. After school, my mom would take my brother, Aaron, and me up the street to a creaky old house that had been repurposed to hold thousands of tapes, categorized by theme and age appropriateness.

Much to the chagrin of my mom, we invariably chose one of three movies: *The Princess Bride*, *The NeverEnding Story*, or *Raiders of the Lost Ark*. (Now that I have a child of my own, who wants nothing more than to watch *Minions* on repeat, I appreciate my mom's purgatory. She laughs at me.)

If we chose *Raiders*, I would sit, rapt, memorizing every scene, every bit of dialogue, every gesture. I can't tell you if it was Egypt, the sheer adventure, or just Harrison Ford, but that movie called out to me.

At that age, I didn't know that no one-size-fits-all fedora exists for archaeologists. We specialize in diverse subfields: aside from a particular time period or regional focus, an archaeologist might study pottery, art, bones, ancient architecture, dating techniques, or even recording and illustration.

I'm part of a relatively new specialism called space archaeology. I am not making that term up. It means I analyze different satellite data sets—Google Earth is one you're probably familiar with—to find and map otherwise hidden archaeological sites and features. It's a pretty cool job, but wasn't an obvious career option when I started taking undergraduate archaeology classes.

Why I do what I do all goes back to my grandfather, Harold Young, who was a professor of forestry at the University of Maine. Every weekend when I was young, while my parents worked late nights at the family restaurant, Aaron and I went to my grandparents' house on a hilly tree-lined street in Orono, Maine. Gram and Grampy had retired, my grandfather from the university and my grandmother from her post there as secretary of the faculty Senate.

Gram ruled the Young household, and the Senate, with an iron fist, so much so that Grampy always gave the same response when we asked if we could go outside to play.

"I'm only a captain," he'd say, smiling. "You'll need to ask the general!" and he'd turn to Gram and give a sharp salute. It ticked her off something awful and sent us into fits of giggles.

Grampy and My Journey into Space

Grampy was in fact a captain, having served as a paratrooper during World War II. Part of the US Army's 101st Airborne Division, known as the Screaming Eagles, he had led a platoon and jumped the day before D-Day. He also led one of only six bayonet charges in the war, receiving a Bronze Star with an oak leaf cluster and a Purple Heart. To plot his landing positions and map where to coordinate his troops, he analyzed aerial photographs, cutting-edge technology at the time.

He took that technology with him when he completed his PhD in forestry at Duke University, developing new techniques to map tree heights using aerial photos. For nearly 30 years, Grampy taught generations of foresters how to use such photographs in their research and became a world-renowned forester.

I was only told about Grampy's careers in snippets over time. He sometimes disappeared, traveling to far-flung places for international conferences, bringing us back carved wooden elephants from Zaire (now the Democratic Republic of the Congo). I later learned he donated his entire forestry library to institutions there. When I was little, I didn't understand what it meant to be a decorated war hero or a brilliant scientist. I just knew him as the kind and gentle grandfather who drove Aaron and me up to the campus to visit the cows in the research barn, where we would get freshly made chocolate milk if we were well behaved, which was rare. To this day I still think chocolate milk comes from chocolate cows.

Most of all, I remember how he'd let us look through his stereoscope,[1] like a set of desk-top binoculars, under which you put two slightly overlapping aerial photographs. The effect is wonderful—the photos jump out in 3-D. It's not something you forget, if you're young and impressionable, and it mapped out the first steps on my path.

Like so many in the Greatest Generation, Grampy never spoke about his war service. I did try to interview him for a high school project, but those days, thank God, were behind him. The forest was safe, and full of trees to map and identify, and that's where he took us, without fail. Grampy ran three miles every day, and still had the strength to walk around the neighborhood the day before he died from cancer.

Three years after we lost him, as I gradually learned more about his research, I increasingly regretted never discussing it with him. By then, his research papers were available online, and my curiosity about his work had deepened to the extent that I took an introductory class on remote sensing in my senior year in college. Grampy had never gotten into satellite imagery—it came into use in forestry about 15 years after he retired—but I wondered just how different it could be from his aerial photography. Besides, most archaeologists had probably already included the technology in their research, especially in Egypt. Right? Everything had likely been mapped. Oh, naivety!

I started to get a clue when I tried to find papers for my final project, using satellites to detect water sources near archaeological sites in Sinai, Egypt. You know you've hit a dead end when the handful of sources cite each other. That one class led to a master of philosophy thesis, which led to a PhD, and now nearly two decades of research. I have my grandfather to thank for my career.

The Hat, My Past, and the Future

As an archaeologist, I felt this connection to my grandfather made a lot of sense. Your quirks, the way you look, your likes and dislikes, are only the surface of the archaeological site of You. Our ancestors are the underlying layers of earth, enhancing our lives in ways we may not even comprehend. So much is buried deep within your DNA, and in the DNA of the landscapes where humans live today and lived thousands of years ago. We just need some perspective to pull back and see the clues and connections between us and within us.

With that perspective firmly supporting us, our dreams can take us anywhere. When I watched *Raiders of the Lost Ark* as a child, if you had told me that I would spend my career becoming a space archaeologist, I would not have believed you. And there's no way that I would have believed I'd ever meet the man himself, Harrison "Indiana Jones" Ford, complete with that hat.

It happened in 2016, when I gave a TED[2] talk in Vancouver in which I described my work as a space archaeologist and my dreams for its potential. By this time I was an archaeologist, just like Indy. I heard a rumor that Harrison Ford might attend the talk, but I was told not to get my hopes up. Well, my luck held, and he came to the conference. My dear friend Tom Rielly, founder of the TED Fellows program, helped organize a luncheon for Harrison to which I was invited. I don't think I slept a wink the night before.

As he approached, my heart raced. He looks exactly like he does on camera—the same craggy, rapscallion handsomeness. While we shook hands, he said all sorts of very nice things about my talk the day before. There was one thing I just had to get out in the open.

"Indiana Jones helped inspire me to go into archaeology," I told him, "and inspired so many in my field. From all of us, thank you."

"You do realize that I was just a character, right? You know more lines from that movie than I do."

"Of course it was a movie, but it was your spirit that made Indy come to life. That was an inspiration from the start. And that's why I'm thanking you, from the bottom of my heart."

Maybe he's just a very good actor, but I genuinely do not think he understood the impact he'd had on recent generations of our field until that moment.

Lunch with him and my husband was amazing. Harrison humored my overexcited archaeo-babble; he's more into wildlife conservation activism than heritage, but he is a very gracious and kind human being, with one hell of a rakish grin. I will always be grateful for his bemused listening.

After lunch, we went outside for photographs, and I produced a brown fedora. Harrison looked at me and shook his head.

"I can't believe you brought the hat."

"I couldn't resist," I said. He laughed.

"Since you're the real deal, you get away with it."

Yes, there is a photo of us fighting over that thing, and I will treasure it forever.

The Scope of Space Archaeology

The human story—the story of us—is evolving at breakneck speed thanks to new technologies. Armed with new data sets, we can spin fresh tales that bring us closer to getting more right than wrong about our ancestors and ourselves.

What we can find with new technologies such as satellite imagery is simply astounding. It is helping us rewrite history. We've gone from mapping a few dozen ancient sites in one summer-long archaeological season to mapping hundreds, if not thousands, of sites in weeks. With advances in computing and artificial intelligence, we are on the verge of achieving those same results in a few hours.

In case you want to be an archaeologist and are worried that we space archaeologists will find everything first, fear not. Knowing the location of an ancient site is only the first step. We still have to survey sites on the ground, a process known as ground-truthing, and then undertake years of excavation to get a better understanding of what is there. And wow, do we have a lot of work to do.

To give you a sense of just how much, and how quickly this field is advancing, I saved writing this introduction until last, to make sure to include any hot-off-the-press discoveries made with satellite technologies. With the chapters done and edited, I thought I could get away with a bit of downtime between big announcements. Dream on, Parcak.

In a recent *Nature* publication, a team led by archaeologist Jonas Gregorio de Souza announced 81 previously unknown pre-Columbian sites in the Amazon basin area of Brazil, using satellite imagery and ground surveys. Based on their findings, they estimated 1,300 other sites dating to between 1250 and 1500 AD in just 7 percent of the Amazon basin, with potentially more than 18,000 others in total. More than a million people may have lived in areas that today seem largely inhospitable.

Their findings included ceremonial centers, large platform mounds, ringed villages, and fortified settlements in north-central Brazil's upper Tapajós Basin, where few archaeologists had ventured.[3] To me, what is extraordinary about this discovery is just how much archaeologists and others had taken for granted about what might, or might not, be there in the rainforest. Satellite data allowed the archaeological team to search large areas in a matter of months, when the job would have taken decades on the ground. All this, from a subfield that barely existed 20 years ago. Although the world is learning more, there's still a way to go in popular understanding. In a recent travel insurance application for my work abroad, I was quoted an insanely high price for one year of coverage, over $50,000. When I inquired why, the team admitted they thought I traveled into space to look down from the actual satellites for ruins. I'm still laughing.

As I write this, I am downloading brand-new satellite imagery of Giza, in Egypt, the site of the last standing wonder of the ancient world. Who knows if I'll find anything previously undiscovered there. The main thing I have learned is to expect the unexpected. New sites and features appear where you hadn't previously thought to look, or, in cases like Giza, have the potential to overturn long-held assumptions about major sites and time periods. In the following chapters, you'll read about projects that did just that.

Mapping sites from space is fun, but getting to explore them is what takes me back in time, often thousands of years, to eras when people believed in different gods, spoke languages now extinct, and lived in places assumed never to have been inhabited—but they were all *Homo sapiens sapiens.* Just like us.

As such, archaeology has the potential to inspire in us great wonder, bringing us together. Today, given the conflicts and unrest around the world, this is very much needed. Some people don't get the chance to experience that sense of awe in person at ancient sites, but I hope the stories shared here will give a sense not only of this, but of how much we assume about past peoples, and how wrong we have sometimes been, given our access to such fragmented information.

There aren't any papers published yet on whether remote sensing can complete the puzzle of what it means to be human and how to avoid the pitfalls of great civilizations that came before us. All I can say is that there is extraordinary wisdom to be learned from previous cultures. It's shaped me profoundly and allows me to place current events in the long arc of perspective. For more than 300,000 years, our ancestors have migrated across Planet Earth, surviving and, in some cases, thriving—being creative, bold, innovative, and, of course, destructive.

This story of space archaeology, its contributions to research, and the tales it helps us tell, only introduces the possibilities of the science. The scale of these new stories, however, should amaze and inspire us. In our history on Earth, humans have habitually pushed deeper into the unknown; as we now begin to focus on exploring Mars, and farther afield, we can imagine 100,000 years from today, when there will be literal space archaeologists traveling from planet to planet, exploring the remnants of our early settlement efforts in other galaxies.

The origins of their field will be many light-years away, but the questions will remain close to those we ask today, about people who came before us. The answers matter far less than those questions. Perhaps it's a start to understanding what makes us human: our ability to ask how, where, when, why, and who, and creating the tools we need to bring the answers to life, on Earth, looking down from outer space.

1

Time Capsule

Nothing prepared me for the moment I saw ancient ruins for the first time. I was traveling to Cairo one afternoon in 1999. Whether by luck or divine intervention, I sat on the left side of the plane, peering out the window as the airplane flew low over the Pyramids of Giza. I gasped in disbelief. Everything I had ever dreamed of lay before me in the form of 4,500-year-old weathered golden limestone, bathed in sunlight, inviting me down—and in—for the rest of my life. Even today, after many visits to Giza, visiting the pyramids shocks my system. As an Egyptologist, I understand the current line on how and when and why the ancient Egyptians built those tombs for the great kings of the Fourth Dynasty, with an estimated 20,000 men. But the intimate knowledge does not dull my amazement.

I had made that trip to Egypt to take part in my first excavation. For the two weeks before the dig started, I traveled around Egypt by myself. (I want to turn to 20-year-old me and ask: "What exactly were you thinking?") It was a grand adventure. Among many wonderful occurrences, I met a group of older Taiwanese tourists on the island of Philae in Aswan, and they invited me on their luxury four-day cruise down the Nile. The tour director charged me only $200 for the entire trip; I was told I would be an "archaeological ambassador." My heaviest lift involved teaching the Macarena to several grandmothers in an art deco–classical mashup themed discotheque.

Weirdly magical though archaeology can be, my work often takes me far from those glamorous heights. I dig for ancient answers in places that do not look like much: a casual bystander might not assume that a modern soccer field next to a school could hold discoveries worthy of global headlines. But even if the site is not as gloriously intact as the Giza pyramids, it is my job to re-create with words or models what time has virtually destroyed.

There's no typical ancient site, even within the same country, and preservation varies from place to place. Only 20 kilometers south of Giza, you see towering, misshapen mud-brick hills, the melting interiors of pyramids built much later that have succumbed more rapidly to the depredations of people and time. Likewise, archaeological sites can range in size from great settlements to tiny campsites in the desert.

Let's just fine-tune the definition of a site, for a moment. Walking through the woods of Alabama, especially near lakes or streams, you might find clusters of arrowheads or other stone tools. Each one of those clusters is considered a site.[1] The same is true if you walk in the deserts of the American Southwest. You could encounter a larger unmapped site, such as remains of a building or even a village, but most likely it'll be a tiny scatter of ceramics, stone implements, or the remains of a small campsite.

Sites Are Filmstrips, Not Photographs

Among the suggestions of what once existed, the promise of our own future demise is readily evident. In English, we say "ruin." The word connotes destruction and suggests something negative, rather than normal or inevitable. In Arabic, on the other hand, my favorite word is *athar.* It can be roughly understood as "archaeology." Linguists would tell you it's more finely translated as "remnant," which suggests the remains of an ancient culture that hint at a hidden completeness. When you say, "Ana doctora athar farony" ("I am a doctor of the archaeology of ancient Egypt"), people understand your profession as Egyptologist. Archaeologists are thus professional "remnant-ologists," dealing in fragments of pottery, bits of amulets, and random pieces of hieroglyphic text, all waiting to be woven together.

The case of Palmyra, the great multicultural Syrian city at the edge of the ancient East-West divide, has sparked a modern confrontation revolving around different interpretations of the word "ruin." In 2015, the Islamic State of Iraq and the Levant, or ISIL, blew up the Temple of Bel and a graceful series of columns at Palmyra. Turning a venue for concerts and tourist picnics into a place of nightmares, ISIL conducted executions in the well-preserved Roman amphitheater and displayed their murdered victims among the ruins, including the great archaeologist of Palmyra, Dr. Khaled Al-Asaad.[2]

Debates have raged in the archaeological community about rebuilding the temple, using archival photographs as guides. Some people think it would be beautiful, and appropriate, to see that glorious old site rise again in splendor. But here's the complication: Palmyra traded cultures many times until reaching its height under the empress Zenobia, whose reign ended in 272 AD. The Roman emperor Aurelian allowed his soldiers to sack the city in 273 AD. Then in 1400, the Timurids razed the city again, reducing it to a small town.[3]

What we see at the site of Palmyra today is a complex series of layers of destruction, the remnants of global power struggles and shifting political alliances—including ISIL's occupation. Some feel that to reconstruct the Temple of Bel is to erase ISIL's atrocity instead of recognizing it and honoring the shattered moment in perpetuity so that we do not forget.

Sites are not static. They are akin to a filmstrip through time, in which building and destruction alternate, sometimes concurrently. As we do our best to capture these partially obscured images, places exist in our imaginations, ideal or ruined, evoked when we first step into the liminal zone of a site. We face past and present, all at once.

Projecting a Single Frame

Capturing a snapshot of exact moments, or even periods of time, is difficult. One reason is that few well-preserved examples of ancient cities exist in the world. The most famous is Pompeii, frozen by a volcanic eruption. Anyone who studies the past must smile, seeing tourists gawk at reliefs of phalli near Pompeii's brothels.[4] It's the sense that Roman Pompeiians and modern oglers share that same reaction, 2,000 years apart.

But even here, there is still something missing. Or rather, someone—a lot of someones.

Ancient sites are ghost towns. If anyone from antiquity happens to be there . . . run. Without a sense of its people, sites become places of monuments, not of activity, however difficult it is to reconstruct the motivations and aspirations of communities who lived thousands of years ago. Context of the material culture they left becomes everything, so we gain insights into use, function, and purpose, to reach the people behind the objects. After carefully collecting the evidence, we study how each piece relates to the others, and squeeze every last drop of data and insight we can from them.

Some people believe sites contain echoes of their former inhabitants. Whatever your beliefs, consider a place like Deir el Medina, the Egyptian New Kingdom village where workers who built the tombs in the Valley of the Kings lived.[5] Today, you see the whole community outlined in mud-mortared limestone walls that survive to a meter or taller. The site tempts you to imagine what happened 3,500 years ago, in the two-story homes that rose from those footprints. Cut off from views of the nearby fertile Nile floodplain, you feel as though you're moving through a secret and sacred place, home to the great artisans whose work fuels feverish archaeological dreams today.

We See Dead People

Archaeologists can find signs of ancient lives if we look hard enough in the thumbprints on pottery, the chisel marks left on stone, and everywhere in the beauty of things designed for people long ago.

But cemeteries, naturally, represent the best bet for finding the actual remains of people. They're typically placed away from living spaces in defined areas for the dead, in some cases near holy sites; think of burial grounds near churches.

Getting to know an actual human being from their bones is not easy: it's the specialist job of physical anthropologists, who also go by the science-fictional-sounding term bioarchaeologists. Skeletons contain a wealth of data about us. If enough well-preserved bones turn up and you know what to look for, you can usually ascertain an individual's sex, height, nutritional status, and approximate age, and sometimes the diseases from which the deceased suffered—and which may have been the cause of death. Even teeth tell tales. Avid followers of the paleo diet would hardly be so keen on the paleo dental plan, which included treating cavities with flint tools.[6]

Also, through the overall health of the bones, the context in

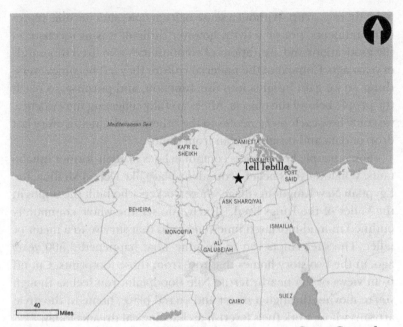

Map showing the location of Tell Tebilla [MAP COURTESY CHASE CHILDS]

which they're found, and any associated grave goods, archaeologists can suggest the social status of the individuals. Repetitive motions over a lifetime leave their mark in ways that inform anthropologists and sometimes reveal occupations. At Tell Tebilla,[7] a site two hours' drive northeast of Cairo, an excavation team led by my husband, Gregory Mumford, came across a case of art brought to life by archaeological evidence.

We excavated a burial of a woman with very strong muscle attachments on her left shoulder. This might have been quite a puzzle, but an artifact in the Metropolitan Museum of Art suggested a cause.[8] The carved wooden image depicted a young woman in a colorful beaded dress carrying an offering atop her head—supporting it with her left hand. Our lady at Tell Tebilla had apparently spent her life carrying heavy loads in a similar way, just as modern Egyptian women still do, deepening the muscle-attachment groove of her larger-than-normal left bicep.

Occasionally we find that ancient people suffered from problems that are usually thought to be modern. In an analysis of 22 mummies at the Cairo Museum, bioarchaeologists found evidence for atherosclerosis, or hardening of the arteries, in more than half the individuals. Most probably, it seems, these people ate too much beef.[9]

By assembling data about the dead from sites of the same time period and looking for patterns, we gain insights into the population that allow us to make inferences about why things happened for that entire culture. Perhaps disease overtook society, affecting specific groups. Or a famine wiped out everyone. Too many skeletons from healthy, strong young men could even suggest war.

Ages at death can, ironically, indicate whether the population is healthy. Physical anthropologists will tell you that they expect to see specific ages represented across the spectrum in a cemetery, and when adult ages skew too young, something significant happened to cause the high number of otherwise healthy young adults' deaths at that time.

Methods like DNA research open new possibilities into understanding the past, such as piecing together family relationships from the interwoven tendrils of our ancestors. A recent study on the mummies of two supposed brothers tells a fascinating tale worthy of any daily talk show. The mummies of Khnum-Nakht and Nakht-Ankh, dating to the Middle Kingdom, around 1800 BC, have sarcophagi with lifelike carved faces. They reside at the Manchester Museum in England.[10]

Using DNA sequencing, researchers discovered that the mummies belonged to mitochondrial haplotype M1a1, showing they had the same mother. But differences in the Y chromosome meant different fathers.[11] I have so many questions. Did the father of the older brother die, leaving the woman to remarry? What struggles did she face as a widowed mother? We'll never know, but the data helps us to imagine the possibilities and allows us to be more empathetic.

Ways to Get Closer to the Past

Reimagining the past requires a leap of faith accompanied by a healthy dose of science. We cannot travel back in time to see people smelting copper or mummifying the dead, but we can re-create past technologies using experimental archaeology.[12] This allows us to rebuild features like ovens or kilns based on archaeological findings and their associated fuel sources, and reproduce everyday tools, pottery, and swords.[13] Archaeologists have made innumerable breakthroughs discovering how and why past people made things, although some techniques remain difficult to re-create, such as the complex inlays in ancient jewelry.

More successfully, Kumar Akhilesh and Shanti Pappu looked at the waste products from the production of lithic stone tools at the site of Attirampakkam in northern India. Dating to the Acheulean era, 1.76 million to 130,000 years ago, the site contained evidence of the production of thousands of lithic tools. The team used experimental knapping to learn more about ancient techniques, and the study helped them to understand decisions past people made about stone sourcing and manufacturing processes.[14]

My Egyptologist colleagues have even conducted real-life mummifications of animals that had died naturally and, for one television show, of a man who had volunteered for the treatment prior to passing away.[15] Maybe when they finished filming that segment, they said it was a wrap!

Another field of study, ethnoarchaeology,[16] focuses on how cultures today may connect to past groups in the same area. Clear differences exist between the pottery workshops of the modern Egyptian Delta and those from ancient sites, yet when I visit, I find potters hunched over their wheels in the same way that's depicted in ancient Egyptian models. Potters today add straw, or chaff, to their clay to strengthen it for firing, just as the ancient Egyptians did; if you peer through a magnifying glass at the edges of ancient pottery fragments, you can see clear chaff imprints.[17]

Cognitive archaeology[18] takes the experiment even further, attempting to deconstruct the actions and thoughts of past people, and how they experienced their worlds. We can gain these insights not only through the study of cultures' material products and architecture, but from their languages and the landscapes that inspired them.

Sometimes, though, we get a fortuitous download of ancient thoughts in the form of letters, and we can imagine the person scribbling away, carefully choosing words. One of my favorite letters dates to 1,800–1,900 years ago, from the Egyptian site of Oxyrhynchus. In the letter, a young boy, Theon, vents his anger to his father that he had left for Alexandria without Theon. He says he will not speak to Dad or even eat, unless he reconsiders taking him to the big city.[19]

You can see him sulking and refusing dinner—then sneaking to the kitchen later on. Doesn't any teenager today throw fits for being kept out of grown-up business?

Panning Out

But to scale up from familial relationships and out to site relationships with the surrounding landscape, we need more perspective. Spatial imagery of all kinds can give us this data. While we cannot see everything as it once appeared, at least we can get enough clues about the ancient locations of rivers, canals, lakes, and the likely size of sites to make a decent reconstruction. Satellites and aerial data can see only so much, and they still require testing on the ground: we can guess from space, but we cannot know what is beneath the pixels.

Unexpected people find things in unexpected places that show us how little we know. In 2004, Abdullah Al-Saeed, the leader of an amateur archaeological group, found enigmatic features in western Arabia's lava fields.[20] He did not realize the extent and scale of these "gates"—a new archaeological site type—until four years later when he turned to high-resolution satellite imagery available on Google Earth and Bing.

Al-Saeed sent the images to David Kennedy of the University of Western Australia, who is well known for his aerial archaeological surveys of Jordan. Kennedy then located 400 of these features up to 1,600 feet long, some of which could be more than 7,000 years old. This concentration of stone structures may indicate large-scale landscape design during a wetter period, perhaps a water diversion or flood management system. Ground surveys are planned to explore them further, but the story shows how new chapters can be opened for areas considered inhospitable and uninhabitable today, all because a single structure intrigued interested private citizens.

This discovery tells a tale of widespread human–landscape interaction over time; but reconstructing a single important episode in human history can only be done with a caveat. "Once upon a time" are the hidden words in every archaeological report. Most of us have a hard time reconstructing what happened last week in our own lives, but archaeologists must try to reconstruct entire ancient life spans.

We are continuously editing our anecdote mechanisms, adapting our sagas for the latest publications and conference presentations—it's something of a balancing act between science and fiction.

Once upon a Time . . .

Here's a story, then, inspired by a surprise discovery from space at Tell Tebilla. It captures the beginning of the end of Pharaonic Egypt more than 2,000 years ago.

The year was 343 BC. An anxious Persian king named Artaxerxes III sailed southwest down a Nile tributary. His history lessons might have taught him that this land was once a swamp, where dense marshes filled with crocodiles prevented foreigners from entering the country. Now, a large river entrance stood clear for him, between islands of reeds, leading straight to a city known as "the beautiful mouth," or Ro-nefer, in the local language.

Artaxerxes commanded a 40-meter-long galley with 200 men, flanked by an armada bearing his army, hungry for battle and the possibility of plunder. This town would not disappoint. Spies had told him of its treasures—gold and incense from Nubia, lapis lazuli from Afghanistan, and luxury wines from the Greek islands: after all, it was the northernmost trade port in Egypt.[21]

Three-story houses of affluent merchants, densely packed, appeared across the reed beds as the ship rounded a bend in the river. And at the city's heart, the huge fortified wall of a temple loomed. Artaxerxes had studied his strategy well enough to know that tearing it out—throwing down the walls and destroying its idols—would break the citizens. His men rowed quietly through the early mist, and the king perhaps allowed himself a small smile. Ro-nefer would not last the morning.

Today, Tell Tebilla appears as a brown mound, rising abruptly from lush, neon-green rice paddies. When you drive onto the site, the only hint of its ancient date is a small cluster of thick-cut limestone sarcophagi near the edge of a defunct water-treatment plant of pink brick. The village of Et-Till sits around the site now, home to a thousand rural souls, a far cry from the ancient cosmopolitan city beneath their feet. Around 200 years ago, the mound measured a kilometer by a kilometer in size. Now it is one-tenth that. Over time, farmers have hauled away most of the phosphorus-rich soil, called *sebakh*, to use as fertilizer.

Archaeological work began at Tebilla in the early 1900s, when French archaeologists found statues of seated scribes dating to ca. 600 BC.[22] Egypt's then Supreme Council of Antiquities brought the site to the attention of my husband, Greg, in the late 1990s, when he mentioned an interest in starting an independent excavation mission.[23] No published work on it had appeared in nearly a hundred years.

Excavating the Beautiful Mouth

Our initial survey confirmed the location of a temple, based on the architectural fragments around the water-treatment plant. Built by the United States Agency for International Development to combat unsanitary drinking water, such plants can be found overlaying sites across Egypt, and their presence often made mounds into targets for further development, including the construction of schools. The unfortunate siting caused heavy losses to the study of urban archaeology.

Construction of the water-treatment plant here had destroyed the temple building's foundations, and we could only guess at what it looked like long ago. Our goal for investigating the site included mapping it and finding out about the ancient city of Ro-nefer and the people who had lived there.

Named for the regional capital, Mendes, some 40 kilometers to the southwest, the Mendesian branch of the Nile flowed by the site in antiquity, but no clues appeared on the surface to tell us anything else. We began our work with coring at and around the site, to get a sense of its past size and the location of the ancient river course. Our geoarchaeologist, or geology specialist, a gray-haired, bearded, energetic imp named Larry Pavlish, carried out the coring and a magnetometer survey to reveal the hidden mud-brick foundations of the buildings underfoot.

Coring is like taking on a layer cake with an apple corer—a narrow round auger is rotated down, allowing archaeologists to see layers of earth without having to excavate. It's simple, but very valuable, keyhole archaeology. Magnetometry is slightly higher tech. Passing a portable magnetometer over a site's surface reads differences in the magnetic properties of buried walls or other features, building up a glimpse of their shape below ground. Both techniques help to target where to dig.

Once Larry generated a detailed map of the highest part of the mound—the "Tell" in Arabic—we selected key areas for excavation.

Our team formed a motley, United Nations–like crew, with members from Canada, the United States, the United Kingdom, and Egypt. We stayed in nearby Mansoura, a beautiful city famous for its riverside walkways and its handsome women. The Marshal Hotel was our home away from home and the source of the mango buffalo-milk ice cream that we craved after a day beneath the harsh sun. We confounded its guests by tramping through the lobby in our filthy dig clothing and, on one occasion, carrying a purpose-built wooden toilet for our on-site outhouse, complete with an antique toilet-paper holder.

To beat the heat of the day, we'd rise at 4:30 a.m. for quiet cups of instant coffee and cookies in the lobby, cursing ourselves for having decided to work in archaeology. It's an ungodly hour to be conscious, yet it is de rigueur for those of us who work in the Middle East in summer months. For the commute, two 1960s Peugeots—one with an exposed propane tank in the back—was how we rolled in the Egyptian Delta. On-site by 6 a.m., we'd drive to the top of the Tell to catch the first pink light snaking through the morning fog. Our local work crew would meet us and shake hands, decidedly more awake than we were.

That summer, we worked hard dispelling the long-held myth that Delta sites, being moister than those in Upper Egypt, have poorer preservation of organic materials. Every Egyptologist knows desert sites—so dry that nothing decomposes—have it all in comparison. Well, that's not entirely true.

In one excavation area, we dug down more than 7 meters, revealing a 2,600-year-old three-story house that had been reused by later Egyptians as a mausoleum. A precarious climb down two sets of ladders, each 4 meters tall, took us to the bottom; the record of 500 years of occupation and abandonment unrolled on our graph paper as we planned the earthen section.

And the finds! The site yielded Greek pottery from the Mediterranean, carnelian from Egypt's Eastern Desert, lapis lazuli from

Afghanistan, and gold from Nubia—all evidence of a thriving international port. Based on the coring data and the landscape reconstructions, we knew that water surrounded Tebilla for nine months of the year in antiquity; this, with its location along the edge of Lake Manzala, made it a prime spot for importing and exporting luxury goods from home and abroad.

It would be unusual for a port town in Egypt's Late Period not to have a wealthy temple with a powerful priestly class. It's an era we hardly hear about on TV or in major archaeological announcements; but if you're looking for ancient examples of cosmopolitan and diverse places that mirror modern times, the Late Period is a good time to start. The arts and technology flourished, with innovations in the use of iron, cavalry, and triremes, and a new form of Egyptian writing, Demotic. Numerous new temples appeared throughout Egypt, including the temple at Tebilla.

Some Historical Context

A brief spin through history helps put this in perspective: after international expansion during the New Kingdom and the rise of the priesthood during the Third Intermediate Period (1069–525 BC), the Late Period began with a Libyan takeover from the west in 945 BC. Then the Nubians of Dynasty 25 came from the south, between 760 and 656 BC.[24] Founded around 664 BC, Dynasty 26 represented the last gasp of Pharaonic Egypt as we know it.

Psamtik, the first ruler of Dynasty 26, threw off Assyrian occupation using Greek mercenaries, stabilized the country, and moved the capital to Sais in the western Delta, only 75 kilometers from Tell Tebilla.[25]

For a time, Egypt had stability and foreign alliances across the Mediterranean and eastern Africa.[26] But for all the international diplomacy, the Late Period eventually brought multiple players to the poker table and left Egypt with a diminishing hand and nothing in the pot.

In 525 BC, the Persians took the country. Egypt kicked them out in 404 BC, and spent the next 60 years resisting a Persian comeback from power bases in the Delta.[27]

This served Tebilla well. In 398 BC, Egypt's capital moved from Sais to Mendes, the large city to Tebilla's southwest. Tebilla likely expanded its influence and wealth over the next 19 years during Mendes's tenure as capital, and merchants flocked to the city to trade in the goods flowing across the fluctuating empires. The temple's riches surely must have grown by the time the capital shifted once again to the central Delta. Four more dynasties had come and gone, but who at Tebilla cared, when the port stood stacked high with goods? They would not have known what hit them that misty morning, some 2,400 years ago.

Tebilla's Downfall

Herodotus called Artaxerxes III "a great warrior," and he was certainly tenacious. He attacked Egypt again and again, first as head of the army and heir to the throne in 359 BC, and then as king of Persia, having knocked off 80 of his nearest and dearest at home to maintain control.[28]

In 343 BC, having had enough of Egypt's refusal to be defeated, Artaxerxes brought more than 300,000 men. He engaged Nectanebo II, the last Indigenous ruler, and his navy along the branches of the Nile in the Delta.[29] Nectanebo ran away to Memphis, crook and flail between his legs, leaving garrison towns and ports like Tebilla to fend for themselves.

The battle did not end well for Tebilla's inhabitants. One humid July day in 2003, our team made a discovery that encapsulated Artaxerxes's triumph—a discovery made possible by 40-year-old photographs taken from space.

These came from a covert program in the United States spurred by the Cold War. The CORONA program gathered thousands of images of countries in the 1960s and early 1970s, freezing them in time prior to large-scale landscape changes caused by the construction of dams, urbanization, population increases, and climate change. Luckily, cameras pointed toward North Africa and the Middle East recorded sites that are now damaged or no longer there—and had so much to say about the archaeology of Egypt's demise.

When I examined the 1972 CORONA imagery for Tebilla, corners of a large rectilinear feature appeared in the north-central and south-central parts of the site. Could this be the temple enclosure wall we had hoped to find?[30]

Magnetometry and associated excavations had given us an idea

*CORONA image of temple
enclosure wall at Tell Tebilla*
[IMAGE COURTESY OF THE
US GEOLOGICAL SURVEY]

of the town's layout,[31] but locating the edge of the wall on the ground
would not be an easy task. Typically, remote-sensing specialists take
aerial photographs and georeference them—which means we connect the photographs to current satellite imagery and give each
pixel an x and y coordinate on the map. You need a minimum of six
recognizable and unchanged points in the aerial photograph for this
process to work. Older, smaller, nondigital images can be stretched
to match up with modern imagery, to achieve the same pins-in-the-
map effect. This process—and I am not making this up—is called
"rubber sheeting."

But georeferencing older images is an imprecise activity where
so much of the modern landscape has changed. Although I tried with
the 1972 CORONA image, there just was not enough of a match, likely
due to distortion caused by the rubber sheeting. Finding the wall on
the ground with that image alone was impossible.

The initial magnetometry work covered several 20-by-20-meter
grids, highlighting buried mud-brick architecture. But this data did
not show a large enclosure, either. We knew the temple walls would
be several meters thick and more than 100 meters long. Locating it
in the remaining month of the dig season suddenly seemed like a
major challenge.

Greg had a brilliant idea: scraping away 10 centimeters of the site's
surface to reach the top of the mud-brick level buried below the silt.
But scraping down *the entire site* would have taken weeks. Instead,
where the imagery gave the wall's broad location on the mound, he

Photograph of excavated enclosure wall at Tell Tebilla
[PHOTO BY THE AUTHOR]

divided the ground into a grid of 10-by-10-meter squares. We then scraped a small window between each. It was like probing between paving slabs to see what was underneath, rather than taking up the whole patio.

Outlines of the buried structures emerged at set intervals. A temple enclosure wall should appear as dense mud brick, with no structural breaks. When we hit an area that fit this description, we just kept scraping until we found two wall edges, some 8 meters apart. Aha! Massive mud-brick wall *here*, and it matched the wall thickness observed in the CORONA satellite imagery. Bingo.

What the Walls Saw

We continued almost 100 meters to the south, until we hit a 90-degree turn to the west. All sorts of interesting things happen in the corners of ancient buildings: foundation deposits, datable material—and we didn't have anywhere to go but down. So, down we went.

Which crew member gets assigned to what excavation unit is always a roll of the dice. This one became my responsibility. I gridded out a 2-by-2-meter unit in the southeast corner and started digging through the dense silt. Surprisingly, the silt did not change in consistency or color as I went down 10 centimeters, 20 centimeters, 30 centimeters. Neither did it contain objects or pottery.

Just as I was giving up on the unit as a bad bet, I struck a strange, crumbling red brick. And another. And another. Instead of forming part of a wall, the bricks sloped downward at a sharp angle. As more of the feature emerged, it seemed as if someone had dumped several dozen mud bricks in the corner and set them on fire.

After planning, mapping, and photographing it, I started to remove the brick layer. But a glint of gold stopped me in my tracks— gold is as rare as hen's teeth in a settlement context. Then a bronze piece about 5 centimeters long came up. As my workmen sieved each bucket of earth, more gold foil appeared, stuck to what looked and felt like charcoal. The trickle of objects turned into a fire-hose stream: bronze, lapis lazuli, beads, carnelian, and almost a quarter of a sandwich bag of gold foil from the sieve. It had our team puzzling over the burning, and this confused scatter of precious objects, going down more than 80 centimeters.

Across the Tell in our tented recording area, while cleaning the objects so that she could draw them, our dig artist-registrar Shakira Christodoulou teased out their meaning. From the encrusted dirt, beautifully cast bronze appeared—crowns of various kinds, plaited beards, ram's horns—all with tenons, projecting pieces for attachment to wooden statuettes.

But not just any statuettes: the gold foil and bronze were all that remained of divine figures. Tebilla's gods had gone up in flames. Gold was the flesh of the gods, and the bronze symbols of their power were made to last forever; these figures embodied the deities, more than represented them. Artisans fitted their eyebrows and eyes in semiprecious stones to imbue them with life. Each day, the priests bathed, anointed, and dressed the statues, not unlike the ritual surrounding temple figures in India today.

It's very hard for us to imagine what their destruction would have felt like to the people of Ro-nefer.

When Artaxerxes and his soldiers swarmed from the river quays to raze the town, the destruction of the temple sent a terrible message. Armed with brutal iron short swords against sleepy civilians, the soldiers burst through the temple's huge double doors. Perhaps the priests on duty tried to fight or hide, but their own walls now trapped them. Down the stone pavement through the temple's center, deep into its heart, the soldiers swept toward the holy of holies and found Osiris, Amun, and other deities defenseless inside their shrines.

Seizing the statues, maybe the soldiers wrenched out semiprecious stones for themselves. Then they ran and set the gods ablaze. Perhaps they committed their iconoclasm on top of the wall, in sight of the citizens, and pushed the fragments over: we know someone in antiquity tossed the statues to the ground, since we discovered the wall's foundation trench just below the find spot. The conflagration fired the mud bricks red and brought them down over the remains, covering them for more than 2,000 years.

What might have taken place in the temple and the town disappeared beneath later occupation; the carnage that day passes from one frame of the filmstrip to the next. The temple was not just a religious center, but an economic engine, a political machine, and an impressive target, perhaps with walls 10 meters tall or more, if it bore any likeness to examples at Luxor. Its destruction was one of many similar topplings as Artaxerxes III wrested away control of Egypt.

How a River Doomed a City

The Egyptians should have been better prepared for a river-borne invasion. But they'd thought they were safe for too long.

The reason why lies with the rhythms of the very river on whose annual inundation they depended. Hundreds of miles upstream, the monsoon rains caused the tributary Blue Nile and White Nile to swell, flooding the Nile proper, which deposited rich, nurturing silt onto the fields for several months each summer. Egypt became a nation-state of islands, on which its towns and people waited for the waters to recede.

On average, the Nile deposited a millimeter of silt across the entire floodplain per year—some years more, some years less—adding up to 1 meter every 1,000 years.[32] Close to the ancient capital of Memphis, near the apex of the Delta, the river split into seven branches with innumerable canals that fed into the Mediterranean. Here, the Nile dumped any silt not deposited along the floodplain, slowly adding landmass.

In time, the virtually impassable swampy landscape of the eastern Delta became livable, and small towns like Tebilla, inhabited since the Old Kingdom, could prosper and grow. If the swamps had remained, so would have Egypt's impenetrability, and Artaxerxes would have failed. However, when the Persian king sailed for Egypt, the country had been opened up to river transport. Ultimately, time and silt, gathering imperceptibly, allowed its conquest.

This story ends where it started: in space. Staring down at the Delta today, satellites reveal that only two of the seven Nile branches remain. Tell Tebilla is more than 60 kilometers inland from the Mediterranean, making it almost impossible to imagine the site along a large river connected to the Mediterranean. In fact, little of Tebilla is left, with more and more of the site being lost to modern encroachment and looting each year. So many other Delta sites face the same fate. Early visitors commented on mounds in the Delta as far as the eye could see, like anthills. Now, it is a half-hour drive or more between the remaining Tells.

Luck favored us when history recorded Artaxerxes III's destruction of Ro-nefer and when the CORONA imagery picked up a major feature on that site that later satellite data could not. Excavation added to the puzzle pieces, though our knowledge of Artaxerxes III's campaign will always be hazy.

With the destruction of sites around the world by climate change and urbanization, we must wonder how many puzzles have been lost entirely.

The good news is, with so many developments in satellite technologies, discoveries are being made more rapidly, across larger areas, and in places we never thought possible. Thousands of hidden stories are out there, about how past civilizations thrived, crashed, and were then reborn. To learn more about them, we first need to delve into how this field came into existence.

2

Space Archaeology

When first encountered, this may seem like a ludicrous, science-fictionalized name for a subfield of archaeology. It sounds like we hope to find evidence of an alien homestead on Mars, extraterrestrial arrowheads, or the mummies of little green men. While this would undoubtedly interest astrobiologists, the gaze of the space archaeologist turns back to Earth, via satellites.

The ground is an appropriate place to start, after all. Visions of gleaming white tents in the desert and scruffy teams kicking up the sand of millennia dance in the popular imagination. Modern archaeological fieldwork now requires pipettes and laser-scanning tools alongside the more traditional trowels and dustpans, but the romantic notion of archaeologists in the field is what first ignited my passion.

Excavating ancient sites is the best part of my job. My inner five-year-old screams with glee whenever I have the chance to use my Marshalltown, a brand of trowel. Every scrape on the ground carries the possibility of discovery. Think of the thrill of a lottery scratch-off game: there is a moment of anticipation, a quickening of the heart, and maybe a letdown. Now repeat 10,000 times a day. You never forget how you felt the first time you found something intact.

Digging for the First Time

In the summer of 1999, after my second year of university, I worked my first excavation at a site called Mendes, the ancient Per-Banebdjedet,[1] in Egypt's Delta three hours northeast of Cairo.[2] We spent most days toiling beneath a hazy ball of heat, exposing 3,000 years of history intermixed beneath an undulating expanse of earth. One moment we'd turn up burnished Predynastic sherds from 3000 BC, and Roman Period ceramics from 100 AD the next.[3] The unit where I worked dated to approximately 2200 BC, Dynasty 8, at the end of Egypt's first great Pyramid Age, the Old Kingdom.

Laboring in the stickiness of a Delta July, my Egyptian team and I had found the edge of a mud-brick mastaba, a classic rectangular tomb. Digging down, a reddish ceramic circle slowly emerged, hints of an ancient vessel. Every second I wondered if what I'd found was going to be intact. As I dug around the pot, the struggle was to temper that enthusiasm, to measure, map, draw, and photograph the object in its original location before I moved it.

Cracks appeared in the pot, showing its broken pieces.

After half an hour of careful work, a 3-D jigsaw puzzle emerged of a flattened beer jar. A ghostly white slip coated its exterior. These jars, common in the Old Kingdom,[4] would not be out of place alongside the stylish serving options for mixed drinks on Bourbon Street in New Orleans. More than just an object, I had a possible story. Perhaps relatives of the deceased had brought the jar to the cemetery. They had said the ancient offering formula, a magical recital ensuring the dead received a bounty of bread, beer, and goods for eternity, and drank to their memory.[5] Looking closer, while brushing the pot for an official photograph, I saw something near its mouth: a fingerprint, from the potter who had made it 4,200 years ago.

In my imagination, the gulf of time separating us compressed.

The print seemed to be from a robust thumb. A middle-aged man appeared, sweat on his brow, bent over the wheel he rotated by hand. The ancient Day of the Dead, the Feast of Wagy,[6] was approaching, and he had a deadline to meet: he would need two sets of fine ware for the mayor and his family and 200 beer jars for the townspeople of Per-Banebdjedet.[7] Nearby, his sons stoked the kiln fires; too hot, and the pots would crack, too cool, and they would crumble. His daughter brought him a small cup filled with cool water, and he smiled, grateful for the blessing of the gods. Praise Djedet,[8] he would make his deadline!

Excavation's Greatest Challenge

Once you taste a drop like this from the spigot of history, you never forget, and your thirst is never quenched. Stories, not things, lie in disjointed sentences below the ground, and it is the job of archaeologists to coax them out and weave them into prose. But when facing a featureless sea of brown silt, or modern fields, or a mound beneath dense rainforest, the challenge is where to begin.

This is the exact question space archaeology has evolved to answer.

On most unexcavated archaeological sites, few hints exist aboveground of what features might be hidden below. This varies widely depending on where in the world you work. In Belize, towering mounds emerge from the rainforest floor, looking out of place in an otherwise gently rolling landscape and suggesting the presence of structures. Stone fragments may appear in straight lines beneath olive groves in Greece, showing the locations of 3,000-year-old walls. Archaeologists feel fortunate when they have these conspicuous clues to guide their excavation efforts.

When the clues are not so conspicuous, we have a setback. While archaeologists may live to dig, they cannot be in the field more than a few months each year, unless they work for a cultural resource management firm or as professional archaeologists for a cultural ministry. Even Indiana Jones taught class. Tight schedules and financial restrictions mean archaeologists must plan for every moment and penny spent: responsible publicly funded excavations do not want to report a fruitless season.

All applications for archaeological funding, public or private, now require well-formulated research questions, state-of-the-art project design, and evidence such as a preliminary site assessment that the team is digging on target.

Some sites are found by luck or by accident. In 1900, for instance, a donkey transporting a gentleman from a quarry in Alexandria, Egypt, fell into an abandoned shaft. What the poor donkey landed in were second-to-fourth-century AD Roman Period catacombs containing hundreds of individuals, now on the list of must-see tourist sites in Alexandria.[9]

Such sites underlie modern towns all over the world. When I was in graduate school, doing survey work in middle Egypt, I needed local help to verify hints from the satellite imagery that an ancient town might be lurking under modern urban landscapes. In the city of Dalga, the priests from a Coptic church led me down two flights of stairs to sacred rooms used for baptisms. They were decorated with sixth-century AD reliefs removed from the earliest Coptic church in the town, located some 20 feet below where we stood. No donkeys were harmed in the making of that little surprise.

Deny it though they might, most archaeologists pray to all gods ancient and modern who might heed our requests for success. It never hurts to spread the love, sample bags in hand! Aside from unexpected discoveries, archaeologists rely on diverse techniques to figure out what lies underfoot.

The simplest is fieldwalking. Moving along equally spaced lines, either in a group or alone, is a way to see how surface remains may change over a site or region. Sudden dense concentrations of slag, the by-product of metal production, may indicate an industrial zone. Tiny limestone chips and bone fragments found together could pinpoint a high-ranking cemetery, with the limestone pieces coming from sarcophagi or tomb structures. Larger limestone fragments in heaps, perhaps with inscribed and/or intact blocks, may locate a long-destroyed sacred or palatial building. And any ancient pottery or other remains flag the range of time periods below.

Fieldwalking—as well as ungulates—may represent an important step in site survey, but only an aerial perspective allows us to see the entire picture, not only of a single site, but of its relationship to the surrounding landscape. Aerial photos have proven invaluable for assessing ancient sites, and those taken from drones today are nothing less than spectacular. However, images from a far greater height, 200 miles higher than the International Space Station,[10] have paved the way for the subfield of archaeology that has already transformed our understanding of the past and of the potential for future discovery.

How Space Archaeology Works

Whenever archaeologists apply any form of air- or space-based data to the assessment of modern landscapes, attempting to locate long-buried rivers or hidden ancient sites, they are doing "space archaeology," also called "satellite archaeology" or "satellite remote sensing." NASA shoulders the ultimate name blame. In 2008, NASA began its "Space Archaeology" program,[11] funding scientists to apply satellite data sets to large-scale archaeological research projects. If NASA calls what I do space archaeology, who am I to disagree?

Interpreting satellite imagery is part science and part art. All remote-sensing specialists must start by learning the language of light, and it is not easy: what appears as a simple high-resolution photograph on your computer screen is so much more. Each pixel on the image is representative of an exact area on the ground.[12] The light composing the pixel represents not only the visible part of the light spectrum, but the near, middle, and far infrared, depending on the satellite-imaging system. Additionally, everything on the Earth's surface has its own distinct chemical signature that affects the light it reflects: much as we all have distinct signatures when we write our names, different materials show up uniquely in the light spectrum.[13]

For example, sand appears very different from forest on the satellite imagery. We can see this easily with our own eyes. When you need to discern different tree species *within* the forest, this is where chemical signatures come into play. A group of oak trees emits a different chemical signature than does a group of pine trees. Visually, they might appear as the same green to us, but using different parts of the infrared spectrum to visualize subtle vegetation health differences, we can perceive color variation.[14]

Remote-sensing specialists can exaggerate these differences by assigning "false color" to the images,[15] to highlight individual classes of surface features. Within remote-sensing programs (like Photoshop color replacement with an attitude), you can choose any color for any cluster of pixels. While it's recommended that users choose classes closely resembling their real-life counterparts—for example, green tones for vegetation, gray for buildings, brown for soils—you can choose any colors you want. Satellite images shown at conferences or in publications sometimes look like bad acid trips.[16]

Scientists shop for specific types of satellite images to suit the data they need. Each satellite is different, and there are over 1,700 of them up there.[17] Most are lower-resolution weather or large-scale satellites, with resolutions of 15 to 30 meters. These are the images most used, not just because they are free, but because there are millions of images going all the way back to 1972 that highlight short- and long-term landscape changes.[18] In addition to these free images, there are high-resolution images recorded by sensors such as DigitalGlobe's WorldView-3 and -4 satellites, with resolutions of between .31 and 1 meter, where a single pixel represents an area between the size of an iPad and a bodyboard.

Everyone looking at satellite imagery extracts pixel-based data to detect subtle short-term versus long-term changes, or to detect features. We tweak and test algorithms depending on our research questions, and eventually, through sheer dumb luck or a moment of genius, we find something of interest, usually because we're scraping the barrel bottom of possible techniques. When it turns out to be dried snot on our computer screen, this being science, we go back to the drawing board and try again.

It Isn't All "Aha" Moments, Except When It Is

People think that remote-sensing work is all about the "Aha" moment, the moment when a single click of a button reveals secrets hidden in plain sight. It isn't. A typical remote-sensing specialist will spend dozens of hours per week in front of a computer screen, often cursing due to program crashes. When something does work, there is additional swearing, because you have forgotten to record the exact steps you took to reach that point. And you must start over. It's about learning, about refining the process.

Then again, "Aha" moments do happen. One of my favorite remote-sensing stories unfolded at the well-known Maya site of Caracol in Belize, which dates back over 1,000 years.[19] In 2008, a new laser-imaging technology called LIDAR, for LIght Detection And Ranging, was just warming up at the starting lines.

Diane and Arlen Chase, a gregarious and generous archaeologist couple at the University of Nevada, Las Vegas, had worked at the site for nearly 30 years.[20] When a keen biologist, John Weishampel, of the University of Central Florida, first asked the Chases about using LIDAR at Caracol, they told him that they were skeptical. They had never heard of it, but they were understandably enthusiastic about the idea of bringing more funding to their site. After decades of toil, they almost hoped they hadn't missed anything major.

They told him to go ahead with his grant application—he could try and peer beneath dense rainforest canopies using LIDAR if he wanted. It sounded like fun and wouldn't do anyone any harm.

John, now grant in hand, commissioned an airplane from the United States to collect the point cloud data, or hundreds of thousands of points from the top of the vegetation down to the forest floor, in a large area surrounding the site.[21] If you were to look at the area on Google Earth, all you would see is rainforest—a sea of green, with nothing suggesting anything ancient, aside from a few well-known limestone pyramids peeking through the tops of the trees.

After he had processed all the data, John displayed the images for Arlen and a small group. Arlen's exact words were: "Holy shit!" The same thing was on everyone's minds. Another astonished colleague said that this was the data to launch a hundred PhD dissertations.

The next day, Diane called John: "Arlen's been stuck to his screen all night looking at the images. And he's missed dinner and breakfast." In a single night, the entire field of Mesoamerican archaeology had changed permanently: Arlen had found more ancient Maya sites than he had in 30 years of combing the jungle. Today, he can find 500 new Maya features before lunch from his desk in Las Vegas.[22]

Such wholesale rethinking is not the product of a single flash of technical brilliance, but rather the result of decades of often serendipitous developments in the field of archaeology. To understand this takes a brief nosedive into the history of seeing ancient sites from afar.

It All Began with Balloons and Airplanes

Technically speaking, one of the first ancient sites to be viewed from an aerial platform was Stonehenge.[23] The famous Neolithic (ca. 2500 BC)[24] circular formation of large stones stands on a grassy down in southern England and is long beloved of modern pagans on summer solstice. Stationed near Stonehenge in 1906, Lieutenant Philip Henry Sharpe of the Royal Engineers' Balloon Section used a tethered balloon to take three photos of the site.[25] Published in the *Society of Antiquaries* shortly thereafter, the photos caused quite a stir. Archaeologists could see the site and its relationship with the surrounding landscape, and curious darker patches appeared on the ground, suggestive of possible buried ancient features. A new world had been opened up from on high.

World War I saw the creation of the Royal Flying Corps, with pioneering aviators flying across Europe and the Middle East. Used for establishing artillery ranges and the enemy's positions, their aerial photography efforts formed the crux of their operations.[26] Photos of the front used to plan attacks have become essential archaeological data today.[27]

Later, Father Antoine Poidebard, who had the rather fabulous nickname of "the Flying Priest,"[28] flew a biplane across large swaths of Syria and Lebanon from 1925 to 1932, recording many ancient sites from above.[29] Aside from these invaluable early photos, he created the foundations for aerial archaeology in the Middle East, emphasizing the importance of timing for revealing ancient structures clearly. Images taken in the morning, for example, when the ground contained more moisture, revealed more sites than those taken in the afternoon, when the drier ground had more uniform colors.

Meanwhile, in England, Osbert Guy Stanhope Crawford, better known as O. G. S. Crawford, pioneered the application of aerial photography to long-occupied landscapes. After serving in the Royal Flying Corps during World War I, he joined the Ordnance Survey as an archaeological officer.[30] While a prisoner of war in Germany during World War I, he had completed *Man and His Past*, a seminal volume emphasizing the importance of maps to define culture.[31] Affectionately called Uncle Ogs by the rising generation of British archaeologists,[32] Crawford located hundreds of previously unknown sites across the United Kingdom.[33] Even today, his aerial photographic archive of Britain remains an invaluable resource for archaeologists.[34]

Crop Marks—It's Not Just Aliens

Most features show up on these early aerial photographs, and later on satellite images, as crop marks. Crop marks do what the name says: vegetation grows faster, slower, or, in some cases, not at all, based on what is beneath the ground, revealing possible buried walls or even entire buildings.[35]

Let's break that down. Imagine the foundations of a stone wall, slowly covered by earth over time. As grass takes root over the top, its roots simply cannot go as deep as the grass a few feet away. Growth becomes stunted and it is less healthy than the other grass. In a time of drought, it might die altogether.

Conversely, over time, a ditch fills in with rotting vegetation. This forms fertile mulch and is an ideal place for new vegetation to grow. Grass and other crops thrive, growing taller and healthier over the ditch than the surrounding area.

The shadows formed by the taller or shorter vegetation can easily be seen on aerial photos, while more subtle differences in vegetation health can be picked up by satellites recording information in the near infrared. Chlorophyll content, for instance, can best be seen in the near infrared—in which all vegetation appears red.[36] Try explaining it that way to your child the next time they ask you why grass is green. My son's response was: "You're a weirdo, Mommy."

These crop marks have a fascinating history, and people can actually see them while walking across fields. In Britain, observant walkers mentioned them over 500 years ago, as noted by British antiquarian William Camden, who named them "St. Augustine's Cross" after the earliest missionary to England.[37]

I regularly receive emails from people in Europe who send me snapshots of crop marks that they have observed on Google Earth, and I am usually impressed. People have great eyes. Straight lines rarely occur in nature, and it is even rarer for them to form rectilinear features, so when multiple connected boxes show up on a satellite image of a field in Britain, France, or Italy, there is a high degree of probability you have discovered a Roman house.[38] Even when a field has been plowed over for millennia, the stone foundations survive and affect crop growth. Despite the pub lunch at the finish line, I can no longer idly go on pleasant Sunday rambles across these fields in England. I'm always on the lookout, just in case.

From World War II to the Start of the Space Age

Following World War II, remote-sensing technologies underwent a great revolution as archaeologists and other scientists recognized the value of emerging color and infrared technologies. In fact, my grandfather, Professor Harold Young, wrote in a 1950 publication: "In a relative sense, the use of aerial photos in forestry has only reached an early adolescent stage. Many research workers are trying to determine the limits of aerial photos, as well as the many ways that aerial photos can be profitably used. Today the possibilities of color film are scarcely known at all."[39]

This was only 70 years ago. Now, we can 3-D scan objects and take thermal infrared photos on sites using our cell phones.[40] These technologies have emerged over only two generations—a blink of the eye of our human history.

During my grandfather's era, archaeologists could access thousands of military images of Europe and the Middle East and use them to plan new surveys. Aerial photography had become a standard archaeological tool, led by pioneers like J. K. St Joseph of Cambridge University. Trained as a geologist, St Joseph learned about the field of aerial photography during World War II, when he served in the Ministry of Aircraft Production. After the war, he commenced major photography of landscapes around the United Kingdom via Royal Air Force training flights, leaving over 300,000 photographs to Cambridge University. He gave wonderful lectures with amazing images but spoke in such a way to earn the nickname "Holy Jo."[41] That's one way to preach from on high.

Expanding interest such as this led to the first international colloquium on aerial photography in 1963,[42] and he published a key tome, *The Uses of Air Photography*, in 1966.[43] With the advent of new military rocket programs, archaeologists could set their sights higher, to spy, in every sense of the word, on the old and the new.

The space race had unintended consequences for archaeologists today. Developed in the 1950s, CORONA, LANYARD, and ARGON were top-secret government spy satellite programs that mapped Russian activities during the Cold War. From 1960 to 1972, rockets launched camera systems into space, capturing large areas of the Earth's surface and producing high-resolution black-and-white photos. A specially designed airplane collected the film capsules as they parachuted back to Earth. These photos had groundbreaking resolutions of up to 1.8 meters per pixel, and they helped to map developing countries prior to their major population growth in the 1960s and 1970s.[44]

Since President Bill Clinton declassified these data sets in 1995,[45] anyone can access them for a small fee, and it is my favorite data set to show remote-sensing students. While archivists in the US government have now fully digitized the imagery,[46] in the early 2000s it arrived as black-and-white negative strips over a meter long and 10 centimeters wide. I love rolling them out and holding them up to my eyes like a spy in a 1950s movie, and the students do, too—most of what they do is on a computer screen, so hands-on adds to the fun. And if telling my students, "Why yes, I use spy imagery for my research," makes them think I'm cooler, I'll take all the help I can get.

All joking aside, for Egyptologists and Near Eastern archaeology specialists, this data is a gold mine. In Egypt, the building of the Aswan High Dam in the 1960s allowed Egyptians to alter radically the Nile Valley and Delta landscapes, expanding towns into areas that had previously flooded. However, this meant leveling numerous archaeological sites. In Syria and Iraq, cultivated areas have also changed, obscuring well-traveled ancient paths called "hollow ways" and river courses that had still been visible only 50 years ago.[47] These archaeological landscapes are now gone forever; without the CORONA data sets, the sites would have vanished without a trace.

NASA's Satellite Revolution

The 1960s brought major upheaval in US history, with riots, protests, marches, the Vietnam War, the race to the moon, and bra burnings. These changes filtered out into the academic community. The United States had already experimented with weather satellites such as TIROS (Television Infrared Observation Satellite), which launched in 1960. The size of a small, very heavy television, tiny compared to satellites of today, and operational for only 78 days, TIROS showed scientists the potential of capturing Earth's surface data.[48] Emboldened by its success, NASA built more TIROS satellites: TIROS-7 lasted a remarkable 1,809 days, producing 30,000 cloud photographs before being deactivated in 1968.[49]

Plans began in 1964 for an imaging system with the capability of mapping the entirety of Earth's surface.[50] Stewart Udall was Secretary of the Interior in the Kennedy and Johnson administrations, and a passionate early conservationist. He had seen power plant pollution in his home state of Arizona from an early space photograph and was appalled. Udall understood the potential power of a space image to share a story and contribute to science, and he took his vision for a global Earth observation system to the Johnson administration. This brought the Department of Interior and NASA together to develop what became the Earth Resources Technology Satellite 1 (ERTS-1).[51] Modern enthusiasts know it as Landsat-1.[52] This time, NASA invited the world to come together, too. Of the 300 researchers and scientists participating in the analysis of the ERTS-1 data, more than a third came from over 100 countries overseas.[53]

It was an extraordinary shift in scientific thinking, especially during the Cold War. In fact, scientists discussing the initial results of ERTS-1 emphasized hopes of developing international, collaborative, remote-sensing programs for everyone to use for global benefit.[54] This collaborative spirit had a profound effect on NASA's more recent data-sharing policies. Amazingly, they have made their database of millions of satellite images free for use by the public.[55] I must have used hundreds of thousands of dollars' worth of their data to date. I could not do my research without it.

With a multispectral scanner, ERTS-1 captured data in green, red, and two infrared bands in the electromagnetic spectrum, with an 80-meter resolution.[56] Not only was 75 percent of the Earth's surface mapped, but every 18 days, scientists could obtain an image of the exact same place to record changes. Such comparative data had immense implications for environmental mapping, disaster monitoring, and resource management.[57]

The scientists behind the program called it the greatest contribution NASA had yet made to the world. In 1976, it even enabled the discovery of a "new" island 20 kilometers off Canada's eastern coast.[58] When Dr. Frank Hall of the Canadian Hydrographic Service explored the newly named Landsat Island, a polar bear took a swipe at him.[59] Needless to say, he beat a quick retreat—from orbit to Ursus, indeed.

NASA's historians may argue that ERTS-1 had its birth in the Cold War, and from a technological perspective, I would agree. But before its decommissioning in 1978[60]—coincidentally the year of my birth—you could say that we can trace its larger spiritual purpose in the rainbow headbands and peace symbols sported by today's septuagenarians: for the first time, the world saw that its landmasses had no true borders.[61]

Modern Space Archaeology

Mary Marguerite Scalera, a NASA intern, receives credit as the first person to predict correctly the future of space archaeology. Writing about six then-current NASA projects in 1970,[62] she gave an upbeat forecast for how NASA's technologies could assist with future discovery efforts.[63] NASA's first historian, Eugene Emme, had supported her interest in researching this report, showing that great innovation in science starts with visionary mentoring.

The 1980s saw the true birth of the field. Landsat data allowed the strategic planning of where to dig by subdividing land, especially in harder-to-survey zones. Unlike today, when a lottery ticket has more value for less effort, my colleagues have told me that then, archaeologists had a 25 percent chance of getting National Science Foundation project funding. But even so, efficiency in project planning made any available budget go further and achieve more. As early as 1981, R. E. Adams published an article in *Science* on using the new data sets to look for possible ancient landscape patterns across the Maya lowlands, a vast area no team could have covered on foot.[64]

And then came "Spacecraft Detects Sahara's Buried Past." I'll forgive you for mistaking it for the title of a Clive Cussler novel, but no, it's the first global headline about a remote-sensing study, led by archaeologist William McHugh. In 1982, the *New York Times*[65] featured his team's extraordinary discovery, first published in *Science*,[66] showing that radar data collected by the space shuttle *Columbia* had penetrated 16 feet below the desert surface to reveal an entire river network in the eastern Sahara. It was a western equivalent of the Nile, dried up since time immemorial. Radar works best in dry environments like sand, so it shone in this sandy field.

By following the river course on the ground, scientists collected a range of remains and stone tools from early hominids—*Homo erectus*, in this case—and the local people whose descendants moved east to kick-start ancient Egyptian civilization. Other finds showed that early sites in the desert had "deflated," gradually becoming smaller, to finally leave nothing but the outlines of stone houses and stone-processing activity areas on the surface or visible just below it. McHugh, in an interview with the *Washington Post*, said: "We've got some sites where there are so many hand axes I stopped counting after I got to 200. It's just incredible."[67]

The excited global reaction said it all: the study showed the tantalizing possibilities of these new technologies and what might be hidden beneath vast, seemingly empty landscapes. A new age was born.

New Beginnings in Mississippi

Meanwhile, the next leap forward came from an unlikely place: Mississippi. A tall, mustachioed, energetic scientist by the name of Tom Sever (not to be confused with Tom Seaver, the former pitcher of the New York Mets) started working at NASA's Stennis Space Center, where his tasks involved broadening the use of NASA space technologies across diverse fields. In a 1983 feasibility study, Sever proposed using a Thermal Infrared Multispectral Scanner and a Thematic Mapper Simulator to map Chaco Canyon, a major archaeological site in the American Southwest.[68]

Since the 1960s, when the new theoretical movement of processual archaeology rattled the field to its core, archaeologists could no longer make grand sweeping statements about ancient cultures without much foundation in their findings. The movement pushed archaeology to become more scientific. Alongside the blossoming subfield of settlement archaeology, the processual wake-up call helped to form modern archaeological inquiry. It drove a change in focus, from concentrating on single sites to considering surrounding landscapes and understanding that the environment played a key role in how and why sites evolved. Advances in dating techniques, chemical residue analyses, and archaeological computing added momentum to archaeological science. These broader trends made archaeologists more open, if skeptical, to the application of space-based technologies suggested by Sever.

Fortunately for my research and, frankly, for all of us in this field, NASA encouraged Sever to move ahead with his proposal and to host a conference that would become legendary.

In 1984, he and his colleague, James Wiseman of Boston University, invited academics from across the United States to Mississippi to hear presentations on new Landsat and radar data sets. Specialists in the archaeology of the Paleolithic period, the Maya and Mexico, the Near East, and the southwestern United States gathered to form one of the most diverse and broad-minded assemblies of US scholars the field had ever seen.[69]

Many of these scientists are luminaries in space archaeology today. Together, they developed guidelines for how researchers should approach remote-sensing data sets, which included using satellites not only to locate sites, but also to study past human–environment interactions; and they emphasized the importance of ground-truthing, or using ground surveys to test the satellite data.[70] When he published the conference proceedings, Sever made it clear that archaeologists had to master the technology before the "pot hunters," the looters, beat them to it. If only more people had heeded his prescient warning.

The Mississippi conference delegates quickly put into practice what NASA scientists had preached. Tom Sever led the way with the detection of previously unknown ancient roadways at Chaco Canyon.[71] Payson Sheets of the University of Colorado Boulder applied satellite imagery to his rainforest research area in Costa Rica, identifying old paths impossible to see with the naked eye.[72] The data could be applied equally well to prehistoric sites: Pamela Showalter of Texas State University used Landsat data to detect previously unknown segments of a Hohokam canal system near Phoenix, Arizona, dating from around 1050 to 1450 AD.[73]

With additional global satellites such as the French SPOT (Satellite Pour l'Observation de la Terre),[74] archaeologists now had their pick of imagery data sets. Resolution improved drastically, moving from 80 meters to 10 meters in 14 years.

But that still mattered little when most features measured a meter in width or less.

A High-Resolution Solution

In 1999, scientists hailed the newly launched IKONOS as the future of satellite technology. It had a resolution of 1 meter, and its ability to image the surface in the visual and infrared parts of the light spectrum meant archaeologists had their wishes answered, save one: cost.[75]

A single IKONOS image could be many thousands of dollars. Now, we archaeologists may be responsible caretakers of priceless archaeological treasures, but our pockets are always empty. We had to be patient. Fortunately, patience is the one resource in which archaeologists are wealthy.

We didn't have to wait long. The field of space archaeology hit warp speed in the early 2000s. Early adopters had taken on a cohort of students, many of whom finished their PhDs during this time. Papers emerged not just on NASA's satellite data sets, but also on the recently released CORONA spy imagery,[76] and finally, here was imagery we could afford.

With the first international conference on satellite archaeology, held in Beijing in the fall of 2004, the field was on the verge of becoming widely accepted. I mention that conference because I attended it as a PhD student, and it is still considered a key moment in the development of the field.

The attendees at the Beijing conference represented the Satellite Archaeology Hall of Fame. Every big name I cited in my thesis was there: Guo Huadong, the director-general of China's Institute of Remote Sensing and Digital Earth; Ron Blom, the legendary Jet Propulsion Laboratory scientist who worked on the discovery of the "lost" city of Ubar, in Saudi Arabia;[77] Payson Sheets from Sever's original conference,[78] and so many others. I was starstruck by these academic superheroes, and our Chinese colleagues had gone all out to welcome us.

With red crushed-velvet chairs lovingly tied with bows awaiting us in the auditorium, tea servers who rushed to refill our cups the moment we took a sip during talks, and extravagant dinners served in exquisite banquet halls, I thought I had hit the big time. Sign me up for this field! I volunteer as tribute! I only learned as the conference wound down that this represented the best conference any of my senior colleagues had attended in their 40-year careers. As a newbie, I was pretty much screwed because I would never have it this good again, ever.

Nonetheless, my extraordinary colleagues at the conference had opened my eyes to a broader archaeological world—one of collaboration, encouragement, and cheering on, and they showed me that there's a big planet to map and plenty of discoveries to go around.

Space Archaeology Today

Since that conference, the scale of discoveries made by my colleagues at sites and landscapes across the globe is simply mind-blowing. These findings have done nothing less than turn heads, make headlines, and help archaeologists to reinterpret several ancient cultures. And that's before we even mention valuable work protecting heritage from looting. Space archaeology deserves its moment in the sun.

In 2016, Greg and I took a bucket-list trip to Cambodia, where we spent a week in Siem Reap visiting the great temples of the Khmer Empire. I'm going to let you in on an archaeological trade secret: the absolute best part of being an archaeologist, bar none, is voyaging to the ancient parts of the world and getting behind-the-scenes tours from your expert colleagues. We had this glorious opportunity in Siem Reap via my friend Damian Evans, who also happens to be the world expert on LIDAR applications in Southeast Asia.[79]

The tour is one thing. It is something else to sit with your colleague as he spreads out an enormous LIDAR 3-D map of the ancient site and shows you all its anomalies hidden beneath the dense rainforest. The ancient Khmer temples that Damian guided us around were strewn in heaps next to mostly intact walls, just awaiting conservation. I saw it as the block exhibit at our great local science center, where our son loves building structures out of soft blue oversized bricks. Just as excited as he gets, I wanted to start stacking the blocks and rebuilding immediately.

Damian had worked in Siem Reap for over 15 years and used LIDAR—the same laser technology used by the Chases at Caracol—to rewrite our understanding of the Khmer Empire's collapse.[80] The lasers showed the bitter truth that the Khmer people relied far too heavily on unreliable yearly rainfall levels, trying in vain to divert water to their fields by altering landscapes on a large scale. In the face of environmental change, time can simply run out for sophisticated societies: no rainfall at all meant that all the moved land in the world would not save them. The rich culture still survives today in dance, music, and ritual, but the great temples and enclosures swarmed by tourists today saw wide-scale abandonment nearly 500 years ago.[81]

These days, it seems there are headlines every other week regarding the use of high-resolution satellite images to discover hidden archaeological treasures. In September 2017, archaeologists announced the discovery of the lost city of Qalatga Darband in Iraqi Kurdistan,[82] a city that stood near where Alexander the Great fought the Persian emperor Darius III.

Archaeologists first noted a potential site in the region using CORONA spy images. Additional on-site drone data showed the outlines of buildings and blocks. John MacGinnis of the British Museum specifically searched through imagery taken in spring, when differences in the wheat and barley growth formed promising crop marks.[83]

As Qalatga Darband is located in a key area between Eastern and Western influences, archaeologists surveying and excavating there targeted their research to unearth evidence for a temple, wine presses, an inner fort, and a large wall fortifying the city. Work on the ground has only just begun, after years of conflict prevented archaeologists from returning to the site.

Full Circle

Space archaeology has come a long way from its very early days of tethered balloons. In many ways, we have come full circle: from airplanes to outer space, and now, closer to the earth again, with semiautonomous, miniature flying machines that give us far greater control over which areas we're imaging. Drones are a new frontier for site mapping, but they cannot yet be used for mapping major landscapes, and in many parts of the world, they are banned outright.[84] Though it may come sooner than we think, we can still only imagine the day when we will be able to map with a resolution of an inch, seeing individual potsherds on a site's surface from 400 miles up in space. How much new information that process will divulge.

Until then, we should ask what ancient features satellites *can* reveal. Pyramids and temples are amazing things to discover, from the air or on the ground. Those features are rare, though, and represent a tiny fraction of what archaeologists find. We are far more likely to dig up a wall, or a room in a small house. It may seem less glamorous, but trust me, those are the findings that inform history, over time. And, as it turns out, satellites are just the thing to help find them.

3

The Promise of
Space Archaeology

Archaeology invites visions of the mysterious and unknown, fueling common misconceptions about ancient societies. Most of the time, rediscovered "lost cities" and intact tombs make global headlines, but that does not mean archaeologists hack through rainforests to help entire Maya cities emerge from the dense vegetation, perfectly preserved. If only that were true! It'd save us all a lot of time and effort.

Cities rise and fall. Their buildings, whether temples, administrative complexes, workshops, or houses, can collapse from natural disasters or human violence, have their stones repurposed by later cultures, and slowly succumb to Mother Nature once abandoned. Discovering a city is only the beginning. Archaeologists want to know who built it in the first place, who lived there, and where its lost inhabitants went. The real gift is the opportunity to search for those answers.

Complex answers to archaeological questions do not make clickbait headlines, but real archaeology doesn't have to be far-fetched to be fascinating. Consider that in most post-apocalyptic movies, you see hordes of bad guys wearing leather, riding motorcycles, armed to the teeth, and living in bad-guy strongholds. I always wonder where their underlying support system is and ask about the thousands of people tanning their clothing, processing the fuel for their vehicles, and working in the fields to feed them.

Whenever a major discovery is announced, archaeologists see

implications about the culture's people—farmers, stonemasons, artists—and its ecosystem as a whole. The media remains focused on the one tomb, the one religious site, or whatever the find happens to be. Alongside the media, museum curators probably carry some responsibility, when they put together displays designed to draw big crowds.

One such blockbuster exhibit toured the United States years ago, on the objects of everyday life found at Pompeii. Here's what I remember from my visit: dismay and disappointment. Instead of the everyday implements that I had hoped to see, the ones that make my heart go pitter-patter, I saw gold. And more gold. And yes, more gold. I'd say jewelry represented 80 percent of the objects on display. This exhibit toured the country and attracted hundreds of thousands of visitors, and the curators missed an opportunity to educate the public on how we interpret the past.

And frankly, the people I saw there had far greater interest in the everyday objects on display, because they could connect them to their own lives. Admittedly, we could see where archaeologists had found all that jewelry and associate wealth with the corresponding individuals or houses. But wealth doesn't portray the richness of society any more than crazies in dune buggies fully represent post-apocalyptic survival. All that the Pompeii exhibit reinforced was the idea that archaeology deals mainly with shiny things and that those things have more value than a pair of tweezers or a carbonized loaf of bread.

Calculating the Importance of Discoveries

Like those everyday objects, 10 "small" discoveries appearing in minor journals can impact a specific archaeological field far more than any headline-worthy discovery. Now, I'm not saying that blockbusters or headline-worthy archaeology aren't awesome, important, or groundbreaking. Headlines fill our classes, remind people why archaeology is cool, and help justify government support. However, let me help put the discovery of a single intact Egyptian tomb in perspective.

Pharaonic civilization lasted 2,700 years, from the unification of Egypt in 3000 BC to the Ptolemaic Period, which ended in 30 AD with the death of Cleopatra.[1] Tombs of elite figures, the type that make headlines, including those for artisans, high-ranking officials, and royal family members, appeared with more frequency during periods of greater stability. You might expect to find well-provisioned tombs from the Old Kingdom (2700–2200 BC), the Middle Kingdom (2000–1700 BC), the New Kingdom (1550–1000 BC), and the Late–Ptolemaic Periods (600 BC–30 AD). Thus, we have 1,800 years or so when we might find richer tombs.

Population estimates of ancient Egypt vary from 3 million during the Old Kingdom, to 4.5 million during the Roman Period (30–641 AD). Since this is hypothetical, let's stick with the lower estimate. Of those 3 million people, that newsworthy elite formed the uppermost 1 percent. So, for every generation, say, roughly 40 years, since the rich generally lived longer, we can expect to find 30,000 tombs that would raise eyebrows today.

Now we follow through with the math.

Over 1,800 years, 45 generations lived and died, with the top 1 percent constructing 1.35 million elite tombs. In the 200-year history of Egyptology, at most, Egyptologists have discovered approximately 13,500 elite tombs—that's just 1 percent of that 1.35 million total.

Consequently, when an announcement is made about a spectacular new tomb, keep a cool head and look for its contribution to our larger understanding of ancient civilization.

I'm not saying I'm immune to our societal obsession with shiny things. A flash of gold fires everyone's wilder archaeological fantasies. Having just returned from a third excavation season at Egypt's Middle Kingdom capital, modern-day Lisht (which you'll hear more about in later chapters), I had the good fortune of finding gold leaf fragments, and even a dense chunk of gold, that came up from an intrusive tomb to the north of the main burial complex. It had heft, and I spent way longer than I should have staring at it. If unrolled, the fragment would probably cover an area of two US quarters put together; it was not exactly the same as Howard Carter peering into Tutankhamun's tomb for the first time. But in the midst of 17-hour workdays, managing a large team, 5,000 miles away from my son, I needed a shiny hit to perk me up. We all do, sometimes.

Fact, Not Truth

The purpose of archaeology is, to quote Indiana Jones, ". . . the search for *fact*, not *truth*. If it's truth you're interested in, Dr. Tyree's philosophy class is right down the hall." The field has evolved in the past century from one focused on things to one focused on the people behind the things, and the forces that drove people to change. Or not to change.

Most archaeologists would tell you we frame research questions or formulate hypotheses, and then develop strategies to answer and test them. We certainly try to tell the truth, at least in our articles.

Every archaeological field rests on some basic assumptions. For example, ancient Egypt became unified around 3000 BC, and someone wrote the last hieroglyphic inscription discovered so far in 394 AD. We know the general order of kings, and we know something about their family trees, the names of their capital cities, and who built what and when. The framework of our Egyptological tapestry survives.

Much of the weft is, unfortunately, missing. Enough of the design remains for us to generalize, and parts are quite clear, but finding the missing threads, and figuring out how we should weave them back together, is not easy.

The story of everyday past people, across the globe, is only now better understood thanks to applying new scientific methods to archaeology. No less than remote sensing, archaeological science was itself new in the 1960s. Now, we can examine past diseases using DNA and bone analyses,[2] and we can learn what people ate through chemical residues on utensils and pots.[3] Innovations in archaeological dating[4] bring a clearer view of chronology.

From these microscopic fragments of thread, the bigger patterns can be extrapolated. I can speak about Bronze Age collapse, across the Near East and Mediterranean around 1177 BC, only by drawing data from hundreds of sites, osteoarchaeological analysis of thousands of individuals, tens of thousands of lab samples, and hundreds of thousands of collective hours spent in the field.[5] Archaeological analysis can be reached only by tiptoeing across the shoulders of swaths of scientific giants.

You have to learn this knowledge assembly young. Because I am an annoying professor who likes to make her students think, I assigned an exercise to my Archaeological Theory class, composed mainly of upper-year anthropology majors, using something I had found in the Metropolitan Museum of Art's online catalogue.[6] It was a square, pinkish ceramic object with a pinched nose and two holes for eyes that looked a lot like my son's kindergarten art projects. I asked my students for information about its cultural context, manufacture, and function. We rarely work on sites where no previous information exists about that culture or time period, but I challenged my students to start from a place of ignorance. Formulating thoughts and ideas about the piece without any additional information proved a large hurdle for them.

No two papers were identical. Some defaulted to the traditional object interpretation that archaeologists offer when we have no clue: "cultic or ritual in nature," with accompanying ideas of just how the culture used it. Each student used the entirety of their archaeological knowledge to interpret the piece; I was fascinated by their responses and impressed with their creativity. One student even hacked the system, putting the object into Google's image search program (outsmarted again!), and one student knew already.

Once they learned what the object represented—an execration piece, buried by individuals to defeat their enemies magically—they had a lot of questions, starting with, "How could we ever have guessed?" Ah grasshopper, you get the point! To know anything about the function of an object requires so much more than the object in isolation, which is why a dig team pools such varied expertise.

How a Dig Works

Every time you go into the field, you risk your reputation, and even your life. You are typically using someone else's money and a whole lot of other people's time, and you have probably spent years preparing your research and applying for funding. Not only that, but you may be navigating another country with associated cultural and linguistic challenges.

Once in the field, as a dig director, you are responsible for the team of specialists there to record the site and its specific data. Each supervising archaeologist takes copious notes and samples from every layer or area dug, typically called a locus, treating each as a distinct 3-D time capsule and recording details about its soil, color, density, material culture, bones, and anything else.[7]

Site supervisors are only the first contributors in the process of extracting archaeological data. Bioarchaeologists analyze human remains, paleobotanists look at preserved plant fragments, artists draw and interpret objects, and cataloguing and documenting finds is the job of registrars and photographers.[8] I have come to believe that ceramists are your most important people.[9] They draw, record, and analyze pottery, and on most historic sites, potsherds beyond number represent the Tupperware of the ancient world. How and why pottery changed over time can be your best insights into the past.

Many others may also join the team, but a spread of specialists like this makes up the core unit on most digs. Ideally, a dig runs like clockwork, with everyone working toward a common goal so you can write articles about the findings, apply for more funding, and do it all again. Another thread gets added to the tapestry . . . if all goes well.

You can imagine maniacal laughter here, because I've been on digs all over the world, and absolutely any challenge imaginable can and does arise. The public never sees this side of excavations—you only see the object in the archaeologist's hand in the perfectly lit glossy magazine photo. Colleagues tell me stories from the field that I would not believe had similar things not happened to me. When our team worked in Sinai in 2004, I came back to the site after breakfast one day to find that our site drawings had become the midmorning snack of a goat from the nearby town. He ran away, and I tackled him, saving about 70 percent of the plans. It took us hours to redraw everything. At the season's end, we had a feast, courtesy of our lovely Bedouin workforce, and the pièce de résistance was roasted goat. No points for guessing which one. I chewed with great relish.

Context Is Everything

If the goat had munched the lot, it would have been a disaster. We have one shot to record every possible fragment of meaning, for to dig is to destroy; once you have excavated a level, or a whole site, it is gone forever. When archaeologists uncover an object, they record its exact location to give context relating to everything else found on that site and other sites like it. For example, finding burned pots next to a flat area that has a stone oven and is covered in plant debris and seeds might indicate an ancient kitchen. If we miss things, or worse, if the site is looted and the pot surfaces for sale, all we can say about it is that it is a "blackened pot."

Archaeological sites are, occasionally, just like a box of chocolates:

you genuinely never know what you are going to get. It is what makes our work so exciting. When archaeologists know little to nothing about a site, we make assumptions based on other similar sites in the region. Sometimes we get it right, but often, we are spectacularly wrong. The irony is that the ingrained awareness of just how wrong we are likely to be is what drives us ahead. Applications to the grant review committees sometimes couch everything we think is there as "maybe," "potential," and "likely," when we perhaps ought to write, "I haven't the faintest idea, so send us there anyway to find out."

What is at stake is nothing less than the sum total of human history and knowledge. No pressure.

To limit needless destruction during excavation, and to keep our work on time and within budget, we dig in the most focused way we possibly can.

If used well, space archaeology can give us a pretty good idea of structures or features at a site, or at least, just below its top layer. Being able to develop hypothesis-driven research on what *is* there versus what *might* be is game-changing.

We can see neither potsherds nor individual occupation levels on satellite imagery. But we can see walls, entire buildings, geoglyphs like the Nazca lines,[10] vanished landscapes, and relationships between site and site, and between site and landscape, in ways we could not 40 years ago, in places we would never have thought to check. With ever-improving use of the light spectrum and new programs to manipulate images, we now can highlight such features, when they would have been easily missed or altogether invisible before.

Satellite imagery allows us to see features at varying scales, from the very small to the overwhelming, and boy, can we use the help. When we spend so much time squinting at the ground, we need some perspective.

Traces of the Vikings

A good place to illustrate this is an island in the North Atlantic, famous for its geysers, Vikings, gender equality, and unpronounceable volcano names. The landscape is as tough as the Vikings' reputation: to survive in Iceland requires extraordinary strength and resilience. Starting in 871 +/-2 AD, the Vikings came to Iceland from their conquest of Scotland's Western Isles to build farms, though whether people lived there prior to 871 is controversial. An Irish monk may have written about Iceland as early as 825, referring to possible settlers there in the late 790s.[11]

Whether from a colonization mission blown off course, or people brought to Iceland by Scandinavian Vikings as slaves, farming communities expanded across Iceland quickly.[12] *The Book of Settlements*, also known as the *Landnámabók*, records a genealogy of the first 430 Viking settlers of Iceland.[13] From that meticulous Viking start, Icelanders are still obsessed with their genealogies:[14] for any concerned Icelanders, there is even a dating app to ensure they don't end up in bed with a close cousin.[15]

You can forgive me for thinking, as an Egyptologist, that I would never in a million years have any reason to work in Iceland. There are fairies,[16] not pharaohs, and the only pyramids you'd find would be those made of snow in sculpture competitions. I do like a challenge, and life is strange, but I still never expected my work to lead me across the North Atlantic.

Small Farms, Big Farms, and Viking Colonization

The Skagafjörður Church and Settlement Survey is a collaborative archaeological project between the Skagafjörður Heritage Museum and the Fiske Center at the University of Massachusetts Boston.

Led by a handsomely bearded archaeologist named Doug Bolender—who would not have seemed out of place in Iceland 1,000 years ago, save for his extreme politeness—the project focuses on Iceland's 9th-century colonization and later development, and how it may have affected the performance of religious and economic units in the 14th century.

I met Doug during the research phase of a BBC TV program I was involved in about Vikings.[17] He and his team, using ground-based remote sensing[18] and coring, were pushing the boundaries of Icelandic landscape archaeology, and he was keen for a collaboration using satellite imagery.

We know a great deal about early Icelandic history because of the famous and very well-preserved medieval sagas.[19] You can see them on display in Reykjavík, in the aptly named Settlement Exhibition

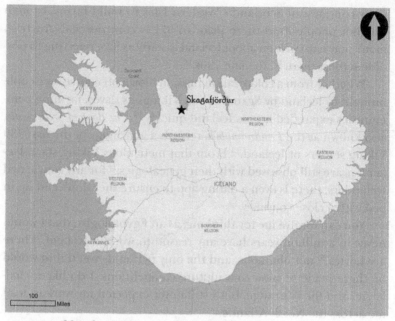

Map showing location of Skagafjörður in northern Iceland
[MAP COURTESY CHASE CHILDS]

Reykjavík 871 +/-2, where visitors can walk around a real Viking long-house and see amazing holographic videos of daily life in early Ice-land.[20]

These reconstructions gave me a few clues as to what I might be looking for from space in northern Iceland, some 200 kilometers from Reykjavík. There, clouds seem to float right in front of you, and the sharp slopes of mountains lead to emerald-green farmland that rolls down to the edge of the ocean, as far as the eye can see.

The early Icelanders typically built structures with cut turf, just like the strips rolled out on golf courses, readily available across the entire country. Unlike Scandinavia, where oak trees abounded for longhouse construction, Iceland had only driftwood and birch,[21] used mainly for house framing, with turf for walls and roofs.[22] Turf is essentially a giant, soft Lego and is very warm; I spent a lot of time petting the walls on the Viking sites I visited. On a freezing cold day, a small fire will keep a turf building quite toasty, and the Vikings used turf for their main longhouses and nearly all their farm buildings.

These larger buildings are a bit easier to see archaeologically, while smaller outbuildings can be more ambiguous. Doug and his team had developed intensive survey techniques to map larger farmsteads, for example, by following ancient trash deposits or middens[23] close to more noticeable central farm buildings, but they had trouble locating the smaller buildings. It was not economically feasible for them to dig test pits every 5 meters, and the chances of missing the outbuildings would still be high.

Putting the Imagery to the Test

My team and I had already searched Iceland using Google Earth, attempting to get a sense of what Icelandic structures looked like from space—we needed to see the full Viking-to-modern range of farm and building types. Ancient field boundaries still in use today are easy to spot, though most of what's visible on the surface is not Viking, but post-Norwegian rule (1262–1380 AD). Many of the sites we "discovered" were already known,[24] but at least we got a good sense of the types of features to look for, their sizes, and their possible spatial relationships to the main farmsteads.

But here's the big problem: typically, in the United Kingdom, you find a ditch buried in a field, or, in Egypt, a stone tomb in the desert. Material X is very different from soil/sand/vegetation Y, and enough of the building material has degraded on the surface to be detectable from space using parts of the light spectrum we cannot see. It is invisible, or barely visible, on the ground. But here in Iceland, my team and I needed to find the foundations of small, degraded ancient turf structures, hidden in massive turf fields. That's a needle in a haystack made of needles.

The BBC thought it would be fun to go needle hunting during a live recording. After we analyzed the satellite imagery, several intriguing spots appeared in the Skagafjörður survey area. Doug selected some of them to search for using a simple auger—a small, handheld drill about two inches across. He explained that it was a million-to-one chance of hitting Viking archaeology with the core.

He and his team had the coordinates of the structure we had seen from space, and they did their best to flag its location by measuring out from the field edges. Satellite imagery can be off by a few meters, which is not a big deal when you have other nearby structures to calibrate distance, but these walls measured less than 1 meter across. Even a small error would mean that we would miss them entirely.

We approached one of Doug's flagged areas. He asked me to stamp down on the core and give it a twist, so I did. It was like my first time on a pogo stick. I got rejected live on camera by the hard ground, which did wonders for my confidence and earned numerous snickers from the team.

"Once more! With feeling," Doug said. Somehow I got the thing in the ground and then twisted. We went down about 20 centimeters.

Doug pulled it up, flipped it open, and cut the turf tube in half. He had a huge smile on his face.

"Do you have any idea what you are looking at?"

"It'd be strange if I did," I replied. He pointed out cool grayish-white lines crisscrossing the turf and explained that each one represented a volcanic eruption.[25] Iceland's volcanoes are consistently lively. Datable by corroboration with ice-core and tree-ring dating, eruptions occurred before, during, and after the main period of Viking occupation, so Icelandic archaeologists can use their evidence in the soil to estimate the date of occupation layers. Doug then pointed to the bottom part of the core.

"What you have here is a piece from a turf wall! Probably medieval."

Talk about reassured. We then dug a quick test trench to expose part of the wall.

While I was disappointed to learn the wall was not Viking, Doug and his team assured me that it was a big step for them. Still, I had hoped it would be easier to spot potential Norse remains, versus medieval, from the satellite imagery. Not helping were all the modern people living on top of ancient Viking farms. Things would obviously be much harder than I had anticipated.

Meanwhile, Back at the Dig House

That night after dinner—though "night" in Iceland during August is a relative term—we gathered in the dig house. Red-and-white survey poles leaned against the walls, surrounded by muddy shoes and coats. It wasn't Egypt, but I felt at home. Doug was hunched over his computer with a team member looking at 3-D reconstructions of the day's excavation work created from aerial photos.[26]

After geeking out at beautiful photographs of excavated burials, I joined Doug's motley crew at a long table, where everyone was at work processing the data they had collected that day. I started reexamining the satellite imagery of the area and noticed the strange image angle—it looked as if a giant had twisted a massive checkerboard.

It made no sense at first. But now, having visited the landscape, I saw how the foot of the mountain sloped gently down to the water. This can cause distortion on satellite imagery. If you didn't know you were looking at it, that would be easy to miss.[27]

Armed with new, on-the-ground knowledge—landscape, vegetation type, and what buried turf actually looked like underfoot—I began to reprocess the satellite data and adapt the processing techniques. The time crept on, but my internal clock barely registered a second. The sand in the hourglass just floated.

As curious shapes started to emerge, I asked the Viking specialists what they thought. Getting instantaneous feedback and encouragement from the experts of a site as I processed the data must have been the most satisfying scientific evening of my career.

Eventually, I had about a half dozen features—walls maybe?—that the team agreed would be well worth exploring. I left at about 2:30 a.m., walking on the thin air of the early morning up the hill to my tiny hotel room. I took a final look at the gray-brown mountains exploding out of the ground, and the absolute stillness froze me in place. It was a land purpose-built for legends, and it seemed appropriate to thank Odin and Freya for their blessings.

Several of those buried features did indeed end up dating to the Viking period.

Finding outbuildings may not seem like much, nor do they make headlines, but they set archaeologists' minds alight. Tiny details matter to us. Outbuildings, collectively, tell us how the larger structures and farms could function. When a central farmhouse has associated buildings like a dairy for storing milk and a smithy for smelting iron tools, chances are good the farm was doing well. A lack of outbuildings adds other details to the bigger picture, and suggests the farmers were poor, perhaps struggling. And if the larger farms had shrunk over time, that shrinkage might be connected to declining resources caused by war, famine, or climate change. Now we don't just have a small building. We have a story.

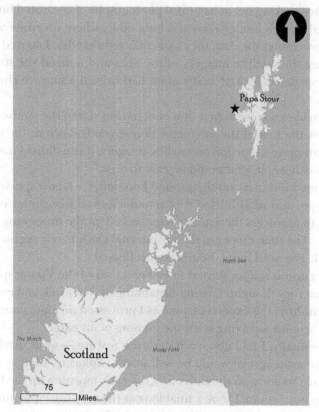

Map showing location of Papa Stour
[MAP COURTESY CHASE CHILDS]

Small walls represent a tiny piece of what satellite imagery can discover. Sometimes an accidental find or something you dismiss as modern can turn out to be so much more.

From Iceland to Scotland

On the northwestern tip of the United Kingdom, the Shetland Isles are a craggy mass of hills, sheep, and fields. Some 1,300 years ago, the Vikings made their way 300 kilometers west from Norway and conquered the area.[28] By the ninth century AD, they had established a stone-built stronghold at Jarlshof, the largest visible Viking site in the United Kingdom, which was occupied for nearly 500 years.[29]

Here, in Scotland, again, my team and I were tasked with locating probable Norse sites. In each case, we'd study the region, poring over excavation and survey reports for what we might discover. Once we determined that a site had potential, we examined satellite databases for local imagery. No imagery, no go.

And it had to be the right imagery. We needed data from the summer or early fall for maximum differences in vegetation health.[30] We chose eight sites for ground investigation. On some, we could see Viking construction clearly. A longhouse is a longhouse is a longhouse.

Except when it isn't. At one promising site in Scotland, we saw a clear curving wall in turf and got excited. When a team went out to examine the location, they found the farmers had cut a longhouse-shaped building out of the modern turf, just to trick us.

A Rune with a View

And then there was the case of North House in Papa Stour. About 50 years ago, Andy Holt and Sabina Holt-Brook moved to a tiny island on the western side of the Shetlands to raise their family. A visionary young couple, they wanted to create a sustainable, organic farm, 40 years before such homesteads came into vogue. Naturally, when people dig their garden, they remove old bricks and debris. At North House, the couple kept finding odd carved stones, which they kept in a basket by the door. One day they discovered a larger angled disk with etched markings.

When they showed the find to local experts, they were excited to learn they had a loom stone, used by Vikings in weaving wool.[31] This one was special: it was marked with runes, Norse writing, showing that whoever had used it was literate. Literacy was rare and elite. Somewhere on their property was a rich Viking settlement or structure.

When our team processed satellite data from Papa Stour, a series of clear straight lines appeared next to North House. My recommendation was to dismiss the site. It seemed suspiciously modern. Given the way we had processed the data, the feature showed up as a lurid pink stripe. It was probably a gas or water line.

We sent all the processed data to various experts for assessment. When I learned the BBC had chosen Papa Stour as their site to film, I was shocked. I emailed them.

On-the-ground photo of the excavated wall near North House
[PHOTO BY THE AUTHOR]

"Hey, that place ranked last for us, eighth out of the eight sites for which we had data. Do you want to film digging up a 19th-century water line?"

I was told the decision was out of my hands and to get ready to fly to Scotland.

Once again an Egyptologist in a strange land, I met the BBC producer in one of the tiniest airports ever. My son's Playmobil airport serves more people. From there, we drove quickly to make the ferry. Beyond the stinging spray of the water, an otherworldly landscape rolled by. Sheep dotted the rugged green outcrops around us, moving like mist-shrouded cotton balls.

"So, have you found anything interesting yet?" I asked the director, Nathan. He gave me a cryptic smile.

"You'll see."

Something I do not understand about the television world is their yen for a big reveal with the presenter, to catch the "Oh my God!" moment of discovery. It frustrated the crap out of me. The team from the local archaeology unit had worked at Papa Stour for two days, but I was in the dark.

We arrived at North House, now a beautiful bed-and-breakfast after its earlier life as a commune in the 1970s, overlooking the gray-blue Norwegian Sea. Normally, B&Bs do not have bowls of Norse artifacts that greet you as you walk inside. The production team kept me away from the excavations in the back garden until I was miked up. By then, the director had a wicked glint in his eye.

The Anomalous Anomaly

Given the mood and joking atmosphere, I anticipated good news, but nothing prepared me for when I walked through the gate and saw the exposed "anomaly" in a 20-by-10-meter garden, with the sea cliffs to the left and the fairy-tale house on the right.

It was a stone structure, some 15 meters long, as if a slate garden wall had sunk a meter into the ground, with additional stone offshoots. I realized, in that moment, that my caution had nearly cost us the chance to see something ancient. The "whoa" from me captured on camera is genuine.

The Regional Archaeologist for Shetland, Val Turner, met me for a tour. Prior to excavating, the team used a simple probe, proving low tech can work just as well as high tech, and had started to dig in two trenches: one near the central part of the wall, and another to the south, where it seemed to disappear. The wall was strongly built, with well-laid slate flooring, while the southern trench had something even more exciting: fragments of soapstone vessels that hinted at the site's Viking date.[32]

Over the next two days, I got to play in the 1,200-year-old sandbox. Digging deeper in the northern trench, we found layers of floor after floor, suggesting that there had been at least 400 years of occupation at the site. During a tea break at the North House kitchen table, Tom Horne, an archaeologist and friend with boundless energy, came bouncing up to me with an impish grin. He whispered to the director, who said, "Outside, now!"

When archaeologists uncover an extraordinary object, the energy of a site changes. Everyone looks like children on Christmas who have gotten exactly what they want. There was an electricity in the garden.

Carnelian jewel excavated at the dig site near North House
[PHOTO BY THE AUTHOR]

"Hold out your hand," said Tom and placed a lustrous orange-brown gemstone into my palm.

"What!" I exclaimed. "How did you see this?"

"I have magic eyes. Just like your satellites."

I held the dime-sized stone between my thumb and forefinger. Faceted and polished, it would not have been out of place in any modern ring. At first it looked like amber, but holding it up to the light, I saw a fiery orange glow.

Carnelian! Even better. It reminded me of my archaeological home some 2,500 miles away, where the ancient Egyptians loved carnelian for their jewelry.[33] For the Vikings, carnelian was an elite item, only found on sites like Birka, in Sweden, a major trading center.[34] It likely was mined somewhere in the region of the Black Sea. Whoever owned that piece, whether set into a brooch or a ring, had been a very important person.

Putting the evidence together, we recognized that we had a potential Norse stronghold on our hands.

In a document written in 1299, a corruption case was brought against a local ruler, Lord Thorvald Thoresson,[35] who had been accused of embezzling rent collections. He wanted to show his innocence, so he invited witnesses to testify. One of these witness meetings may have happened in the living room of the future ruler of Norway, Duke Haakon, somewhere on Papa Stour. Prior to our work there, archaeologists had pinpointed the duke's farm as the Biggings, an excavated 12th- and 13th-century AD structure.[36]

But this new Viking structure, located in a strategic position next to a beach, could actually represent his home. After a few days' excavation, we had barely scraped the surface, literally, and had already uncovered numerous rooms. Walking on the beach below, I could see obvious stone walls exposed along the cliff edge, showing that the site was once far bigger. Sadly, I had to leave, and the excavation was backfilled to protect it. More discoveries await us there in future.

Amped for Amphitheaters

I admit when I am wrong, and now that I am the mother of a very loud and opinionated five-year-old, I am reminded often when I am. The Papa Stour case kept me on my toes and has since made me question all my ambiguous results.

However, the most embarrassing moment of my career took place six years earlier, when I was expecting that five-year-old. On a previous BBC program, I had the chance to collaborate with a team in Italy that turned my own perception of new technologies, both space and ground based, on its head.

Flying into Rome's Fiumicino airport, you can look down and see a strange hexagon amid the urbanized landscape and fields.

Just a stone's throw from the runway lies one of Italy's most fascinating archaeological sites, Portus, where some of mapping's hottest technological developments are being applied. Portus was Rome's great trading center about 1,900 years ago. Located along the Mediterranean coastline in antiquity, it was founded under Emperor Claudius in 42 AD and expanded by Emperor Trajan during his reign between 98 and 117 AD, serving as a key redistribution center connected to the major port of Ostia nearby.[37] Today, the ancient coastline is 4 kilometers inland, as silt deposited over time by the River Tiber has gradually filled in the large, protected harbor.[38]

The ancient site had a great deal in common with an Amazon warehouse of today. Goods flowed into Portus from across the Roman

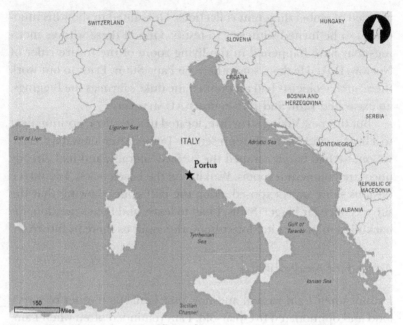

Map showing location of Portus [MAP COURTESY CHASE CHILDS]

Empire, from Egyptian wines to Arabian perfumes. Sailing into the harbor, ships were guided by a lighthouse designed after the famous lighthouse of Alexandria. The vessels then eased into the hexagonal basin to dock at warehouses and off-load. Boat repair sheds also dotted the basin, one-stop shopping for captains and warehouse managers. Goods were loaded onto smaller boats, which sailed northeast toward Rome along the Tiber. Because of its bustling shipping business, Portus was a thriving community, with housing, warehouses, roads, a cemetery, and a marble quarry.[39] And probably a dozen brothels, speaking of delivery.

There is a rich history of archaeological exploration at Portus. Today, Simon Keay, an affable professor based at the University of Southampton, leads the excavations there. For over 30 years, Simon and his team have used a wide range of ground-based remote sensing tools to map large areas of the site. In many ways, they have rewritten the book on approaches to landscape archaeology for ancient Rome, while their discoveries, such as the function of the boat repair sheds, have cast light on international trade.

Modern land use has created unusual challenges for them. Today, Portus is a complex place amid a mishmash of modern buildings and mixed-use fields. The central part sits within an archaeological park, but the rest lies outside it, and the amount of planning and detailed work required to map this disconnected landscape is enormous.

The excavators had been working with ground-penetrating radar (GPR), aerial photographs, and magnetometry so far,[40] but not high-resolution satellite imagery. Simon asked if I would like to collaborate. I was apprehensive. Simon is an absolute legend and a lovely human being to boot, and I don't like to wave imagery at site directors in areas about which I know little or nothing. But he told me he had been searching for a major amphitheater at Portus for years, and to date, had not found it.

Finding Roman Sites Is Not as Easy as You Think

A word on Roman sites: Rome, with its rich empire and monumental construction, leaves obvious, massive stone foundations easy to find at a glance. Just like the Colosseum, right? Wrong.

With rapid urbanization, reuse of stone, and field tilling over 2,000 years, many sites have been partly or completely covered over. Ancient texts might describe a theater, amphitheater, or hippodrome (a horse-racing stadium), yet they may be invisible to modern archaeologists. Those that remain well preserved survive mostly by luck or accident. If modern towns have absorbed the sites over altogether, this raises significant issues when processing satellite imagery. Differentiating a solid signal from background noise can be the greatest challenge for space archaeologists.[41] Knowing what *should* be at a site or in a landscape may seem like the correct archaeological process, going from the known to unknown, but it can bias our perception.

And it can even lead us to find shapes where there are none—a psychological phenomenon called pareidolia; put technically, after spending hours processing satellite data, your eyes go funny. You see things where there is nothing, or miss things entirely. That's why working in a team is crucial, so you can cross-check each other or just tell a weary or overenthusiastic colleague that he or she is smoking crack.

But this project arose before I really had my team together. I knew enough about ancient Roman structures to get me in trouble, having written half my dissertation on Late Roman Period Egypt, though not enough to feel confident about my imagery processing. But I had to start somewhere. After familiarizing myself with Simon's findings from his publications, I ordered a GeoEye-1 .5meter resolution satellite image from the summer of 2010, during a particularly dry period. This imagery had visible data as well as an infrared band.

Since most of the construction at Portus was of stone, and there were old river channels to be found as well, I was happy with summer imagery and hoped for good crop marks. And did it produce! Houses, large rectangular buildings, roads—over a dozen structures appeared. I was quite proud of these discoveries and sent them off to Simon and his team, expecting to be showered with praise. My poor swollen ego was burst the next morning.

"It's great the satellite imagery picked these up!" Simon said. "We've known about them for years." Sadly, I must have missed a publication or two before my hours of work.

After the primal scream, the Ball of Shame under my desk, and lots of chocolate, in that order, I did not know what to do next. Surely the processing I had done had revealed all that could be seen there from space.

If at First You Don't Succeed . . .

Perhaps a slightly different image from a different time of year might show more. And I got lucky: DigitalGlobe's WorldView-2 satellite image with a broader spectral range had just become available from the previous September, during the driest fall that part of Italy had seen in years.[42] This data had visible bands, called "red edge" bands, covering the light spectrum between the visible red and the infrared, and two infrared bands. With eight bands of data instead of four in the earlier satellite imagery, the WorldView-2 imagery allowed us to do a better job of detecting subtle differences in vegetation health.[43]

After I processed the data to emphasize those differences, a curious 40-meter-wide ovoid shape appeared in the fields to the northeast of the hexagonal basin. With eastern and western entrances connected to an east-west road, and rectangular buildings on the shape's northern face, it was so clear that I dismissed it as likely something modern, probably some type of 19th-century water cistern. But, just to be safe, I sent it to Simon to get his opinion.

WorldView-2 processed satellite image of amphitheater feature
[IMAGE COURTESY DIGITALGLOBE]

He got *very* excited. A magnetometry survey there had revealed nothing like what the imagery showed, and they had not yet been able to do ground-penetrating radar. But this looked just like an amphitheater, with possible training barracks attached. Looking at nearly 80-year-old aerial photography taken during a similarly dry period, we realized we could see its faint outlines there, too.[44] Now that we knew what to look for, it became obvious. Finally, we had an exciting result!

Simon, his ground survey specialist, Kristian Strutt, and I wrote a paper about our results, comparing the satellite imagery to ground-based remote sensing tools such as magnetometry and GPR, as well as aerial photography.[45] As excited as I get about space imagery, I know it has limitations; used together with ground-based remote-sensing tools as force multipliers, it becomes even more powerful.

Simon and his team plan to explore the amphitheater in the future. Chasing it down was an essential lesson for me in not giving up and being willing to go back to the drawing board.

If you apply the right analytical techniques from the right time of year, space archaeology can highlight an astonishing range of sites, no matter where you're looking or which ancient culture you're hoping to find. From the very large to the small, using everything from

.3-meter to 30-meter data, you can crack the discovery code by understanding the landscape and its geology, and the building materials that environment provided.

These discoveries are mere hints of the insights now available to archaeologists thanks to new technologies, but it is never just about the discovery, or even new theories. This is about shaking archaeological foundations, testing new ideas that sometimes work well and sometimes leave more questions than answers.

4

A Risky Business

Archaeology tells us who we are, where we come from, and how we got here. The temptation to tilt at the windmills of archaeology is huge, though, even when there is just the tiniest chance of success, and I know this from experience. After years of good fortune in my chosen field of work, I had my own Don Quixote moment of taking aim far outside my area of expertise.

But let's start at the beginning. If you are intrigued by those grand questions, it's important to learn how you take up archaeology in the first place. For some, it's a family occupation. Others took a class in college that changed everything. Most have known since childhood that the dirt, and the past, called to them. But the reality is far different from any Hollywood fantasies: hard work, sacrifice, and lots of luck are needed in abundant measure to get an archaeological job, and any groundbreaking discoveries come after years of staring at laptops or scrabbling down dusty holes, both often with a good deal of physical discomfort thrown in.

Who even gets to call themselves an archaeologist is confusing. Sadly, as far as I am aware, no Archaeological Fairy Godmother exists, ready to bless you with your own trowel when you have gained enough experience points. (Though if she were real, I think she would wear a lot of leather.) Most archaeologists in North America start by majoring in anthropology, classics, Near Eastern studies, or art history. In the United Kingdom, archaeology and anthropology are separate, though aligned, fields. In Europe and in many universities around the Mediterranean, you study archaeology as part of your main field focus, for example, Turkey or the Roman Empire. Often, across the world, students study for a tourism degree alongside the archaeology degree, as the field pays so little in comparison to other professions.

With so many struggles awaiting you, you'd be forgiven for wondering why you'd bother. Kent Flannery, the granddaddy of today's archaeological generation, wrote a piece satirizing his 1980s colleagues, in which he describes an "Old Timer," a hero, a true for-the-love-of-it digger, who famously describes archaeology as "the most fun you can have with your pants on."[1] For so many people I know, the intoxicating nature of discovery and the idea of protecting heritage are worth the trade-off against financial stability.

So You Want to Run a Dig?

Some people I meet think that becoming a dig director means you have achieved the greatest glory possible. All I can say is, be careful what you wish for, because it is a long and lonesome road. You start as a project volunteer, learning the ropes for a few seasons. You may become an area unit supervisor, and after that a field supervisor or a field director, with the responsibility of managing all the excavation work. Depending on your graduate research, you may be the on-site specialist in seeds, animal remains, or epigraphy—drawing and translating ancient inscriptions.

In time, and if you're lucky enough to have funding, you formulate original research questions and might strike out on your own, at a smaller part of your supervisor's site or at another site entirely. In that case, my condolences, er, I mean congratulations!

Most of us work up that way, step by step. Long before I directed my own dig in Egypt, I learned by watching others. I was lucky to see Greg in charge of projects in Sinai and the Delta, before, during, and after my PhD. At the time, I relished the chance to focus on my dig square. No one bothered me the entire day as I worked with my crew, recorded my notes, drew my site plans, and watched Greg deal with a hundred messes to which I should have paid far more attention.

I didn't appreciate how difficult managing a team in Egypt is. When finally leading my first dig, I went from a happy digger straight to a stressed-out, ancient-world CEO, something I don't think anyone is quite ready for. Fortunately, I had a small team to start and a wonderful husband to help me when I was falling flat on my face.

Customarily, about six months before every dig season, I spend the better part of a month putting together my application. Every team member needs to submit a CV and a passport page and fill out a security form. Bungled paperwork can and does prevent team members from taking part. Endless correspondence follows—coordinating, planning, sorting plane tickets and airport pickups—all in preparation for one month of work in the field. I'd like to go for longer, like in the old days, pre-job, pre-house, pre-child, but life gets complicated.

Then there are the innumerable Skype calls with my Egyptian foreman to plan meals, secure a work crew, and manage the transportation of the supplies. Even reviewing the supply inventory involves chains of international emails: trowels, Sharpies, graph paper, clipboards, good compasses . . . it's all time-consuming to find in Cairo and must be shipped in. None of this can get started until after my grant transfer has cleared at the bank, which always happens at the last minute. And you have no idea how finicky you have to be, juggling airline weight allowance bag by bag, to transport an excavation.

Then we have the busy Cairo runaround. I arrive four or five days early and set up meetings with all the appropriate government officials to share season plans, get feedback, and sign my official paperwork. By this time, team members are flying in from all over the world and can help with the massive, pre-dig shopping spree. Our carts fill up with a mix of the mundane and eclectic, from solid wooden desks for our registration team to toilet paper and even cases of tonic water. I mean, this is Egypt, which contains both G and T, and 5 p.m. comes fast every day. We have a tradition to uphold.

Once the dig begins, I'm a combination hotel manager, menu planner, nurse, and diplomat. I also manage the budget, which, thank goodness, Greg helps with. Every day I do rounds with my senior staff to make sure they have everything they need, and I meet with whichever officials or colleagues have visited that day.

Our food on-site is always wonderful, as we have a great team of local cooks who take pride in feeding us well. I am a foodie and appreciate how true is the saying that an army marches on its stomach. Accommodations on digs vary, but even a good room one day can turn into free bathroom waterworks the next. And then weather. Ah, weather. Egypt is all sunshine, if you discount the heavy winds, sand-storms, and unexpected winter rains.

And whatever happens, people need taking care of. I have a core staff of 15, a main Egyptian professional digging staff of 8, and a workforce of more than 70, including day labor, police, and guards. The buck stops with me. Running an excavation is the biggest and most awesome responsibility I have ever had, and getting your own trowel in the ground can sometimes be frustratingly far down on the to-do list.

But here's the thing: as director, you do all this to get the best work possible out of your team. Gathering world-class experts, mak-ing sure they are healthy and happy and that your work crew is well paid and safe is all in a day's work, because in the end, that's what you need to achieve your vision and your dream—lots of help. So you celebrate and honor both your professional staff and your workforce in all your talks and publications, and you never forget that you could not do it without them. It's the best damn job on the planet.

With all this at stake, you now have a sense of what drives people in archaeology. We are always struggling on to the next step in the yellow brick road: the PhD, a postdoc position, a job, tenure, a pro-motion, a grant. Most people work their whole lives to retire and travel; we archaeologists keep working to keep digging, and we would all do it for free. Most of us have worked for free, at some point, though we shouldn't have to.

If only all the press of dramatic discoveries translated into real-world funding or university support. Fame is not the driver in archae-ology, and it hinders as often as it helps. Instead, we are driven by insatiable curiosity. Our inner child keeps asking the universe, why? We're always impatient for just one more trowel scrape. You never know. It could happen. The pieces might just fit together, this once.

To Boldly Go . . .

Bold claims require bold testing. When doing high-risk science, you increase your chances of getting funded from impossible to maybe 1 in 1,000 by creating testable hypotheses with a solid research design and building an outstanding research team. Caution is key. Despite the high stakes, you must make it clear to all stakeholders that the chance for success is narrow. The reward comes from the contribution you *might* make to history. Even if it seems like madness.

Last chapter, you might have been wondering what the heck I was doing, as an Egyptologist, making a TV show looking for Vikings in cold places, so let me give you the backstory. In 2013, when our son was not quite one year old, I had just completed a documentary with the BBC on the Roman Empire. The History Channel show *Vikings* had just begun, and a blockbuster Vikings exhibition and conference at the British Museum was opening. Perhaps sensing a trend, the BBC proposed the new program.

I responded with a polite email asking if, perhaps, they had forgotten my specialization. I did pyramids, not longhouses. With my research on the Late Roman Empire, moving a bit east, west, and north to find Roman sites was reasonable, but searching for Viking sites seemed like a leap too far. I laid it out straight: given that I had a small child, most of my days were already taken up searching for diapers and wipes.

I thought that had ended the matter and soon forgot I'd ever been asked. Until the next summer. Greg and I were visiting dear friends in London, and somehow the BBC caught wind of it and asked me to have a quick lunch with an executive producer to discuss a potential show. Over fish and chips and a very loud toddler, the executive producer tried to sell me on the idea of looking for potential Norse sites in Canada and elsewhere. Again, I tried to dissuade him. At that time, I taught a module on the Vikings in my introductory archaeology class, but that was it. Then he incanted certain magic words: "We'll pay for all the research costs."

Ah. My weakness. An offer like that does not often come along. Maybe I needed a bit of a change. Maybe it was the hard cider over lunch—I do love a pint of cider. Maybe I was so jet-lagged and toddlered-out that I'd temporarily lost my mind. I do not remember saying yes, but I obviously did, because when we got home, I was greeted by all sorts of budget-related emails about the project.

I already had a team at home to help with the project. Dave Gathings, a magnetometry specialist conversant with obscure mapping solutions and the entire Beatles output, and Chase Childs, a techno whiz kid fresh from a Cambridge MPhil, were on call to dive in. And I had a very excited husband, who had nearly majored in medieval archaeology at university and could not wait for the chance to visit Viking sites and help with background research. There were countless Norse specialists on whom I could call and with whom I could collaborate. What could go wrong?

Well, everything.

Thousands of other explorers, adventurers, and archaeologists have searched for evidence of Viking presence in North America. In Minnesota, people claim to have found Viking runestones.[2] In Maine, a legitimate discovery of a Viking coin at a Native American site suggests some form of contact with or perhaps transitory exploration of New England.[3] Many people also think there are more Viking sites to be found in eastern Canada and, perhaps, along the northeast coast of the United States.[4] They're not wrong to hope.

To picture Norse expansion from the fjords of northern Europe and Iceland, imagine how rapidly Iceland filled with farmers and how their sons and daughters carved up more and more of the arable land.[5] Naturally, it led to tension and competition.

Legendary Viking Erik the Red, perhaps named for his hair color as well as his temper, got into a nasty fight, killing two men called Eyjolf the Foul and Hrafn the Dueller.[6] This got Erik exiled from Iceland in 982,[7] so he took a group of people westward to Greenland and founded its first Norse settlement, the remains of which can be seen today as a crumbling church and stone house foundations.[8] More than three thousand people lived in the Eastern and Western Settlements, adapting and surviving for over 400 years in a new land.[9] Though the descendants of the first settlers abandoned the place around 1450, losing their livelihoods to climate change as the Little Ice Age swept in, it was still an extraordinary accomplishment.[10] But that new land was not enough to quench their thirst for exploration.

We know so much about the Norse adventures to North America thanks to the Icelandic sagas.[11] The *Saga of Erik the Red* and the *Saga of the Greenlanders* describe five separate trips to a place they called "Vinland," between 999 and 1017.[12] Also, we see other references to Vinland in the Icelandic *Landnámabók* and in Icelandic annals.[13]

Where and what is Vinland remains a subject of much debate in the Norse world,[14] and I barely have the guts to dip my pinky toe in the ongoing discussion. If you thought the Vikings were fierce, you should see Norse specialists debating each other.

As the Norse sailed west and south from Greenland, they encountered three diverse landscapes. The first, Helluland, or "flat slab land," was known to have rocky coasts and no trees, and today, archaeologists believe that area corresponds to Baffin Island in Canada. Markland, or "forest land," located south of Helluland, is associated with present-day Labrador, where dense forest runs for many miles along the coast. Vinland, the third, is supposedly somewhere farther south.[15]

Even the translation of the name is up for debate. The "Vinland" could be a place where the Norse could grow grapes for wine,[16] but it could be named for the large number of berries in Newfoundland and elsewhere along the Gulf of Saint Lawrence that were good for making wine, as they are today. Or the vines could be just vines.[17]

What we do know is that after sailing south from Helluland, the Norse established more than one settlement, with at least one in Newfoundland.[18] The big question is just how far south they sailed, and how far south they would have settled, if even for a single season. This question is the one my team and I decided to put to the test using satellite imagery.

First Contact

While so many searches for Norse sites had failed, one succeeded beyond anyone's wildest expectations—and changed North American history in the process.

It began in 1960 with a Norwegian couple, Helge and Anne Stine Ingstad. In reading the Norse sagas, they thought that Vinland likely referred to Newfoundland, as its northern coast would have been the first logical area for the Norse to make landfall when sailing south from Labrador.[19] After they spoke about their search to George Decker, a local fisherman, he led them to a series of foundations made from sod and covered in grass that had a similar shape to Norse longhouses.[20] This goes to show you that locals everywhere know what is what.

Over the next few seasons at the site, called L'Anse aux Meadows, what they excavated was so astounding that it took years for the larger community of Norse scholars to believe them.[21] Out of the houses came a spindle whorl made of soapstone, essential for spinning wool to make woolen garments.[22] Iron boat rivets suggested that larger boats had made the journey there.[23] Excavations in other areas revealed a forge, where iron was smelted and iron items manufactured,[24] but it was the discovery of a typical Norse metal ring pin that quieted the naysayers.[25]

Radiocarbon tests provided multiple dates around 1000 AD,[26] with the buildings having an identical shape to those in Iceland and Greenland from the same time period.[27] It appeared the Ingstads had discovered the first evidence of the Norse in North America.

After the Ingstads came legendary archaeologist Birgitta Wallace from Parks Canada.[28] She and her team worked in the swampier area of the site next to the beach, where they found pieces of worked wood.[29] Significantly, they also uncovered a butternut, along with wood from a butternut tree, which is a species of walnut not found in Newfoundland. That's a strong suggestion that the inhabitants of L'Anse aux Meadows sailed across the Gulf of Saint Lawrence, cutting down trees for wood and exploring.[30] The evidence added up to show that the Norse lived at L'Anse aux Meadows for a short period of time, with a maximum population of about a hundred people.[31] Curiously, no animal bones appeared in the archaeological record, nor was there any evidence for stables.[32]

Given all the trips described in the sagas, surely there had to be additional settlements. L'Anse aux Meadows could have been Vinland, or Vinland might have been a description for the entire region. The more we investigated, the more we realized that no one had ever conducted a search for potential archaeological sites along the eastern coast of North America using a systematic approach with remote-sensing technologies.

It wasn't just Norse sites that offered exciting potential. The eastern coast of Canada and the Gulf of Saint Lawrence were home to fascinating ancient native cultures, including the Dorset,[33] Beothuk,[34] and Maritime Archaic.[35] Discovering further traces of these peoples[36] would provide valuable additions to the archaeological record.

As we prepared our research design, we wanted the most unbiased approach possible. We were not seeking any particular ancient site, but rather wanted to test the remote-sensing science to see if it would work in identifying any ancient sites, period. Studying Indigenous ancient cultures gave my team and me a good sense of the range and type of structures we might encounter. We also studied Norse longhouse and farm construction from Iceland, as well as the standard types of construction from 18th- and 19th-century settlers in the area.

A Lot of Land to Map

At this point, we had budget enough to pay for Chase's and Dave's time and a bit of satellite imagery. For site mapping and discovery, we normally focus on one small area, but getting high-resolution imagery for the entirety of Canada's eastern coastline, plus down into New England, would have cost tens of millions of dollars. We had to seek an alternative approach.

Thank God for Google Earth and Bing, two open-access imagery platforms, with at least 60 percent of eastern Canada's coastline available as high-resolution data. However, in areas with low population density, the quality of imagery can be patchy, as there is simply too little demand for the data. Lower-resolution imagery showed trees but no smaller details.

Weeks of searching followed, hours on end scrutinizing the edges of the coastline and the shores of lakes and rivers nearby. Any curious shapes or features got marked with pins for team review the next day.

About 50 sites of interest appeared around Newfoundland, our most likely hot spot for any ancient sites. Rather than purchasing high-resolution satellite imagery, which would have cost us about $30,000—still way too expensive—I found high-resolution aerial photographs from a government environmental mapping agency. A bargain at $1,000. Although these images did not have multispectral data, they did have a resolution of 25 centimeters, allowing us to assess if the features were worth more exploration.

That took us from 50 sites to 6, a number for which we could afford to use multispectral imagery. On closer inspection, four hit the cutting-room floor in swift order; for reasons of elevation or vegetation growth, putative features from the aerial photos turned out to be nothing. That left us with two sites: one about 20 miles to the west of L'Anse aux Meadows, and another about 700 miles to the south, at Point Rosee, almost on Newfoundland's southernmost tip.

That tip, covered with lighter vegetation, jutted out from a dense forest into the Gulf of Saint Lawrence. In a 120-by-240-meter area of

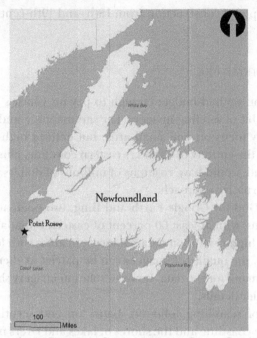

Location of Point Rosee [MAP COURTESY CHASE CHILDS]

the satellite image, a series of dense black lines appeared, possibly the faint outlines of a few structures 8 meters wide and 20 meters long. In the south and east, a narrow black dotted line surrounded nearly all the "structures," forming what looked like an enclosure wall of a farm. Something like farmed ridges appeared to the east.

The BBC took us up on the suggestion of further, noninvasive investigation on the ground. At this point, I had to figure out how the permitting process worked, because you cannot just show up on a site in Canada and start surveying. It's against the law. I emailed Martha Drake, who heads the Provincial Archaeology Office of Newfoundland and Labrador, with a report of our initial results.

Sure that I would be dismissed as a crackpot, I dreaded her response, but I could not have been more wrong. Martha was charming, gracious, and very sympathetic to the idea. On the phone, she told me she was supportive not because she thought we would find anything per se, but because we would test a new methodology for the archaeology of eastern Canada, and Newfoundland in particular.

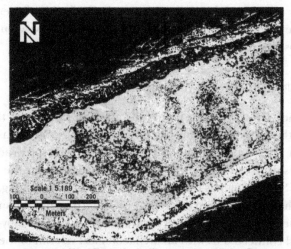

Processed WorldView-2 satellite imagery of Point Rosee
[IMAGE COURTESY DIGITALGLOBE]

Permit duly acquired, that October Dave and Chase flew from Birmingham, Alabama, to Deer Lake Regional Airport, about a three-hour drive from Point Rosee. I did not appreciate the real-life consequences of putting together two brilliant people so different from one another. Chase was up early, raring to go, while Dave is more of a coffee-fueled night owl.

Even finding Point Rosee had turned into a disaster and would have been impossible if it weren't for the help of a kindly store owner, Edwin Gale—known locally as Hockey—whose emporium contains everything from groceries and bait to guitars. He lent Dave and Chase a 4×4 and told them how to avoid the bears. Newfoundland is still wild. Up to my eyebrows in teaching back home, I got occasional texts from Chase, with encouraging messages like, "Dave nearly died today." The forest we had seen in the satellite imagery was virtually impenetrable, and wind gusts of more than 60 miles per hour nearly blew Dave off the side of a 50-foot cliff.

Nobody ever said this was easy.

Somehow, Dave and Chase set up the necessary grid for Dave's magnetometer survey.[37] After the standard procedure of strapping the magnetometer on his back had turned him into something like a sail in the high winds, Dave had hacked a safer way of carrying it, and they completed the work in the week they had budgeted. Good thing they finished when they did: the day they left Newfoundland, Point Rosee was blanketed in several feet of snow.

Tantalizing Clues

When they returned, both thankfully alive, we sat around the computer as the image processing began. Anxiously, we watched as a series of darker lines appeared with a half-dozen magnetic spikes across the site. These spikes matched with what we had seen on the satellite imagery. Something was there, something worth investigating.

We shared the data in our report with Martha, and she suggested doing a season with limited test excavations in a series of 2-by-2-meter units and connected us with an archaeological veteran of the region, Fred Schwarz, for planning and digging. Fred told us he thought what we had found so far was probably archaeological, but we needed to know if it was an 18th- or 19th-century settlement[38] or a trace of one of Newfoundland's Indigenous cultures.

We also shared the initial results with Doug Bolender, of the University of Massachusetts Boston—the same chap we'd worked with in Iceland. Doug was cautious but excited, explaining that, no matter what, we'd developed a sound scientific approach to mapping potential archaeological anomalies in Newfoundland.

In the short time before the planned June 2015 season, we dove into the settlement history of southwest Newfoundland[39]—as you do, when you're an Egyptologist. No homes or settlements could be found on any maps close to Point Rosee. All we could do was hope for the best.

A Grand Adventure

I arrived in Newfoundland a few days after Greg, Chase, Dave, and Fred had started the season. Newfoundland can deliver some brutal temperature shifts and weather changes. I had read about the "wreckhouse winds," which were so powerful they could knock a train off the tracks, so I was a little wary. But, along with the unfailing kindness and generosity of the Newfoundlanders, I will always remember the smell of the air on the coast, like a Christmas-tree farm along a beach. The freshness and cleanness and sheer wildness were breathtaking.

Every day, our team set out from Hockey's store on foot, tromping about 3 kilometers over extraordinarily varied terrain. While one of us drove a 4×4 with supplies to the site, the rest hiked through lightly wooded hills, passing sprays of pink, yellow, and white flowers that dotted the landscape. Walking up an old logging road, we entered dense woods with muddy ruts for us to leap over, and then spilled out onto sloping grassy hills that rolled down to the ocean cliffs and deep bogs.

Point Rosee jutted out into the ocean in the distance. So we kept walking, through dense bushes and small trees hugging the coast. Seals sunned themselves on the rocks below. On a really good day, we spotted whales. Finally, we'd enter the point, where knee-high grass and wet sod earth grabbed at our ankles and pulled us down.

Archaeology is all about the details, and any good excavation starts with a grid system for later reference. Greg and the team had begun a grid that measured 120 meters by 240 meters along the western half of the site, based around a 1974 Canadian Geodetic Survey marker, part of an ongoing 100-year-old Canadian government mapping program.[40] We had trouble pinpointing the magnetometer spikes and possible satellite imagery features on the ground to test-excavate them, but it was nothing daunting.

We set up our assorted units, while Dave conducted more magnetometry. Fred, a gruff but kindly man with over 30 years' experience excavating every possible site in eastern Canada, dug a test unit in an area where nothing had appeared on the satellite imagery, to establish the layers of natural soil on the site. Chase and I worked away to the north, where a 1-meter-wide potential "wall" feature had appeared. After a few days, Dave confirmed a find from the initial survey: a major spike of 250 in the magnetometer readings, when other areas ranged from −2 to +2. This suggested a subsurface magnetic anomaly; perhaps an area of burning or a ditch.

We set up another small excavation unit there and immediately uncovered an ovoid boulder, the tip of which pierced the ground surface. When we removed the heavy grass and roots covering the area, the boulder seemed to have been fire-cracked, with dark metal lumps that looked like they had been soldered on starting about 5 centimeters below the top ground level.

We did not think much of it at first. But further down, harder pieces the size of a quarter popped out of the ground as Fred and I

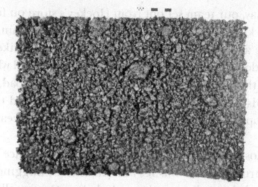

Bog iron from Point Rosee [PHOTO BY GREG MUMFORD]

dug away. We cleaned them off in one of the clear puddles nearby. They seemed to be burnt bog iron. Bog iron is found in swampy environments, when concentrations of ore form together in clumps. The Vikings smelted down these impure deposits, after various heating processes, to make iron for nails and tools. In our case, some of the chunks had what looked like bubbles—potential evidence of processed metal. Fred told us that in all his years of working in the region, he had never seen anything like it.

This was a major moment for us. We could have found an area where someone in the past had intentionally heated bog iron and left waste. We expanded the unit to follow the deposit.

Digging Deeper

Since the start of our dig, it had rained nearly every day, with North Atlantic winds and freezing cold. The site, and our team, spent most of the time soaked. Rubbing my hand against the boulder, I noticed a veneer of black come off—maybe charcoal residue. The waterlogged ground had caused lots of organic material to disintegrate, and there were hundreds of what appeared to be tiny charcoal pieces no bigger than a splinter in the earth, which left black streaks against my hand if I ground them against my palm. We sampled everything we could there.

Chase and I found a roughly circular hollow ringed by stones, set into the ground at close intervals, and placed beside a boulder. Inside were nearly 20 pounds of bog iron, going down 20 centimeters. We

*Potential furnace feature
at Point Rosee*
[PHOTO BY THE AUTHOR]

noted that a thin gray layer covered the deposit, which looked just like ash. We tried not to get too excited.

But Fred was finding that hard. None of the Indigenous ancient cultures known from Newfoundland used bog iron; all the known tools from the Dorset and Inuit people were made from meteoric iron, and there surely would have been some other sign of Indigenous activity, such as flint working, if this were one of their sites.[41] Nor did European settlers smelt bog iron, since they imported metal items on the ships they sailed from Europe.[42] And if the site had been an 18th-to-19th-century settlement or even a single house as Fred had suggested before we broke ground, we would have found pottery,[43] the standard debris from every other known French and English house on Newfoundland.

This left one possible origin: Norse.

With a beach a kilometer away, and a protected inlet, this seemed like an ideal location for a small camp, if not a transitory settlement. We started to dream we might have found the westernmost and southernmost evidence of Norse occupation. L'Anse aux Meadows probably did not stand in isolation: one saga referred to a place called "Hop,"[44] which was warm enough for the Norse to cultivate grain, at a settlement next to a protected inlet connected to a river. Coincidentally, the Codroy Valley, where we were working, is the one place in Newfoundland known today for its farming. Conditions might have been warmer 1,000 years ago, but not enough for all of Newfoundland to be farmed.

It was easy to start connecting the dots. And more dots appeared. Greg was working in a unit just south of our "furnace." When Doug Bolender joined us for a few days at the end of our season, he opened up the area between Greg's unit and ours, where the darker feature had appeared in the satellite imagery. As he scraped away, exposing the unit, we heard him mutter, "It's not possible. I don't believe it."

He had apparently uncovered the remains of what seemed to be a Norse turf wall—undulating strips of angled brown and black sod. Doug had seen hundreds of them. I later saw examples in Iceland, and they looked the same as what we found in Newfoundland.

While we did not come up with much beyond the bubbled bog iron, this was not surprising. All the specialists with whom I had spoken said Norse sites did not have many artifacts, just as at L'Anse aux Meadows. We left Point Rosee in high spirits, determined to return with a bigger team the next summer. Our test season seemed victorious.

New Dating Evidence

Greg and I returned home with our samples to post them out to specialists, and Greg then spent hundreds of hours doing the postseason write-up and data analysis. Later that winter, we got back the radiocarbon dating results from the rock-top bulk carbon sample. To obtain it, we had scraped the carbonized material from the top and side areas of the rock that had clear evidence of burning. No other rocks on-site had anything like it.

With a 95 percent probability, we got a date range of 1255–1287 AD, which fell within the period we would hope for Norse activity. It was 250 years later than L'Anse aux Meadows, in fact, leaving room for speculation about just how long the Norse were in Canada. We also got a radiocarbon date of 764–886 AD. A withered tree root sample from below the ground surface gave us a date in the early 17th century, which meant that the tree took root before any Europeans were known to have occupied that part of Newfoundland and the ground had been undisturbed since.[45]

We asked a geologist at my university, Scott Brande, to analyze the similar "burnt" material from around the rock top, and bog ore beside the bottom of the rock, to determine if the separate areas reflected the same time period and activity. And indeed, they did. Additionally, as a longtime Birmingham resident, Scott had studied the city's iron industry in detail and told us that a temperature of 1,250 degrees Celsius would be needed to smelt iron, way outside the range of a grass fire.[46] Also, some of the bog ore and rock-top residue samples he tested had an iron concentration of 75–85 percent, quite rich and useful for smelting.

After consulting with a Norse metallurgy specialist at Aarhus University in Denmark, Thomas Birch, we learned that we had not found slag, as we had initially thought, but what preliminary indications suggested to be the first part of the smelting process, roasted bog ore. If you put bog iron directly into a hot fire, it will explode, due to its water content. Gently roasting out the water at a lower temperature prepares the ore for the next stage. This seemed to explain why some of our bog iron, which would normally fall to pieces in your hands with gentle pressure, displayed bubbling and was difficult to break.

Yes, it appeared we had indeed discovered the first clues to potential Norse activity at Point Rosee. But this is science. And science can be cruel.

Back to Newfoundland

After sharing our results with several Norse specialists and Martha Drake's office, we returned with soil scientists, Norse settlement specialists, an authority on ancient plant remains, an archaeological-dating specialist, pollen specialists, and an additional surveyor. We spent months designing the excavation and survey plans, making sure they met with the approval of the experts.

And then the cards of the house we had built fell one by one. As we expanded the unit around the "furnace," what had initially appeared as a turf wall, matching the width of the satellite data perfectly, kept going. And going. It turned out to be not a turf wall after all, but instead a rare soil feature caused by a combination of water movement and bedrock gradient, the likes of which our enthusiastic local archaeologist Blair Temple said had never been seen in eastern Canada before. We were hugely disappointed. Quite soon, Blair's resilient good cheer was all that kept us going.

The "furnace" feature, given how badly it had been waterlogged the summer we first uncovered it, had lost all evidence of what we believed to be charcoal. At the time, we had to bail out our units several times a day, which is about as destructive a process as archaeology can experience. The feature had nothing more to give.

We found a lot more bog iron, which had been densest around the furnace, but it spread out over a larger area than expected, having formed there naturally. All the other features that had been suggestive of walls in the satellite imagery turned out to be natural, as did one clear, rectilinear dark-green patch of vegetation. The imagery had let us down, and we ended the season very low in spirits.

Samples, endless samples—we took half of Newfoundland back to be tested in labs. Chiefly, we sent five "burnt" sandstone and quartz samples contained within the bog ore to a top University of Washington lab run by James Feathers, for dating using thermoluminescence (TL) and optically stimulated luminescence (OSL).[47] These techniques are invaluable for archaeologists. TL dating tells archaeologists when a mineral was last heated to more than 500 degrees Celsius, which would indicate that something was burned intentionally. OSL can be used on quartz in a similar way.

Up until spring 2018, we had only radiocarbon dates from the "hearth" feature. We knew that if the OSL and TL dates taken from the same context had virtually identical date ranges, then we could say someone intentionally burned bog iron in a roughly 40-centimeter-wide, naturally occurring bowl. We could see no other discernable "burning" outside the bowl, which would have been present with, say, a broader brush fire or a lightning strike.

In late April 2018, we received OSL and TL dates back from Dr. Feathers via email. I admit, after the disheartening 2016 season, I had written them off and braced myself for more bad news.

Except it wasn't quite what we expected. The first OSL date from the finer-grained samples had a calendar age of 921 ± 130 AD, which means a possible date range of 791–1051 AD. The second series of samples, taken from courser-grained material, had a date range of 1200 ± 300, or 900–1500 AD. Alas, the OSL analysis did not confirm any distinct burning against the boulder itself or in an adjacent area beside the "hearth." Thus there was no conclusive evidence for the ore or the feature we hoped might have served to heat or process it.

Norse, or No Norse?

That confusing bombshell allows us to say we have four dates from the same archaeological context, all independent and closely matching, from 764 to 1500 AD—admittedly, in addition to several earlier radiocarbon dates. The best "Norse"-linked material coating the rock top is indubitably associated with the lower "hearth" feature.

I have no idea why the vegetation gave such misleading readings, and we are still looking for answers. For some reason the grasses growing across the site and the strange "turf wall" soil were a bit healthier and displayed some linear patterns. Something in the soil perhaps, a mineral content or interaction between plants; the striped soil type did seem to retain more water than the surrounding soils. Perhaps it was just sheer chance that the promising longhouse shape in the northern part of the site was the same size, shape, and orientation as other known longhouses. It's important to push boundaries and figure out why things appear or do not. We still have a lot of pondering to do.

There is enough evidence here to suggest that one or more groups came to Point Rosee 1,000 years ago, more or less, at the latest, and may have displaced or gathered sufficient bog iron to coat the rock top and fill a stone-edged hollow. Our initial observations suggested enough heat to burn or embed a fair amount of iron into the rock, using charcoal, despite none of it surviving well. I know what I saw with my own eyes.

Maybe we found the first evidence of the local Amerindian or Dorset groups burning bog iron purposefully. That would be groundbreaking. Alternatively, we may have found ephemeral evidence of the Norse pulling up, roasting enough bog iron to smelt elsewhere for a few nails to repair their ships, and then retreating. It would not leave much to be found.

Birgitta Wallace of L'Anse aux Meadows fame was kind enough to come and visit Point Rosee with her husband, Rob. They are just fabulous human beings. Birgitta is one of the grandes dames of archaeology—kind, generous, and wise, and responsible for mentoring several generations of archaeologists. She sat me down for a chat at the end of our season and told me that while the site was not what we had hoped for, we had created a very high bar for future archaeological investigations in the area to jump over.

"It doesn't matter what you found," she said. "You used state-of-the-art technology and an excellent digging strategy, and you brought together interested experts. You threw the kitchen sink at the site. That's what every search for new Norse sites recently has lacked. Hold your head high."

This gave me food for thought. If Point Rosee had turned out to be an obvious Norse settlement, it would have meant years of work at the site, major funding applications, and close work with the Canadian government to develop the area for tourism, none of which would have been a bad thing. We still need to run additional analyses of the possible roasted bog ore and strange-patterned vegetation. But for now, the site is suggestive at best, and it may always be.

After all this work, I feel that Vinland was not a single place, but Newfoundland and the Gulf of Saint Lawrence in its entirety. Using an aerial laser mapping technology like LIDAR might reveal Norse campsites or even settlements farther inland, near good farmland, and potentially near Point Rosee, but presently hidden beneath vegetation.

Science has its foundations in an approach to experiments that can be replicated in the future, not just impressive findings. With advances in mapping technology, an accidental discovery, or just more searching, I believe that more Norse sites will be found in Canada in the next decade. It is equally likely that some of the modern settlements along the western coast of Newfoundland cover Norse sites. After all, settlers 300 or more years ago would have chosen the best possible locations just as the Norse may have done, and people usually continue to live where people have always lived.

Both Greg and I are sorely tempted to return to Newfoundland. If the windmill is shiny enough, I'll charge. Armed with LIDAR, and knowing what we know now, I think we could do far more rapid testing of potential sites. Yes, I am inviting more risk and potential failures, but I do so with lots of experience. My colleagues have told me that this search has reignited interest in archaeological surveys of the area for potential Norse sites, and this is great for its warm, hospitable people, who were excited to learn more about Newfoundland's past. The game is afoot. Expect surprises.

5

Digging in the Wrong Place

S ometimes you get an archaeological site on the brain, like an earworm, but nestled deeper, and impossible to budge. Aside from *National Geographic Magazine* and library books, I first got to "see" archaeology in action on TV, from occasional documentaries on public television to movies like *Raiders of the Lost Ark*. I obsessed about Egypt. For a seventh grade project, I made a sarcophagus out of a refrigerator box, correctly decorated, and wrapped myself in toilet paper. I rose out of the box and proceeded to showcase my mummified organs to a class half horrified, half amused. Instead of getting professional help, I opted for the profession, period.

When watching *Raiders* as a child, what I loved most was the Tanis scene—a map room, a lost city laid out, hiding the secret site of the lost Ark of the Covenant. And despite the Nazis' evil plots and sweeping excavation, Indy's friend Sallah can write off their archaeology with one pithy line:

"They're digging in the wrong place."

You could say I've had Tanis on my mind for some time, simmering away in the place where you store childhood dreams.

The Story of Tanis

Hollywood didn't quite get Tanis right. Tanis, biblical Zoan, is located in the eastern part of Egypt's Delta, about a three-hour drive north

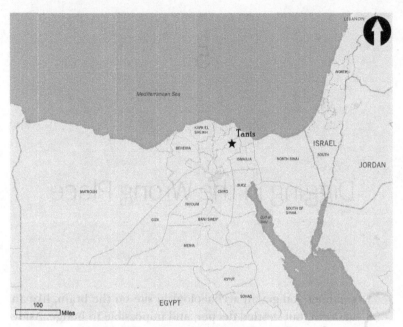

Location of Tanis [MAP COURTESY CHASE CHILDS]

of Cairo. It grew along the Tanitic branch of the Nile, south of the Mendesian branch where Tebilla is located. We know from textual evidence that occupation of its nearby predecessor Pi-Ramesses at Qantir started in Dynasty 19 (1296–1186 BC), but we have virtually no archaeological data at Tanis prior to Dynasty 21 (1070–945 BC).[1]

Through the streets and alleys of San el Hagar, the modern community overlying part of ancient Tanis, twisting and turning by car, you have no idea you might be above a long-abandoned metropolis. Outside town, what looks like a rambling white vacation house greets you. Lush pink bougainvillea line the walkway to the entrance. When you reach the veranda out back . . . your breath leaves you. A seemingly endless ocean of dusty hills spreads out. At their base, white stones form a large temple complex.

Few sites like Tanis are left in Egypt. Shaped like a tilted South America as seen on Google Earth, the site defies all large adjectives: it is a decaying megalopolis. Measuring more than 2 kilometers long and 1½ kilometers wide, the site has an aboveground volume I would estimate at 22 million cubic meters. At a rate of 4

General landscape of Tanis [PHOTO BY THE AUTHOR]

units per season, it would take archaeologists working in standard 10-meter-square units over 55,000 years to excavate.

As you approach the middle of the site, mud-brick debris comes into view, piled 10–15 meters tall in places. The soft layer of silt that covers the site can make it hard to walk, especially in the rainy season when you end up with pounds of mud making platform shoes of your hiking boots.

The main sacred area is in the northern end of the site, where the topography rises gently. It has temples to Amun-Re, Mut, and Khonsu—a typical god-goddess-son triad—and is possibly a cult center for Re.[2] There, a promenade of upright 4-meter-tall statues and stelae greets any tourists who make the special day trip.

Tanis was the capital of Egypt for more than 350 years, from 1070 to 712 BC, home to two dynasties of Egyptian kings, 21 and 22, at the dawn of the Third Intermediate Period.[3]

As Egypt's great age of empire, the New Kingdom, fizzled out, Libyan tribes began to enter Egypt's Western Desert. Anxious people fortified their towns against increasing unrest.[4] Ramses XI, the last king of Dynasty 20, ruled from Pi-Ramesses some 20 kilometers south of Tanis,[5] and high priest Smendes was his right-hand man in the Delta.

When Ramses XI's reign staggered to an end, Smendes assumed the kingship of northern Egypt, thus launching the Twenty-first Dynasty. He moved the capital to Tanis and practically took the light-bulbs: the Tanite architects robbed Pi-Ramesses for blocks and other building materials so thoroughly that archaeologists long mistook one city for the other.[6] Later in the dynasty, King Psusennes I (1039–991 BC) made his own innovations, building his tomb inside the temple complex at Tanis to take advantage of extra security and the associated royal cults. By ancient Egyptian standards, this was pretty radical.[7]

Sheshonq (945–925 BC)—Shishak in the Bible—the first ruler of Dynasty 22, built a new royal residence at Tanis[8] despite civil war in Egypt and a power grab by the Libyans at Mendes and in the western Delta. It was all going wrong. In Dynasty 24, ca. 712 AD, Tanis was no longer tenable as a capital city.[9]

Early Exploration at Tanis

The site has an incredibly rich history of exploration, starting with Napoleon's savants in the early 1800s. An archaeologist named Pierre Montet continued the tradition of French excavation by making what I and others in my field consider to be one of the greatest Egyptological discoveries of all time.[10]

In the early part of the 20th century, Montet and his team had toiled away at Tanis for 11 seasons, hoping to find Pi-Ramesses—as I said, a mistaken urban identity. He noticed that the outer enclosure wall of the temple of Amun did not run neatly parallel to the temple wall, but instead veered to the southwest. That seemed, well, radical. Exploring mud-brick structures in that corner, he and his team found nine tombs, five of which belonged to kings. The deeper his team dug, the more they uncovered.

Psusennes I's tomb was among them, not only inventive in its construction, but largely undisturbed. This was the age when pharaohs were laid to rest in coffins of silver; unlike gold, which could be imported from ancient Nubia, silver had to be imported from the eastern Mediterranean or western Asia, making it much more valuable.[11]

Montet found a solid silver sarcophagus. While the Tanite mummies had decayed in antiquity and there had been some looting, the tombs contained innumerable treasures and jewelry every bit as beautiful as Tutankhamun's.[12] Gold bowls, offering tables, necklaces, bracelets, and pectorals, which hung from the neck like Olympic gold medals: it was the stuff archaeologists' dreams are made of. Most had fine inlays of lapis lazuli, carnelian, and turquoise, detailing hieroglyphs or scarabs. My favorite piece is a gold falcon pectoral with individual inlaid feathers.[13]

But Montet had terrible timing. This was 1939, just as Nazi Germany absorbed the world's attention and stole Tanis's thunder.

By the time the world began to recover from the horrors of war, Tanis was a distantly remembered news story. Today, when tourists visit the Museum of Egyptian Antiquities in Cairo, they often miss the Tanis display, tucked behind King Tut's treasures. It's the hidden crown jewel of the collection, but then again, I am a bit biased.

Compared to other known capitals in ancient Egypt—take Memphis, Amarna, or Pi-Ramesses—we know little about the settlement of Tanis. Usually, at a site like this, we deal with multiple phases of occupation, either layered or jumbled together like a mixed-up puzzle. Without knowing the layout, it is that much harder to make hypotheses about the city's settlement, administration, population, class structures, and daily life. Trying to get a grip on the site's importance is like trying to understand the Eastern Seaboard of the United States without maps of New York or Washington, DC.

However, unlike so many sites, the Tanite settlement evidence is not beneath a modern town. Out in the open and largely unsurveyed, Tanis opens the door to possibility.

Tradition both grounds us and holds us back in archaeology, especially at large and complex sites like Tanis. Until the 1970s, Egyptologists mainly worked on excavations of temples, tombs, and pyramids. An archaeologist focusing on everyday life in Egypt was a rare beast. Then, with shifts in archaeological thought and practice, archaeologists started delving into settlement archaeology, or the study of ancient settlements,[14] and more projects focused on Egyptian cities, even if most stuck with temples and tombs. As settlement work developed, we gained a new understanding of what it was like to live in ancient Egypt. This 50-year-old subfield still presents many complexities, as the hundreds of individual layers on a site are never easy to reconstruct. But that's what makes it fun.

Breaking into the Map Room

I had my first look at Tanis from space in 2010, a decade after I had visited it for the first time as an undergraduate. I remember being impressed at the site's size and the number of statues out in the open, reused from the time of Ramesses II, but that's all. In other words, I did not expect to find much; maybe I'd find additional rooms in one of the temples.

At that time, high-resolution satellite imagery had not come down in price. The cost-prohibitive nature of the data meant few archaeologists had applied it to locating smaller features beneath the surface of sites. I got a great deal on DigitalGlobe data as an educational user, and that made all the difference.

However, although DigitalGlobe's database held many images, the company did not have the range and number of satellites in orbit that it does today. I couldn't be picky about my data, so I just had to use what there was.

Work I had done previously using lower-resolution data suggested that imagery taken during the winter months allowed easier detection of entire sites. I thought the same theory would apply to finding features as well, and I got lucky. Two images appeared in the database taken in January 2010 from the WorldView-1 and WorldView-2 satellites. The first usefully had a .5-meter resolution in the panchromatic range—which, counterintuitively, is black and white—while the second was multispectral, with eight bands going into the near-infrared range, at a lower resolution of 1.84 meters. The multispectral data could show more, but only if the feature was bigger than a double bed.

I downloaded the data in my university lab office, and it took forever. While waiting, I opened Tanis maps in my archaeology books, which I hadn't done in years. Right away, the large blank areas in the central and southern parts of the site jumped out. The temples in the north overwhelmed the site. If you did not know better, you'd say the site was a sacred space for worship and nothing else.

When the data was finally good to go, I loaded the multispectral WorldView-2 image into my main processing software, ER Mapper, and opened up the site and the fields surrounding it. As I zoomed in, the large Amun-Re temple walls showed up, a bit blurred, with limestone blocks in the center glowing a bright white. I scrolled south, toward a known Horus temple.

About 100 meters south of its outline, I could make out a cluster of fuzzy lines, suggestive of subsurface architecture. Playing around with the data, trying different combinations of the light spectrum bands, showed a little bit more detail, but the image remained mostly ambiguous. For me, though, this was already a success. The data had shown some potentially buried walls across a 600-by-800-meter area I knew, from on-the-ground experience, to be unremarkable-looking brown silt.

Next up, the WorldView-1 JPEG image. Instead of manipulating the black-and-white data, I decided to use a technique called "pan-sharpening."[15] It may sound like a death-match cooking competition, but here's how it works: 1.84-meter-resolution data will not pick up smaller features, but you can supercharge it by merging it with higher-resolution panchromatic data. The result is higher-resolution multispectral data. I know, it sounds like magic. It kind of is.

Think of it this way: a lower-resolution color image shows the vegetation in an agricultural field, while a higher-resolution black-and-white image shows the internal agricultural field divisions. By merging them, you get the vegetation information at the same time and with the same resolution as the important field subdivision data. Lower and higher data sets do not even need to match perfectly in terms of geographic area: areas that match will be pansharpened automatically.

I waited while the imagery merged, not expecting much, then zoomed in on the new imagery, starting in the north. Temple walls appeared with slightly more clarity, but the limestone still glowed brightly. Satellites take these images in the late morning, so you cannot do much about bright stone reflecting light.

Tanis Strips Off

I scrolled down. And then I almost fell off my seat. I thought I was hallucinating: an entire ancient city leapt off the screen. Ambiguous, faint streaks that had appeared in the multispectral image now emerged as clear buildings, streets, suburbs . . . everything.

If you get one discovery like this in your lifetime as an archaeologist, you have led a blessed life indeed.

But that wasn't all the tricks up my sleeve. After the pansharpening came the fiddling, like tweaking the radio to get the best possible signal. You can take so many different approaches, it is overwhelming. But armed with the season of the imagery, its resolution, the geology and soil type of the site, and the materials and size of the structures you seek, you can narrow things down.

A thousand data points affect what buttons you push. Some techniques enhance the subtle differences in the brightness of pixels next to one another, and others broaden the total range of values a pixel can have.[16] Also, what works well in one part of your image might not work well across the entire thing.

After trying dozens of different processing techniques during the afternoon and into the evening, I ended up with a crisp image showing the outline of the main city of Tanis, almost like the map room in the *Raiders of the Lost Ark* scene, with only a little more imagination needed. My headpiece of Ra was a multispectral satellite, and my expression was the same as Indy's, wonder that a great ancient secret had revealed itself to a patient archaeologist.

Today, looking at Google Earth, anyone can see outlines of the structures in central and south Tanis on satellite images, which currently have a resolution of .3 meter. That's smaller than your average laptop. But in 2010, that was not the case (a resolution of .5 meter, remember), which shows how dramatically the technology has developed.

At home, when I went to show the images to Greg, I just about dropped my computer as I took it out of my bag with shaking hands.

"What's going on?" Greg asked. I opened the laptop and pulled up the imagery.

He stared. And then said, "What is this?"

"What do you think? It's Tanis! All of it!"

He grabbed my mouse and scrolled around the processed satellite image, zooming in and out. I pointed out all the details and their implications for Egyptology, at which point he informed me that he *had* worked in Egypt since 1988. Sigh.

We discussed the next steps for how to proceed. First, we had to digitize the data, drawing every individual building on the computer to see them more clearly. I thought I could draw the entire map of the city, which measured 800 square meters, using my mouse and the line tools in a program called ArcGIS, which allows the user to store layers of maps and connected information like census data.

Well, I tried. And failed miserably. The lines appeared straight when I zoomed out, but when I zoomed in and looked close up, they had blobby edges of differing thicknesses. After six hours of everything going wrong, I gave up. There had to be an easier way to capture the varying details.

Greg had the brilliantly simple idea of drawing the town plan by hand, the old-fashioned way. We would print out a massive poster of the satellite imagery for the entire central city, and then cover it with transparent plastic sheeting, to draw in every detail in pen. It's one of the ways Egyptologists record scenes from blocks or temple walls. I took the image to a print shop and asked them to expand it as much as possible, on one piece of paper. I got looks.

The final map measured 2 meters by 1 meter and covered our entire dining room table. It took us more than two months to draw it all, a little at a time. Greg let me fill in the wall lines. He's not sexist—just protective of his artwork. As you might have gathered from my ArcGIS wobble, I manipulate technology, but I can't draw.

We estimate it took more than 50 hours of work during those eight weeks. After discussing the tiny details and making sure we drew the clear features and dotted the ambiguous ones, we could do no more. It gave us a far deeper insight into the distinct buildings and the three phases of the city's occupation than we'd seen in publications before.

Better Than Ground Survey—or at Least Cheaper

For fun, Greg and I decided to compare the efficiency of satellite imagery versus ground surveys. We chose magnetometry as an example; that's the same subsurface mapping technology we applied in Newfoundland. A good magnetometry surveyor, with an assistant, can map 80 square meters in a normal workday, if the site is flat and there's no vegetation to get in the way. For every five days of mapping, specialists need a day to process their survey data. At Tanis, the central city covers an area of 640,000 square meters, and there's an additional area of 20,000 square meters to the south with clear structures, for a total of 660,000 square meters.

So that's 103 days to survey all that. Assuming a standard month of work—longer periods are generally not possible for technical specialists, since they often have other job commitments—103 days is five full seasons. With an average cost of about $1,000 per day for a magnetometry survey, including the expert team's airfare, room, board, and in-country travel, surveying the entire settlement of Tanis carries a $200,000 price tag.

This assumes that you have permission from the Egyptian government to conduct the survey, cooperative customs agents for importing the necessary equipment, functional equipment once it arrives, and survey specialists who manage to stay healthy. None of these is ever guaranteed.

Compare that to $2,000 for the satellite imagery, and only, say, 60 hours total of our time. It was an enthusiastic thumbs-up for the satellite data, even if magnetometer results might have had a bit more detail. But oh, the things we could see on the dining room table from 600 miles in space.

In the distinct occupation phases of Tanis, there were roads, the full economic range of houses, and large administrative complexes. Some structures have to have been elite homes or palaces, bigger and more elaborate than other buildings at the site. And there appear to be at least three of them.

The satellite map allows us to travel to the past, and for the first time, to really understand how the city might have functioned. Its implications are wide ranging, primarily because Tanis represents one of the largest and most well-known capital cities in antiquity.

Digging Down

When we find things from space, we must always ground-truth them, either via excavation or survey. Even when the maps looked great, and "showed" things clearly, we had to verify if what we saw on the surface of Tanis represented what lay beneath. Thanks to a collaboration with the French team that worked at Tanis through 2014, led by archaeologist Philippe Brissaud,[17] we had a chance to put the data to the test.

I got in touch with Philippe right away. To ground-truth, Philippe would have to apply to the Egyptian government for permission to do a test excavation in the south, though having never used satellite imagery before, he was skeptical about our results.

I arrived on-site during the full swing of the fall excavation season. History hangs heavy at Tanis, inside and out. The French dig house goes back almost a hundred years, with photographs of every archaeological team that has ever worked there on the walls. Philippe, an enthusiastic and gregarious dig director, welcomed me with proper French hospitality. Delicious as lunch was, I did not, however, partake from the bowl of chicken feet on offer, especially after he shoved one of them in my face, to peals of laughter from his team.

Philippe gave me a fantastic tour, showing me ongoing work in the temple of Mut, where they had uncovered a series of gorgeous carved blocks. My favorite bit was visiting the storeroom on-site, full of intact and reconstructed pottery vessels from the last 100 years of French excavations. The pots told the history of excavation at the site as much as the site's history—had Montet himself held some of them in his hands?

In the central area, where a clear 20-by-20-meter house had appeared just south of the Horus temple, the team had worked for several days to uncover walls up to 2 meters thick. A smaller room appeared in the middle of the house, only a meter wide—a storage area perhaps—which the satellite imagery had not picked up. Curious. I asked Philippe for his impression. He looked at me with a big smile.

"It works! With 80 percent accuracy, I think. The imagery just did not pick up the smaller rooms, and there is a 20-to-30-centimeter offset between the edge of a wall and its true corner."

The team had dug down about a meter into each room, finding different phases of house construction, some of which matched the other building phases around the house that we had seen on our dining room table.

We also examined the edges of the excavation unit and the depth of the surface silt, and tried to determine what quality had made the buildings pop so clearly. At Tanis, the silt covering the site is slightly sandier than at most other settlement mounds in the Delta. That sandy soil contrasts with the crumbling mud brick of the building foundations, and the mud bricks gain an even more distinct color when they absorb water during the winter rainy season. Although I am aware that what worked so well here may not give the same results at other sites, I felt much more confident after that visit about the use of satellite imagery in general, and about beginning to reconstruct this ancient city in particular.

Digging at Tanis with Philippe Brissaud's team [PHOTO BY THE AUTHOR]

Daily Life at Tanis

People of every kind lived at Tanis: kings and queens, priests, administrators, artisans, architects, soldiers, and a large working class to support the temples, palaces, and main town.[18] Like every major city today, it had a bustling central section. The Tanitic branch of the Nile curved around the northeast part of the site, facilitating the transportation of carved blocks for the temples and artisan workshops. Given that geography, there must have been more than one harbor area,[19] with marketplaces dotting the riverside. There, ship captains and traders hawked their goods from across the empire, from Israel in the north to Nubia in the south. We know of similar marketplaces at Luxor, the southern city associated with the Valley of the Kings.[20]

The priests lived in housing located in the northern section, close to the temples.[21] The temple's size suggests a staff of hundreds, from high priests and their assistants to the cleaners. People brought food and offerings into the temples all day; and during festivals, thousands of Tanites would have crowded the exterior court of the temple enclosure, hoping for a glimpse of the king or some good fortune from the gods.[22]

Moving just south of the Horus temple, in the central part of the site, we found an area full of homes, each measuring 20 square meters, lined up along streets. The houses seem to have four to eight internal rooms, with at least one larger in size than all the others. They seem similar to the large homes of royal officials at Amarna, which was Egypt's capital 300 years earlier.

If you had business in the home of a Tanite official, you were ushered into a central room or the public area of the building. Alongside the official, scribes were there to prepare any necessary letters following your conversation. The walls were probably whitewashed and painted, with stone or wooden columns to hold up the ceiling.[23] Servants awaited orders, ready to pour imported wine from Palestine to quench your thirst.[24]

The back of the house was private and included the kitchen, bedrooms, and even a separate bathroom area[25]—not bad, for 3,000 years ago. As at Amarna, these houses may have had upper stories. Best of all, given the central location of the homes, the owners had a five-minute stroll up the street to get to the temples and administrative buildings, or a two-minute hop to the palaces. The Nile brought cooling breezes to their homes, giving this part of Tanis a more pleasant smell than the poorer neighborhoods. It was prime real estate, if you could afford it.

Just south of this desirable neighborhood were the 20-to-30-room villas and palaces occupied by the elite and two dynasties of Egypt's kings and queens.[26] Nearby, artisans toiled away in their workshops, producing stunning jewelry and fine objects,[27] and chefs prepared delicacies with spices and goods from across the Mediterranean, always ready for a feast.[28] Emissaries from foreign lands waited for the city's top officials, hoping for the king's ear on pressing diplomatic matters. The quarters of the royal family, located away from the prying eyes of the court, housed the queens and royal family.

In the throne room, maybe with a beautiful painted floor depicting birds and wildlife along the Nile and symbols of Egypt's dominion over foreign lands, the king held court, surrounded by his vizier, head of the treasury, chief general, and countless scribes.[29] Even in Egypt's last Intermediate Period, the pharaoh lived as a god on Earth as he attempted to balance the forces of the universe in Egypt's favor.[30]

In the spit of land forming the tail of the mound, the southernmost part of the site, we can see several dozen 8-by-8-meter homes, built next to one another in more organic fashion. The area immediately appears less affluent.[31] Each house seems to have one or two rooms, so perhaps families lived in adjacent one-room dwellings.

These could have been homes for the people who worked in the palaces. Without excavation we cannot tell, but we can fairly confidently say that this area was the poorest zip code of Tanis, farthest removed from all the amenities on the doorstep of the wealthier district. And it does appear to be a distinct neighborhood, aligning with the second phase of construction observable in the satellite data.

Reconstructing the Landscape and Population

Figuring out the population of this bustling community based on the satellite imagery is tricky. We know that major cities like Alexandria had an estimated population of up to 500,000 some 700 years later,[32] and these numbers could be a clue. Here at Tanis we can see dozens of houses, and we have the total area of the central city. The Delta has experienced great archaeological loss due to the growth of modern cities and the mining out of soil by farmers, so we have to wonder just how big the city was.

In the fields surrounding the city, many suggestions of structures show up beneath the surface as crop marks. Some lines indicate earlier field boundaries from modern times, while others trace out structures with the same size and shape as the clear features in the satellite imagery. I spoke to farmers from surrounding villages and the town of San el Hagar, and all described in detail the mud-brick structures they encountered while digging, as well as the dense ceramic debris.

In the 1960s, a decade from which we have good CORONA satellite imagery, Tanis seems to have been about 50 percent larger than today. Modern agriculture has cut into much of the lower-lying site to the north and east, and San el Hagar has grown by 500 percent. We have also lost the evidence of the ancient relic watercourses to the east and south.

The site would have looked quite different 200 years ago, during the Napoleonic expedition. The *Description de l'Égypte*, the expedition's 23-volume report, was published between 1809 and 1829 and included a detailed survey of the entire country. This extraordinary volume can now be found online.[33] In the online map of Tanis, the site appears to be twice as large, although that is only a rough estimate.

It might help if we imagined the landscape surrounding Tanis

3,000 years ago, in which many smaller sites formed a network of villages and estates supporting the capital. During the yearly inundation of the Nile, the main city became a large island surrounded by smaller islets. We will not know the extent of this network until archaeologists carry out a campaign of coring and noninvasive surveys around Tanis, which will take years to complete.

The Bigger Picture

Understanding the nature and extent of Tanis and its wider community has major implications for the study of Egypt and of the Near East, where we see the earliest foundations of modern city living. For the first time, having established a map for Egypt's largest and most continuously occupied capital city, our satellite work fills in a big missing puzzle piece. But when we look closer, we see other puzzles to solve. We can create all the hypotheses we want about the spatial construction of the settlement and the nature of urban life at this specific capital, but to go further will take careful excavation.

We archaeologists have made so many assumptions about major sites around the world. The more satellite technology advances, the more we find out how little we know. My team and I got WorldView-3 satellite imagery recently, with .3-meter data and an even farther reach into the middle-infrared part of the light spectrum, and we can see twice as many structures at Tanis as in the WorldView-2 data.

For instance, when we originally analyzed the house that the French team excavated with what we had available, one small interior room showed up. Using the more powerful WorldView-3 data, with a higher resolution, *lots* of smaller rooms appeared there, and in all the houses of Tanis. Hundreds of houses and structures appear across the site, in parts of our original data that we assumed were blank. We're now busy doing a 3-D reconstruction of the new houses at Tanis, which will help bring even more life to the site.

But no one data set catches everything. The usual rules of times of year, or maybe drought versus an unusually rainy spell, apply. Those palaces in the original imagery that allowed us to imagine the daily lives of royalty 3,000 years ago are completely empty in the higher-resolution WorldView-3 data. Once again, the season the imagery was taken, and the weather, have played their parts; the newest imagery seems to be from a slightly drier time of year.

Just to keep us guessing, additional phases of architecture in the central city we hadn't seen before do pop out in the new data set. After seeing the differences between old and new, we want to test data of varying resolutions from different seasons. That will take time. And now we have WorldView-4 imagery to test[34] and dozens of new Tanis images. Our headpiece of Ra is multifaceted and not as easy to use as the one that Indy just had to stick on a pole of the right length.

At the very least, this more powerful imagery helps archaeologists choose more carefully and productively where to excavate. With the improving quality of the data, we can write far better grant proposals—or increasingly, do better pitches to private donors—to show with a high degree of accuracy what we'll be focusing on during our field seasons. Being able to say, "This season, the team will excavate two elite and two poorer houses at Tanis, to compare living conditions and access to both food and materials in a wealthy city," and then show the exact outlines of the chosen houses . . . well, that's convincing to any interested party.

A Clearer View of Modern Cities and Their Future

Cities like Tanis give us insights into our own societies, and make us wonder what crumbling remains of our own cities will be left for future archaeologists to excavate. It's hubris to think our society will survive in perpetuity. Look at Tanis now, and just imagine telling a Tanite of 1000 BC that the city's entire footprint would be lost.

Our cities will evolve alongside our concept of what makes a city and what about it is worth keeping. As I write this, many cities across the United States are experiencing a revival, from Detroit to Nashville to Birmingham, but we do not yet know why. Maybe it's the under-40s returning to urban centers to start their own businesses, or the craft brew movement that kick-starts redevelopment in the most unlikely of places. Maybe it's outside investment. When we do unravel this organic process, the potential for cities once thought to be irredeemable is limitless.

But our rural towns are now crumbling instead, and society is debating whether to save them or let us become a nation of cities. Big questions, and we can get the framework for answering them by diving into our deep human history.

o   o   o

My Hollywood fairy tale came full circle, from discovering an ancient city on our now-ancient VHS player, to seeing the same city come to life for real on my laptop with a godlike eye from the heavens. I've learned that the power of understanding the past in new ways is ultimately a balance between figuring out how to use new technologies and coming up with better questions to push the technology to its limits. Sometimes it works, sometimes it doesn't, and that's okay.

We occasionally get answers to our questions, from the brush of a trowel, a drop in a pipette, or a new, applied algorithm, but answers are momentary, like a cool breeze on a hot day in Tanis. All we can really do is hope we are digging in the right place.

6

A Grand Tour

On the streets of Birmingham, Alabama, one of my favorite things to do is to peer down street-repair holes. I should probably get a better hobby, but I love seeing the layered streets that have built up over time. A few stretches of cobblestones remain around our town, and walking there, I imagine horses, buggies, and the people from long ago. History lurks beneath our feet almost everywhere.

What we may not appreciate is the sheer number of sites, or even civilizations, lying beneath deserts and forests that archaeologists have not yet discovered. Finding a new feature on a site, or a new site altogether, is one thing, but now, using space archaeology we can find hundreds, thousands, or even tens of thousands of new sites and features.

This enormous scale is transforming archaeology so rapidly we have to formulate new questions to ask as we go. A century ago, or even 20 years ago, archaeologists could not have imagined the size of these data sets. Analysis of big data like this is itself quite a young field, but computer scientists are beginning to collaborate more closely with archaeologists to formulate mapping and modeling approaches.

Figuring Out What We Don't Know

Also, we have no idea how much we have left to find. Archaeologists certainly consult inscriptions, ancient texts, and papyri for clues to lost palaces or the whereabouts of a king's missing tomb. German archaeologist Heinrich Schliemann's obsession with the *Iliad* from a young age, and his later search for the city of Troy, is probably the most famous example of discovery through the study of ancient literature. Determined to find the city, Schliemann began work at a site called Hissarlik in Turkey in 1871, obliterating many levels from later time periods in his excavations. Today, we know the site as Troy, and you can still see the massive Schliemann trench. But there are limits to what written sources can tell us.

We have tax records from Roman Egypt that list dozens of ancient town names, but the names of modern towns may not be similar enough to give any hints of where the old towns and cities might be. If it is so easy to lose a town important enough to appear on the tax rolls, good luck finding the smaller places that never ranked a mention. In fact, I am often asked how much from ancient Egypt is left to discover. This is an impossible question—my favorite kind.

If only 1 percent of Egypt's wealthier tombs have been discovered, we can easily extrapolate this to all the poorer cemeteries, the settlements, vanished temples, industrial areas, quarries, and military outposts. And then just take that to the world, to unexplored and inaccessible lands in the Middle East, Africa, Central Asia, and the Far East. Consider the rainforests of Central and South America, the wilderness of Canada, the deserts of the American Southwest, and the Arctic plains. Millions of square kilometers currently lie beneath oceans, previously exposed during ice ages and covered over due to climate change or geological forces.[1]

What we do not know about the surface of our own planet is astounding, so we shouldn't really be surprised when archaeologists make new discoveries every week—massive cemeteries, previously unknown ancient cities, or even proof that the Neanderthals created cave art.[2]

America's Undiscovered Archaeology

We can start pretty close to home to get a sense of how much is out there in the rest of the world. Even the earliest European occupation of the United States is still not mapped fully. In 1540, Hernando de Soto and his band of conquistadors apparently explored all the way to North Carolina from their original landing spot in Florida,[3] with some potential evidence uncovered in McRae, Georgia.[4] Even today, the exact location of sites such as Mabila, where de Soto fought the legendary Chief Tuskaloosa somewhere in Alabama,[5] is the stuff of mystery and near fisticuff-level debates at yearly conferences at the University of Alabama, so I've been told.

Only 350 years ago, the skyscraper forests of our cities were real, untamed forests. Prior to European colonization of North America, Indigenous occupation stretched back 18,000 years. Evidence from mitochondrial DNA suggests that there was just one migration into the Americas at that time, and that all modern Indigenous people are descendants of that original population.[6] Known sites of human occupation so far are 14,000+ years old.[7] Six hundred generations—that's tens of millions of people—lived there before the first documented historical contact with Europeans in 1492.

Maps show original names and locations of these Indigenous groups, and others whose names have been lost. They reveal a well-traversed land.[8] Some groups moved seasonally to hunting or fishing grounds, extending the reach, and potential traces, of their cultures.[9] In Northern California, Siskiyou County alone has more than 10,000 sites,[10] and the county is 1/26th the size of the state. Assuming similar site densities throughout California, that means there could be a quarter of a million known archaeological sites in that one state, and that means tens of millions of known sites in the United States.

In the United States today, there are 567 federally recognized Indigenous tribes, 229 of whom live in Alaska.[11] Canada has 634 First Nations groups.[12] Each of these countries is nearly 10 million square kilometers: not easy to search, with dense tree cover over 40 percent of the continent, mountainous landscapes, and areas covered by snow for many months of the year.[13]

From the 1700s onward, the western movement of settlers across the United States, and the following displacement of millions of Indigenous people, led to the destruction of countless native sites.[14] Remote sensing is beginning to give us a sense of what was lost. In the Toolesboro Mounds National Historic Landmark in Iowa, archaeologists Melanie Riley and Joseph Tiffany, from the Georgia Department of Natural Resources and the Office of the State Archaeologist at the University of Iowa, embraced LIDAR to give them new perspectives. The Toolesboro team searched for a reported enclosure from the Middle Woodland culture of 200–300 AD, and traces of destroyed burial mounds.

Success! They located the enclosure, eight mounds, perhaps a ninth, and two anomalies.[15] The landscape in question is mainly forested, with only two visible mounds. It certainly shows you can't judge a site by its tree cover, and certainly not the size or scale of archaeological sites by what is out in the open now.

Farther south, in the Everglades of Florida, where pine forests, sawgrass marshes, and dense mangroves make a standard archaeological foot survey nearly impossible, LIDAR helped archaeologists locate earthworks dating from 1000 to 1500 AD.[16] Remote sensing's potential for our understanding of the diversity and richness of native cultures is immense. Equally, our understanding of European expansion is rapidly opening up thanks to recent advances in drone imaging and more availability of low-cost or free LIDAR data from state agencies.

Such open-access LIDAR data from southern New England allowed archaeologists Katharine Johnson and William Ouimet to identify a number of previously unknown building foundations, farm enclosure walls, and old roads dating from the 18th century to the 1950s.[17] This is an area mainly covered in forest today, which begs the question of how many thousands of other farms are out there.

Discoveries like this can enlighten dark times in our social history. While we have written accounts of slave-owning plantations, the archaeology on plantations in the United States is opening our eyes to the daily lives of slaves. In Maryland, LIDAR helped create 3-D maps of plantation sites at Tulip Hill and Wye Hall. New revelations included a potential terrace, embankment, slave quarters, and garden beds, though the archaeological team responsible has emphasized the need for test excavations to confirm those discoveries.[18]

All this, and yet archaeologists have completed surprisingly little remote sensing work in the United States and Canada, in comparison to the rest of the world. We're learning so much as this changes.

All Aboard

We've probably only mapped about 10 percent of the Earth's land surface for archaeological sites, and far less of the ocean floors. There's still a lot to see, so let's get a taste of the work being done globally, and explore the extraordinary scope of my colleagues' wide-ranging discoveries abroad. I think you'll soon share our field's excitement for the future potential of space archaeology.

In the 1700s and 1800s, wealthy young people from Europe and America would embark on grand tours of the Mediterranean and the Middle East, marveling at the wonders of the ancient world and coming home inspired. We don't need to limit ourselves, and we'll travel in style, by luxury cruise liner, and by air. No dress code for dinner, but do wear *something*. Enjoy the boarding gin and tonic—for medicinal purposes, naturally.

Mapping the Maya

Sit back in your deck chair and relax, but not for too long! We're heading to an area some might argue is the hotbed for remote archaeological discoveries, receiving the lion's share of media coverage over the last few years, and rightly so: it's not often you find tens of thousands of new features at well-known ancient sites. We're sailing south, to Central America.

It is home to the Maya civilization, located in an area of over 300,000 square kilometers, 43 percent of which is covered with dense rainforest and other vegetation.[19]

Given the landscape in the area, archaeologists must use LIDAR data to look for sites, and they are racing against time. Alarmingly, deforestation plays a role in the destruction of archaeological sites, as well as the environment. We can track the trees that have been lost through illegal logging, the use of chemicals in farming, and drug production, but we have no idea of the number of ancient sites that have disappeared.

As you saw earlier, the LIDAR revolution began with the work of Diane and Arlen Chase in Belize. As part of the same study, the Chases used LIDAR to map a 9-square-kilometer area in west-central Mexico around a site called Angamuco, which was built by Aztec rivals known as the Purépecha. Their findings showed a major urban settlement with hundreds of residential areas connected to monumental architecture.[20] After those astonishing results, other Mayanists soon received funding for their own LIDAR mapping efforts.

With that, I invite you all to board helicopters for a bird's-eye view of the stunning landscape the Maya occupied. On the way inland toward Guatemala, you fly over the rainforest in Belize. Looking down at the sea of green, you realize just why fieldwork there, in the company of jaguars and fer-de-lance vipers, is not for the faint of heart. I had the chance to work on the Belize Valley Archaeological Reconnaissance Project there as an undergraduate, and for two glorious weeks, I lived in the rainforest, helping to map cave systems used by the Maya for burials and ritual activities. Even walking through the buttress roots, vines, and creepers was a struggle.

As you enter Guatemalan airspace and approach Tikal, arguably the country's most well-known site, limestone pyramids peek out from the canopy just like in the scene from *Star Wars: The Empire Strikes Back*, but with the beautiful addition of noisy scarlet macaws. The movie was filmed here, and the view is otherworldly. No imperial storm-troopers to worry about in reality, but the botflies, which lay maggots beneath your skin to chew out on hatching, are far more terrifying.

It's hard to see anything except the monumental structures from above, and on the ground, the rest of the site is obscured by dense vegetation. In early 2018, a major announcement focused on the area. Using the largest LIDAR data set ever collected for archaeological research, a team of archaeologists analyzed more than 2,100 square kilometers in 10 distinct areas within the Maya Biosphere Reserve in Central America, targeting Tikal, Holmul, and other large Maya sites in Guatemala. To date, they have mapped more than 60,000 previously unknown buildings.[21]

In case you are wondering, that is insane. When I saw the news, I yelled so loudly my husband thought our cat had jumped on my back.

Those results are all part of a three-year project run by the PACU-NAM LiDAR Initiative. which has plans to map 14,000 square kilometers of Guatemala. Fundación PACUNAM is a not-for-profit focused on conservation and research in the Maya Biosphere Reserve. Francisco Estrada-Belli, one of the project co-directors, described to me the perils of ground work near Holmul.

In the middle of the night, he was awakened by something moving beneath his air mattress. Lifting it up, he found a five-foot-long snake coiled beneath where his head had just rested. The worst part: he had to put the mattress back down over the snake to get his pants on before getting help. And you thought only the archaeology was exciting![22]

Assuming similar densities of features, there could be as many as 400,000 previously unknown structures in the surveyed area alone. Maya civilization covered more than 300,000 square kilometers at its peak in about 800 AD, which means nearly 8.6 million potential sites and features could be hidden beneath the lush rainforests of Central America. And that's not even counting the vast landscape reshaping the Maya achieved. As my students say, I can't even.

The Secrets of the Amazon

After so many new sites to see, relax onboard ship for a while, while we sail along the coast of Brazil, and past the Amazon rainforest, which has an area of around 6 million square kilometers.[23] Starting more than a hundred years ago, a new age of archaeological exploration took root in its diverse regions. The disappearance of Percy Fawcett in 1925 in his quest to discover the city of "Z," as he called it, a mythical place somewhere in the Amazon, is one of the most well-known tales.[24]

Whatever happened to him, Fawcett was partially right, as Michael Heckenberger of the University of Florida found. Working with Indigenous groups, he and his team located 28 previously unknown plaza towns and villages in the Upper Xingu headwaters of the Amazon.[25] These settlements included a series of ditches and could be connected by ancient roads.[26] Though the team did not make these discoveries using satellite imagery, they showed the intensity of pre-Columbian occupation in the Amazon. We can only imagine what remote sensing will show in the region.

Also in Amazonia, in the Acre district of western Brazil, a team led by Martti Pärssinen of the University of Helsinki used aerial photographs and Google Earth to identify more than 200 new geoglyphs. Like the Nazca lines, these figures or geographic patterns are created on the ground by humans out of natural materials such as stone, or by clearing away stones, on a sometimes epic scale. In Acre, they are signs of a "new" civilization dating between 200 and 1283 AD. The satellite imagery, taken after deforestation occurred, allowed the team to map the sites in great detail and revealed curious shapes with diameters from 90 meters to 300 meters—one to three American football fields—which could have been ceremonial, defensive, or both. Work on the ground led researchers to suggest a population of more than 60,000 in a region once considered too marginal for intensive exploitation. With the limited coverage of Google Earth, the team believes they've found only 10 percent of the features in the region. That means there may be nearly 2,000 other monumental structures there.[27]

It shows the region's extraordinary potential for archaeological discovery. The Amazon might once have been as densely occupied as the Maya region in Central America. I hope LIDAR can be applied broadly there soon, and I expect big headlines.

As we sail around Cape Horn, things could get a little dicey onboard. Load up on the seasickness tablets, because we're on our way to Peru! You might be familiar with the epic tale of Hiram Bingham's 1912 investigation of Machu Picchu, which is now considered to be the top tourist destination in South America, but that was a hint of what was to come.[28]

Across Peru, high-resolution satellite imagery and drones have allowed both archaeological discoveries and the mapping of looting across many ancient sites.[29] Peru has a long history of looting, and, sadly, you can see thousands of looting pits at many ancient cemeteries. Looters sift through graves looking for bright colored textiles to sell, and they're often successful. Recently, I made a quick search of eBay under "antiquities Peru textiles," and it revealed dozens, from the Chimú, Huari, and Chancay cultures. None of the listings had site locations, which suggests very strongly their sketchy origins.

To map threatened Peruvian sites enables archaeologists to begin safeguarding them. One team, led by Rosa Lasaponara, used a combination of QuickBird and WorldView-1 satellite imagery to reveal evidence of potential buried adobe features at the Piramide Naranjada, which they later confirmed with ground-penetrating radar and magnetometry.[30] Elsewhere, archaeologist and former vice-minister of culture for Peru, Luis Jaime Castillo, has used drones to create beautiful and awe-inspiring 3-D models of dozens of sites, making Peru perhaps one of the most thoroughly drone-mapped countries in the world.[31]

Polynesian Preconceptions

We have some time to rest as we cross the ocean, so a bit of an introduction before we disembark for our next site tour at one of the most well-known archaeological islands in Polynesia. Today a part of Chile, Easter Island has more than 900 large stone statues called moai, the famous standing humanoid sculptures, located within a landscape of only 163.6 square kilometers. One of the reasons I love the story of work here is that it shows how satellite technologies have upended long-held assumptions about how and why the Rapa Nui civilization "collapsed." Things are often more complex than they seem.

Walking around the island, you'll be struck by its light green landscape outlined starkly against the backdrop of the Pacific. It seems so cut off, especially after what you saw in Guatemala. The stone sentinels themselves are square-jawed, stoic, and challenging, daring us to wonder how they came to be.

Europeans came to the island for a day in 1722 and again in 1770, and found a population of 3,000 people. The general assumption about the Rapa Nui was said to be a lesson for us today: when they occupied the island, they overexploited its natural resources, destroyed the forest, and drove their animals to extinction. Earlier archaeologists had assumed Easter Island was first occupied between 400 and 800 AD, but using radiocarbon dating of seeds, archaeologists Carl Lipo of Binghamton University and Terry Hunt of the University of Oregon have found evidence for a much later colonization, after 1200 AD.[32]

Using high-resolution satellite imagery, Lipo and Hunt mapped the roads on which the ancient moai were transported across the island.[33] During their survey work, they discovered 62 moai along roads leading from the source quarry. Based on the resting positions of the statues, the team proved the hypothesis that they were "walked" upright by groups of people on either side—not dragged—to their final positions.[34] The discovery dispenses with the fixed idea of mass deforestation just to create rollers to move the moai. The Rapa Nui exploited their own ingenuity, not their forests, to move their greatest works of art.

Where deforestation happened for agricultural purposes, the people preserved the land's productivity by crushing volcanic rocks and adding them to their gardens like mulch.[35] Based on recent geospatial analysis, it appears the Rapa Nui built their *ahu*, or megalithic platforms on which one or more moai can be found, close to freshwater sources, potentially indicating a display of territories connected to a limited natural resource.[36] Rather than bringing about their own demise, the Rapa Nui were decimated by disease brought by the Europeans.[37]

As we leave the island behind us, alone in the wild sea, you can wonder what else the West has misinterpreted about Indigenous groups across the globe to fit preconceived notions rooted in a colonialist mentality. Remote sensing, it seems, could provide a more factual interpretation.

The Silk Road

Across the ocean, west into Asia, we see endless landscapes unroll in front of us, with equally extensive opportunities for remote sensing. It's a huge area: vast regions of the Silk Road remain unmapped, yet Chinese archaeologists have already created a database of 51,074 sites dating from 8000 BC to 500 AD, taken from site maps of 25 Chinese provinces.[38]

The Silk Road, used for over 1,500 years, stretched across land and sea from China, to India, into Indonesia, across Iran, through the Middle East, to East Africa, and on to Europe. Not one road, it was many routes that fluctuated over time based on access to water and other resources. The full scale of the sites along the Silk Road, and the number of roads in this network, are still emerging. Many sites along the Silk Road can be differentiated according to time period by their shape and size from space, without a ground survey, which throws open the potential for future remote-sensing efforts to reveal and date many hundreds of additional archaeological treasures there.

In one study, CORONA and Google Earth data helped archaeologists N. K. Hu of Shaanxi Normal University and X. Li of the Chinese Academy of Sciences expose 70 previously unknown sites in northwestern China around the Juyan Oasis, dating primarily from 1028 to 1375 AD.[39] Imagine the other oases, the trade posts and junctions on the routes, that still remain to be mapped.

Sailing west, we round Thailand, Vietnam, and Cambodia, filled with the magnificent temples of the Khmer. The rainforests of Thailand and Vietnam have not yet been mapped, but I've heard rumors that new LIDAR campaigns are about to be launched. Adventure awaits.

New Beginnings for the Indus Valley

And here we are in India. Vibrant, varied, and ancient, it's a country with some of the greatest remote sensing potential on Earth. A big part of this tempting prospect is the Indus Valley Civilization, relatively unmapped from space, unlike similarly ancient civilizations Egypt and Mesopotamia. Larger than both, the Indus Valley Civilization swept across India, Pakistan, and beyond.

Results of recent mapping lead us to expect great things. One team, led by Cameron Petrie of the University of Cambridge, has used remote sensing and ground surveys in northwest India[40] to visualize relationships between ancient sites and the rivers close to them. The team mapped more than 10,000 square kilometers of ancient river channels using medium-resolution satellite data sets. They created a 3-D model of the landscape's topography and have very kindly provided their code for all researchers to use.[41]

Another team, led by Ajit Singh of the Indian Institute of Technology, Kanpur, and Sanjeev Gupta of Imperial College London, made a global splash when they used radar-derived elevation models and Landsat data to locate an ancient channel of the Sutlej River, known as the Ghaggar-Hakra, in northwest India. For over a century, archaeologists believed that the densest concentrations of Indus Valley urban settlements relied on a major river with its source in the Himalayas. They were so convinced, they claimed that when the river dried up or moved, the urban sites declined and were abandoned between 2000 and 1900 BC.

This is a tidy story, but the remote-sensing work and subsequent coring and dating efforts overturned it completely. The new research proved that the river actually dried up by 6000 BC, long before the rise of the Indus Valley Civilization around 3000 BC. This suggested that Indus Valley settlements appeared along the relic river channel because of its relative stability, free from unpredictable flooding.[42]

I'm very excited about what will be found right across Asia in the next few years. We can sit back and contemplate that as we sail across the Indian Ocean to South Africa. We'll need to enjoy a few vineyards to recover.

Our Earliest Ancestors

This is where it all gets dusty, and hot. Much of the African continent remains unmapped and unexplored archaeologically. It would take volumes to even begin to describe the extraordinary diversity of cultures and peoples who have lived there since the first *Homo sapiens*. Going further back, our family tree looks more like a dense bush, and new ancient human ancestor fossil sites sometimes appear in unexpected places. We have barely scratched the surface in understanding our human origins, and I think Africa represents the greatest frontier for archaeological discovery in the world.

Large regions of East and South Africa are ripe for exploration using satellite imagery, and contain some of the best-known sites where early human fossils have been found. And plants, not artifacts, lay our trail here. Paleoanthropologist Lee Berger, from the University of the Witwatersrand, in South Africa, used Google Earth to find wild olive and stinkwood trees, which tend to grow near the entrances of caves in South Africa.[43] Perhaps ideal sites for our early ancestors' shelters, those caves can contain new species of early humans.

Around the Turkana Basin, in Kenya, the son of world-famous anthropologists Louis and Mary Leakey, Richard, and his wife, Maeve, made many of their famous discoveries. Today, their daughter Louise continues the family tradition. Hyperspectral cameras and other remote-sensing tools might assist such evolution explorers in the location of other sites. Fossils emerge from the ground after rains or as a result of erosion processes; when they could be scattered across areas measuring hundreds of square kilometers, a ground-based surveyor is limited to lucky finds and happy accidents.

However, high-resolution maps, created by hyperspectral cameras, showing exactly where other fossils might emerge, would better target their search. In a collaborative project with Louise Leakey and her team in the Turkana Basin, I was proud to help develop such mapping. While the results are largely preliminary, the cameras did detect areas with the same spectral signatures as other fossil-rich deposits. The mind boggles at how such new data might assist in our understanding of our own evolution.

Zimbabwean Achievements

It's a long, long trek overland, north and east to our next stop. The massive stone-built ruins of Great Zimbabwe, capital of the Zimbabwe people, is a UNESCO World Heritage site and has recently been remapped using high-resolution satellite imagery. From 300 BC to 1900 AD, Great Zimbabwe had five phases of occupation. Unfortunately, archaeological work had to stop altogether in the 1990s because of the political situation there.

Thanks to Shadreck Chirikure and his team at the University of Cape Town, work has recently resumed, and already, satellite data has shown previously unknown terracing, unmapped walls, and three routes up the main hill complex of the site.[44] Perhaps an additional satellite survey will add to our knowledge of the 200 or so smaller Zimbabwes, other stone enclosures such as Mapela Hill in southwestern Zimbabwe, showing that the region had a far greater political importance than previously assumed.[45]

We're back into tree cover again in Central Africa, where a rainforest measuring millions of square kilometers stretches through Cameroon, Gabon, Congo, Uganda, and up into the Central African Republic. In West Africa, too, dense vegetation blankets the landscape. It's largely unexplored for archaeology, with work beginning only in the last 50 years.

Exploration on the ground is difficult in the region because of ongoing wars, disease, and lack of infrastructure. Given the region's rich history, though, and recent discoveries of new sites and features in the rainforests across the Atlantic, the area is crying out for LIDAR work. Who knows what could be found; maybe even large-scale farming or other signs of entirely undefined civilizations. If I could pick anywhere in the world to turn my archaeological all-seeing eyes, this would be it. Discoveries there could shake up our perceptions of the continent.

Familiar Territory

Northward up the east coast of Africa, we come to the great snorkeling opportunities of the Red Sea. Its crystal waters are rich with coral and brightly colored parrotfish and angelfish, and the seafood is great. A project led by Matthew Meredith-Williams using radar and high-resolution satellite images has revolutionized our understanding of more than 4,200 shell-midden sites in the Farasan Islands and Dahlak Archipelago, off the coasts of Saudi Arabia and Eritrea, respectively.

These middens show up as hills of hundreds of thousands of shells, measuring up to 6 meters in height, and they are common throughout the world where people depended heavily on the fruits of the sea. Archaeologists knew of only 20 before, so this is a wealth of new information. The mounds range in age, but most probably formed more than 5,000 years ago,[46] which suggests that there could have been many more people than were previously assumed living in the area.

Inland, through the dry desert river wadis carved down through the sand and rock, we come to ancient Nubia, in modern Sudan and the far south of Egypt. It was one of the greatest civilizations in Africa, and has received less attention and less satellite imagery analysis than its more famous northern neighbor. Rising waters from dam projects in Sudan prompted major surveys in the 1960s, leading to numerous archaeological discoveries. Today, similar dam projects threaten vast tracts of land, which archaeologists once more have limited time to survey.

The promise of satellite imagery for detecting sites shines at the archaeological sites of Karima and Gebel Barkal, 350 kilometers north of Khartoum. Archaeologists located relic courses of the Nile, created high-resolution 3-D site maps, and found a wealth of features for investigation in future seasons at Gebel Barkal.[47] I cannot stress enough the urgency of using satellite imagery here—this part of Sudan may contain hundreds of unknown sites, and development, including gold mining, also represents a serious threat.[48]

As we pass by Egypt through the Suez Canal, we can look west to the Nile Delta. I had adventures to last me a lifetime of dinner parties during my survey work there, including the time when a man demanded that I marry his toothless son. I told him his son would not be able to enjoy my cooking, and the father answered, without missing a beat, "Do not worry! He can enjoy your soup!"

Beyond the Delta lies the barrenness of the Western Desert, which is the gateway into the Sahara. Here, 9 million square kilometers have witnessed countless changes in climate, from wet to semiarid to dry and back again. It spans 10 countries, with large areas too inaccessible to explore, so the best way to search for its hidden treasures is from space. Unless you happen to be a camel, in which case, go for it.

An ongoing project in southwestern Libya led by David Mattingly and Martin Sterry from the University of Leicester has located more than 180 cemeteries and 158 new settlements amid the sand. Using high-resolution satellite imagery, drones, and photos taken from kites, the project has led to new insights about the Garamantes, a so-called lost civilization that flourished from 300 BC to 500 AD.[49] The team's efforts in Libya and Tunisia have revealed thousands of other forts, settlements, roads, and cultivated areas, showing the true scale of occupation in the region.

Sites Under Fire

As we sail along the coastlines of Israel, Lebanon, and Turkey, you're seeing the landscapes of the other great remote sensing revolution in the world. While Central America is leading the charge for the use of LIDAR, archaeologists in the Middle East have found sites at a jaw-dropping scale.[50] We've barely begun the archaeological interpretation of all this new data. In 23,000 square kilometers of northeastern Syria alone, a Harvard University team looked at lower-resolution satellite imagery and digital elevation models using data sets from several different seasons and detected 14,000 archaeological sites.[51] Given the ongoing conflicts in Syria, parts of Iraq, and Afghanistan, remote sensing has been an invaluable way for archaeologists to continue their mapping work.

In Afghanistan, David Thomas of La Trobe University in Australia has focused on the use of Google Earth for site mapping and planning. In 2008, he noted that only 7 percent of Afghanistan—46,000 square kilometers—had high-resolution Google Earth coverage. In that small area, archaeologists knew of about 250 sites, but only 33 of them had detailed architectural plans; the countrywide database stands at only 1,300 sites at present.[52]

Working in a country like Afghanistan carries major risks. Thomas described one incident in 2005 where his team's chartered plane didn't show up when they were trying to get back to Kabul. They had to drive all the way back, a distance of nearly 500 kilometers, and nearly crashed into an artillery canon casually left in the dark outside one village, in the middle of the road. When he asked the airline why the plane didn't show up, they told him, "Stuff happens."[53] Stuff is not the word I would use here.

His team looked at 45 medieval sites, only 8 of which had available plans, and used satellite imagery to draw their above-surface features. They discovered 451 additional sites, which included campsites, dams, enclosures, dwellings, and hamlets, giving a site density of 0.32 sites per square kilometer in the Registan Desert region alone. Afghanistan has a total area of 653,000 square kilometers; if the entire country was occupied to the same extent, there could be more than 209,000 additional sites.

This is not surprising. The country is at the crossroads of East and West, valued by conquerors, ancient and modern.[54] Ongoing work at the University of Chicago's Afghan Heritage Mapping Project has discovered numerous new settlements, caravan rest houses, and relic river channels, tripling the number of known sites.[55]

We can follow those caravans west to Jordan, a country roughly one-eighth the size of Afghanistan, but with an equally rich history. Here, we see the work done over the past three decades by David Kennedy of the University of Western Australia and Robert Bewley of the University of Oxford, using tens of thousands of aerial photographs.[56] In an area of western Jordan, where only 8,680 sites were known to the Jordanian Department of Antiquities, they found more than 25,000. At their estimates, 100,000 sites could be there.[57]

With high-resolution Google Earth imagery now covering almost all of Jordan, Kennedy and Bewley are continuing their efforts via the Endangered Archaeology in the Middle East and North Africa project. Based at Oxford, this project aims to map the ongoing threats to sites across the region.[58] The MEGA-Jordan website,[59] supported by the Department of Antiquities, has a database of more than 27,000 known sites,[60] meaning a site density of 0.3 sites per square kilometer. And that's just the known sites.

The World's Most-Mapped Countries

We'll continue east, stopping off in Rome for some gelato and pasta. Time to stretch our sea legs—we've traveled some 60,000 kilometers!

Italy is basically one gigantic archaeological site, since people have occupied its landscapes intensively for thousands of years. Led by Rosa Coluzzi and Rosa Lasaponara of the Istituto di Metodologie per l'Analisi Ambientale, a team there used LIDAR to discover a medieval village in southern Italy, revealing buried structures[61] and mapping ancient river channels in the Apulia region.[62] Also, multi-spectral and aerial photographs combined with ground-based remote sensing helped reveal a detailed outline of the Roman city of Altinum near the Venice Lagoon.[63]

Europe has a long tradition of using remotely sensed data sets, and many archaeologists there were early adopters of satellite imagery. But despite large areas of Europe being so well mapped, we keep getting surprises like new hillforts, Roman villas, and medieval churches.

As we head through the Mediterranean and north, we're nearing the end of our journey.

If we were to say that the Brits love maps and mapping, that would be a wee understatement: the United Kingdom is one of the most well-mapped countries in the world, and it even forces its London cabbie-wannabes to memorize and take tests on the "Knowledge," more than 25,000 street names and 20,000 places of interest, plus 320 routes between all those locations.[64] It takes three to four years to pass.

It's unsurprising that the United Kingdom has more than 190,000 listed archaeological sites,[65] and for a country of 243,000 square kilometers, that is a *lot* of sites. And there is more to map—try 17 kilometers of Roman roads in Lancashire.[66] LIDAR data is now available across a large part of the country, going back to 2008, and ranges in resolution from 25 centimeters to 2 meters. The availability of those data sets sheds new light on known sites and is already changing British archaeology. In the summer of 2018, due to unusually low rain levels, crop marks appeared by the bushel in fields across the country, prompting archaeologists to launch drones to capture the ephemeral hints before they disappeared again.[67]

Across the Channel in Belgium, similar efforts with LIDAR have revealed a potential Iron Age hillfort as well as Celtic field-and-barrow complexes beneath forests. The technology has allowed the team from the Flanders Heritage Agency to combine management for wildlife with ancient feature preservation.[68]

Underwater Archaeology

On our return voyage across the Atlantic to New York, look down into the depths of the ocean. I'd be missing our eighth continent if I did not point out underwater archaeology and its great potential. While satellites cannot see through deeper water because of the reflection of light off its surface and the water's movement, cutting-edge applications of remote-sensing underwater technologies are making progress. I've heard estimates from specialists of three million shipwrecks remaining to be discovered globally. Given the challenges of searching deeper waters for wrecks and sites submerged as the result of earthquakes or higher water levels, satellites and drones might be our most cost-effective tool for finding all sorts of underwater features.

Google Earth is a simple but valuable tool, with imagery taken during low tides capturing a 1,000-year-old stone fish trap off the coast of Wales.[69] NASA scientists have already shown how free, lower-resolution Landsat-8 imagery can reveal shipwrecks in coastal waters by identifying sediment plumes, streamers of sand and dirt from the sea bottom pushed to its surface by the movement of currents over submerged objects.[70] Drones are now being deployed to help find shipwrecks beneath the surface of Lake Huron in the northern United States.[71]

Since that kind of imagery is only able to capture features close to coasts, ocean drones like the OpenROV,[72] a briefcase-sized machine that anyone can purchase and use, will contribute much to archaeological discovery and shipwreck mapping. In the future, additional spectral bands in satellite imagery might improve mapping below the surface of oceans and lakes. I volunteer first for any related survey work in the Greek islands. You all know it will be a huge sacrifice for me.

So What Is Left to Find?

Let's rephrase the question posed at the beginning of the chapter: Can we suggest the total number of sites left for us to discover globally? Such a guesstimate could fuel a new generation of explorers and new developments in archaeological technologies.

Here goes. From broad-scale discoveries in previously unmapped parts of Asia, to new LIDAR data sets revealing features in already well-mapped countries, we've seen just how much is being discovered at present. And those are just the larger-sized features visible through remote sensing, not the small-scale sites that are still the domain of the sharp-eyed on foot.

There are nearly 40 million square kilometers of habitable land on our planet. Just looking at larger-site densities per country, in areas that we have discussed above or those elsewhere, we get figures ranging from 0.3 sites to nearly 1 site per square kilometer, but that depends on how each individual country defines what constitutes a site. Even if we go with the lowest density of sites detectable from space published in larger area surveys and expand that to the globe, that's 12 million potential sites.

Extrapolating from this and from some of what I know will be announced in the next few years, I'll go out on a limb:

I believe there are more than 50 million unknown archaeological sites, from major settlements to small campsites, left to discover globally, above and below water. And that's on the conservative end of my calculations.

The scale and pace of discovery, and the big new questions it allows us to ask, put us firmly in an archaeological golden age. And it pales in comparison to what we could find with better sensors. Imagine the day when we have a space-based laser-mapping system like LIDAR, and we can map beneath all of the Earth's vegetated areas.

We've been recognizably human for around 13,800 generations, and 108 billion people may have lived in the last 50,000 years.[73] That's a lot of human activity to trace. With my estimate of 10 percent of the Earth's surface already explored archaeologically, we still have close to roughly 36 million square kilometers of habitable area remaining,[74] without counting shipwrecks or inundated sites under oceans, seas, lakes, and rivers. I could be horribly mistaken, by the way; the number of unknown sites could be far higher or far lower. I'm counting on one of you to prove me wrong.

When we have a better sense of the global range and type of archaeological sites and can collect the data from their surfaces and below the ground, what we find will grant us access to new insights about how and why civilizations emerge, rise, collapse, and, with resilience, rise again.

Bronze fittings excavated at Tell Tebilla
[photo courtesy Greg Mumford]

Photograph of the landscape of Skagafjörður
[photo by the author]

Processed WorldView-2 satellite imagery of Tanis showing the extent of the ancient settlement [courtesy DigitalGlobe]

General photograph of the central area of Tanis, showing the silty landscape where the bulk of the city appears in the satellite imagery. Virtually nothing is visible on the surface. [photo by the author]

WorldView-2 processed satellite image of feature at Papa Stour, North House
[courtesy DigitalGlobe]

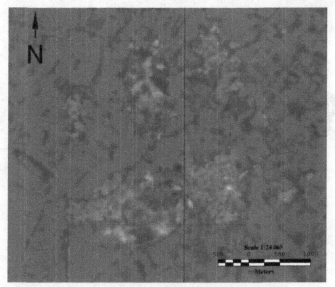

*Processed Landsat-7 satellite imagery, showing multispectral analysis
of a site in Egypt* [imagery courtesy NASA]

Analyzing the core samples at Lisht with Dr. Zaghloul, Dr. Bunbury, Dr. Bader, and Louise Bray from the BBC [photo by the author]

Digging the tomb of Intef at Lisht [photo by the author]

Image of an ancient face from Lisht [photo by the author]

Intef's name and title [photo by the author]

Eye inlay from Intef's tomb [photo by the author]

Completed excavations at the tomb of Intef [photo by the author]

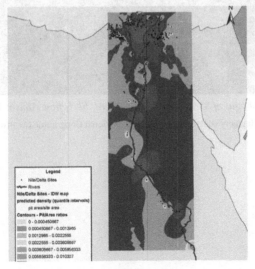

Looting density across Egypt [image by the author]

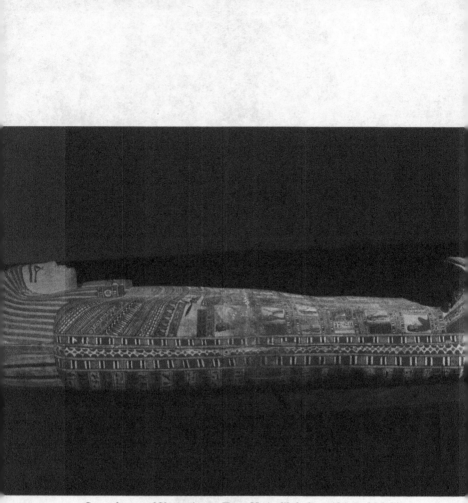

Sarcophagus of Shesep-Amun-Tayes-Herit, likely from Abusir el Malik
[imagery courtesy Rebecca Hale, National Geographic Creative]

7

Empires Fall

Now that we've toured a world of archaeological discoveries, I know you're jet-lagged. Let's park ourselves at the Mena House Hotel for a while and enjoy a drink, gazing at the Giza pyramids that rise just beyond the hotel's lavish gardens. Pull up a thick-cushioned chair to a low brass table. A waiter in a red tarboosh will take your order; I like an ice-cold hibiscus juice after a long day out—fresh, tart, and a little sweet.

A View of the Past, and a Lesson for Our Future

After 4,700 years and without their original limestone casing, the pyramids still command our gaze, even on a hazy day, from downtown Cairo some five miles away. They make us ask questions of ancient Egypt and of ourselves, including why pyramid building at such an immense scale stopped, and why Egyptian culture rose in the Old Kingdom, ultimately fell, and rose again in renaissance during the Middle Kingdom.

We also wonder if anything from our own time will last through future millennia. Our impermanence is laid bare in the presence of the pyramids; they hold lessons for us today as we try to keep our footing in a world that seems ever more turbulent.

When those monuments stood as gleaming white sentinels along the banks of the Nile, the Egyptians surely did not imagine the empty, eternal ruins they would eventually become. They were busy people, building, trading, plotting, learning, caught up in the everyday affairs of being human in a world of increasing complexity. Like us, they wrote on walls and obsessed over cats.

After looking down and gathering insights from space, putting ourselves into the sandals of past people can give us a different perspective, especially as your seat in the Mena House bar looks out over the desert, where a vast cemetery hides a multitude of clues to ancient lives.

Clues Woven into Stories

From human remains, we can spin out a whole life, such as that of a poor girl from Tell Ibrahim Awad, a site in Egypt's northeast Delta. We'll call her Meryt, the beloved. We don't have her real name, just the excavated bones of an adult woman. You never know what you'll find beneath the ground, or the stories it will allow you to tell, especially after a few of the Mena House's excellent G and Ts.

○　○　○

Meryt wound reed stems together, dangling her feet in the canal. Just another twist, and the reed boat's prow would lock tight, ready for sailing. Or racing.

"Hurry up, little sister! Ours are finished already!"

Meryt shouted to Teti to go ahead. Two years older, he'd want to win anyway, guiding the boat past papyrus thickets alive with birds, to where the bank shallowed and the king's cows came to drink. "Meryt, now! Or I'll come and stomp on it!"

A distant thump: her oldest brother, Seneb, had hit him with something, but Teti was giggling.

"If you do, I'll bash you!" Meryt shouted back. Five years old or not, when they played stick battles, she could hold her own. She set the boat into the water's quiet gurgle.

Downstream, a tail-whisking sea of horns and glossy coats sploshed down the riverbank, prodded along by her father. She waved.

"Boys, don't let a crocodile eat her," he called. "And don't forget the fodder needs cutting. If you want us to trade for meat, you'll help get it in."

"Yes, Father," they groaned. Teti fished his boat out.

"And you said it'd be good, having our own field."

Rolling his eyes, Seneb wrung the hem of his kilt.

"So it'd be better to have nothing to sell to the estate?" Teti thought about it. Absently he rubbed his stomach as they set off, and Meryt wound her arm through his.

Their house was nearby, through the royal pastureland, the date groves, and their small plot. Mud-brick houses staggered uphill from the town wall, out of reach of the annual floods. Several thousand neighbors jostled the temples and the governor's enclosure.

Seneb grabbed some fodder for the donkey snoozing in the stable built onto the house. Inside, Mother was preparing lunch. When Father came home, they sat together and ate bread and stewed vegetables.

"Hotep, would you take Meryt with you to town?" Mother asked, smiling at Teti shoveling in the last beans. She glanced through into the only other room, at the loom's shroud of half-woven linen, and Father nodded.

Later, Meryt held tight to Father's hand as they wound through narrow streets and up to the Nubian soldiers beside the governor's gate. One waved at her, but kept to his post.

"Taxes?" asked a scribe who saw them in.

Inside the lush courtyard, Father leaned down to Meryt.

"Stay here, darling, and don't make a nuisance of yourself," he whispered.

Not a short man, he looked very small disappearing inside a house that rose three times taller than their own and spanned wider than their field. Meryt squatted down to watch scribes sitting cross-legged, their accounts stretched across their laps. Their kilt fabric was a costly weave that Mother had tried to teach her. But a man came out wearing linen so fine his belly button gaped from behind it like an empty mouth.

He stood over the scribes, and the gold-beaded collar across his chest flashed.

"His Majesty is pleased with the year's taxation. He will honor your Lord with a burial place at Saqqara." A steward looked up, mid-correction of a junior's addition.

"Will he really, sir? Our province gives its humblest thanks." But the steward did not get up, and soon turned back to the figures.

Awkwardly, the dignitary paused, and then left with a nervous squint at the soldiers.

"Come, Meryt!" Father reached down to hoist her into his arms. She laughed and bit into the cake he had placed in her hand. "A treat from the governor," Father said, smiling. "Now, shall we see about racing your brothers' boats?"

The Prosperous Old Kingdom

Meryt and her family start out in a time of relative peace and prosperity in the later Old Kingdom, around 2700–2200 BC. During that long sweep, we see overall growth and consolidation of state power, with kings ruling as gods from Memphis, just south of present-day Cairo,[1] and overseeing the infrastructure necessary to unite the country's people and resources.[2] Egypt's renowned bureaucracy develops, with scribes and administrators as well as architects and artisans becoming essential parts of Egypt's societal fabric.

Major pyramid building kicks off in Dynasty 4 with the Red Pyramid at Dashur, when King Sneferu (2615–2589 BC) completes what becomes the quintessential royal tomb design. For such megaprojects and rapid state growth, Egypt has to reach out: Sneferu sends numerous expeditions to Sinai for copper and turquoise, to Nubia for gold, and to Lebanon for cedarwood. Dynasty 5 (2498–2345 BC) looks even farther abroad, to places such as Punt, probably in Eritrea, where traders and emissaries collect gold, incense, and baboons.

Wealth pours in from home, too. The establishment of new cattle estates in the Delta gives the court and pyramid builders alike regular access to beef and creates employment for generations of families like Meryt's. Royal agricultural settlements, including those granted to mortuary cults, feed workforces tens of thousands strong and still generate surpluses.[3]

To organize an increasingly complex national administration, and more significantly, its tax dues, a provincial system of nomes—similar to states or provinces—divides the country into 22 Upper Egyptian and 20 Lower Egyptian units. They are led by nomarchs, or regional governors.[4] It's possible that the nome designation originally referred to areas of good cattle pasture, similar to where Meryt and her family live. Cows and their welfare are that precious.

But far enough from court to consolidate power, local officials farm homegrown influence, too. Change and decentralization of power begin under King Djedkare Isesi (2414–2375 BC). Instead of loyally deriving influence by constructing their tombs around the royal pyramids, nomarchs are buried in their own provinces with private mortuary cults. Commoners also gain religious privileges normally reserved for royalty and noblemen.

And far to the south, Nubia starts to flex its muscles. By Dynasty 6, new and stronger Nubian cultures rise, and diplomatic contact is left to governors in Aswan, rather than the king's officials.

By the time Pepi I (2321–2287 BC) takes the throne, the massive, decorated tombs of self-eulogizing provincial officials display unashamed wealth and power, when for generations, royal pyramids had shrunk in scale. The Pyramid Texts—wall-to-wall esoteric prayers carved throughout the royal burial chambers—are their crowning glory.[5] Nevertheless, the texts required less manpower, and, being hidden from sight, they hardly made the same statement as the massive earlier monuments.

Pepi eventually tries to join what he can't beat, marrying the daughter of a provincial official from Abydos in Upper Egypt. That sounds pretty shrewd, but he wasn't consistent: he also granted a tax exemption to the mortuary cult of Sneferu at Dashur when the king's cut of any royal mortuary cult was too valuable an asset to simply give away.

The silt hits the alluvial fan, so to speak, when Pepi II (2278–2184 BC) inherits the throne at the age of six and rules for nearly a century. More tax exemptions hemorrhage wealth and cripple the central administration, and rule becomes hereditary in the provinces, no longer granted by the king himself. Worse still, massacres of Pepi II's troops occur in Nubia and Sinai. Any idea of expansion is kicked out of bounds.

The Final Frontier

There's no better evidence for mission-abort abroad than an Old Kingdom fortress on the western Sinai coast, on a beach by the Red Sea. I was lucky enough to work there on Greg's mission between 2002 and 2010, until a latter-day Intermediate Period rendered Sinai too volatile. It's a beautiful site—we very much hope to return one day. The site is a circular stone structure that measures 40 meters in diameter and has walls 7 meters thick and more than 3 meters tall on the northern side. It housed an Egyptian expedition during a series of seasonal missions to mine copper and turquoise.[6]

Egypt's broad-scale growth created demand for exotic raw materials. Anyone of means wanted amulets or jewelry fashioned from turquoise, since it was sacred to Hathor, the goddess of love and fertility, and everyone needed copper. From stonemasons' chisels and carpenters' tools, to knives and axes, personal accessories such as mirrors and razors, and statues and vessels for cultic equipment and even makeup, copper ore, not stone, built Egypt. Access to the mines was essential.

Over the course of our fieldwork at this unique fort, we estimated that at least four or five expeditions had used it prior to a catastrophic storm surge that partly destroyed it. As "storm surge" suggests, these waves form in the Red Sea during extreme weather events. The seaward walls were covered in a cement-like coating of salt spray, and the western bastion, or quay, was partially churned up, with beach pebbles and shells mixed with broken construction blocks.

Presumably to prevent the fort from being reused by potentially hostile locals, or possibly just to relocate it, the Egyptians dismantled some of it prior to 2200 BC. They thinned the walls to 20 centimeters on the southern side, walled up its western doorway, and used grapefruit-size cobblestones to close its interior entry passage. And then they abandoned it.

None too surprising, in hindsight. With the major damage sustained during the postulated wave, and reduced confidence in reinforcements arriving from the mainland, it was time to get the heck out of Dodge and go home to face an uncertain future. It's a sobering thought that we might have found evidence for one of Egypt's last mining trips to Sinai, prior to the fall of the Old Kingdom.

Around the end of Pepi II's rule, in an increasingly fragile Egypt, only a final straw was needed to bring the central government down.

o   o   o

"Meryt, not there." Seneb yanked his hoe back, just as Meryt hopped from one mound of silt to the next. "And not there, either."

Scraping the ditches clear, Teti grinned. Another front tooth had recently fallen out. Giggling, Meryt jumped down into the dry field.

"Sons," Father said, panting, "we must get this finished today." Lean, wiry, and drenched from the furious summer heat, he smashed his hoe down into soil dark as his sunburned skin. "Meryt, please fetch some water."

She found their jar beneath a sycamore fig. Irrigation canals stretched all the way to the river. Mounds stood ready to trap the precious water after it rose; inundation had made it up to these fields since before Seneb was born.

That night, Mother prepared extra beer to celebrate. She tied her dark curls back into a knot, laughing at Father's silly jokes, and the oil lamp lit her smile. Falling asleep, Meryt puzzled over the sand-brown lines on Mother's teeth, when her own were pale and smooth.

o   o   o

"Little sister, wake up."

She blinked. It was long after bedtime.

"Teti?" He sat her up, pointing at the window.

"Look. Sopdet is rising again. Inundation will be soon—we'll race boats all the way to the fig tree." Through heavy eyes, she stared at the brightest light in the sky—the star Sopdet never lied.

But the next day, when the town gathered at the riverside where priests inspected the notched pillar, the river showed no sign of flooding.

A week later, at the same spot, people held their children close, their voices hushed, and the priests seemed pale. Returning home, Meryt's family passed a docked ship loaded with sweet-smelling lumber. Half the deck was empty. Grave faced, a dignitary and a troop detachment disembarked and headed toward the governor's enclosure, while a deckhand secured the mooring stake. Father greeted him in surprise.

"Nakht? How long has it been?"

"Hotep!" The friends embraced. "Years. Years, since I last sailed to Byblos." He frowned at the cedarwood. "I'm not sure why we bothered. There was a time His Majesty's name meant something."

"Are things that troubled, at Memphis . . . ?"

Seneb hovered nearby, listening, but Meryt pulled on Teti's hand. Down the stone steps, by the pillar, they squatted down, measuring finger spans from the water to the second-lowest notch.

"Mother! Come and see how low it is!" But Mother didn't seem to want to. She gazed downriver toward the cemetery.

Father had his hand on Seneb's shoulder when they climbed back up. The older boy's face was no more cheerful than the dignitary's.

"Teti, leave that now. I want you both to come with me to the granary."

"But it's still full," said Seneb. Father shook his head.

"It's time you learned to measure grain carefully." Meryt looked up at Mother, feeling her fingers grow tight around her hand.

"And I must teach you to weave, my love."

Settlement Patterns in the Delta

At this moment, we need to zoom out to understand the importance of Tell Ibrahim Awad, Meryt's home, for our story. My remote-sensing project in the Delta in the early 2000s only added a layer to the 700 archaeological sites known from previous excavations and surveys. In the summer of 2003, while we were excavating at Tell Tebilla, weekend sorties to verify my findings on the ground gave valuable opportunities to explore the larger settlement patterns within the site's immediate 50-by-60-kilometer surroundings.

Rather than restricting myself to "new" sites highlighted by the satellite imagery, I also investigated some of the known ones; for so many, all we have is a dot on a map, with no dating information. A fieldwalking visit to those "blank pages" seemed useful, to collect, record, and date pottery or any other visible evidence of material culture on the surface.

I then looked for parallels at other sites, consolidating my findings with known dating evidence from sites in my survey region and from the entire Delta. It was the Delta's first large-scale settlement-pattern overview. What I found was puzzling.

From everything collected in the eastern Delta, we know of Old Kingdom remains at 29 archaeological sites.[7] That settlement evidence confirms ancient texts and reveals expansion that coincided with the state's increased stability, prosperity, and growth. But when I looked at the site evidence during the Old Kingdom's immediate aftermath, I found evidence for only four settled sites. Across the whole Delta, east and west, we see 36 Old Kingdom sites drop to just 11 in the First Intermediate Period, between 2160 and 2055 BC.

Something caused wide-scale abandonment in my survey area, while the Egyptians struggled on in only four places. Mendes, the regional capital to the south of Tell Tebilla, has a residential area apparently dating to this time,[8] Tell Sharufa has surface pottery,[9] as does Tell Akhdar,[10] and Tell Ibrahim Awad, the home of Meryt and her family, contains a cemetery.[11] I started sifting through all the archaeological and textual data to find out why these places remained settled, and the answer has startling implications for why and how Egypt's great Pyramid Age ended.

o o o

Men passed water jars from hand to hand, irrigating the thirsty crops. What cattle remained must be fed, somehow. Sores glared, red and angry, where empty hide draped from their shoulders and hips.

Now 10 and 12, Teti and Seneb together could just manage the huge jar Father passed. Beyond the work chain, the fields looked as if nothing was ever there except for thorns and tough grass that the cows could not eat. After the workday, no daylight would be left for the family to water their field.

Where fodder used to grow, there was dust. More blew away with every breeze, and Meryt had no time to help, working from dawn until sundown at her loom beside Mother's.

The low-flood year had been hard, the granaries emptied, by the time Sopdet finally dragged the river from its bed last summer. A better year followed, a little respite. But a month ago, when the star's brilliance lifted the town's hopes, no floodwaters came at all.

The governor strode along the line with a scribe behind him. He paused.

"I've considered your idea, Hotep," he said quietly. Father bowed his head.

"Thank you, sir. If we can repair the canals upstream . . ." The governor nodded, and the scribe unrolled blank papyrus and wetted his brush, awaiting the governor's decision.

"The canals to the pasturelands belong to the royal estate." Father pressed his eyes closed, strain in his thin shoulders as he hauled the next jar to Seneb.

"I'm sorry, sir. It was not my place—"

"And I see no reason why we should not maintain them. If the king sends no one to do so." Father looked up.

"Then we can cut a new branch from them, get water back to the higher fields?" But as the governor agreed, the jar slipped from Teti's hands midtransfer and poured water at the man's feet. Blushing under Seneb's whispered rebuke, Teti bowed double and apologized. The governor smiled slightly, considering the boys' limbs, no meatier than a gazelle's.

"Hotep, if your sons are to do a man's work, they should have a man's ration." Gesturing to the scribe, who scribbled quickly, he walked up the chain.

Within days, the governor organized the project. Soon, crops began to grow, and greenness returned to the pasturelands. When harvest came, so many had worked on the new canals that rations poured into every family's granary.

Meryt paused while weeding their vegetables, moist from the new branch ditch that Father and Seneb had cut. Her slight body tired quickly. Breathing deeply, she bared her canines, reflected in the black ditchwater. Striped, like Mother's. Meryt smiled; something else to share with her. In three years, she had become a skillful weaver, however little she had grown.

"Are you finished, love? Come and help me thread the warp." The call rang from the door, past the empty stable.

"Coming, Mother." She stabbed out another water-stealing weed and stood up.

Her eyes narrowed. Dust rose like an ostrich plume from the road beyond the fields.

"Mother! Mother, come!"

Hurrying up onto the flat roof, they looked out. From north and west, roads were choked with people. Families, or what was left of them; some clutched possessions, but most lacked the strength. Every bone showed through their skin. Mother pressed a hand to her mouth.

"Meryt, you know how we offer to your aunts, in the cemetery?" Meryt frowned. Mother's muffled voice sounded so strange.

"The little-girl aunts?"

"Yes, my love. No older than you. This is why." She wiped her eyes. "Come, we are all children of the Nile. We must gather food and take it to the town entrance."

"But Seneb says our granary is less than half-full . . ."

"Do you want our hearts to weigh heavy on the balance? We must uphold *ma'at* . . ." She turned toward the stairs. "Even if the king does not."

When the Nile Fails . . .

You've probably heard that Egypt was the breadbasket of the ancient world. If this was so, then the Nile was the bakery. The country's fortunes have long been intertwined with the river, its canals, and the agricultural fields and desert resources flanking the Nile Valley.[12]

The Blue Nile originates at Lake Tana in the Ethiopian plateau, and the White Nile at Lake Victoria farther south; they converge at Khartoum in Sudan.[13] The Nile flows year-round due to the rains that fall nearly every day in the equatorial lake region,[14] but the two sub-Saharan lakes are only filled by annual monsoon rainfalls, welling up in Asia from late May to June, before blowing east to Africa. The lakes' swollen waters flood the Nile tributaries.

Before the construction of dams in Aswan to control the flooding, completed in 1902 and 1970, the monsoon waters gushed northward into the Egyptian Nile. Nilometers, or built structures for measuring the waters' height, can still be seen today on the ancient island of Elephantine in Aswan, while the elaborate decoration of the Islamic Period Nilometer on Rhoda Island in Cairo shows the flood's enduring importance. Yearly flood levels were recorded, high and low, as well as the general water level.

While too high a flood caused destruction, good flood levels meant a plentiful harvest, good fishing, and better pasture, both watering the soil and nourishing it with silt. Since taxation was based on the flood height, it also directly affected the royal treasury.

But the well-organized system of dikes and canals that extended the land suitable for agriculture broke down when flood levels were low. If a poor monsoon rainfall blew in from India, the Ethiopian highlands produced a much-decreased peak flow of water, which meant low floods in Egypt and reduced crop yields. Famine wasn't always inevitable: in their tomb inscriptions, local governors and leaders proudly celebrate their efforts to manage scarce water resources.

As the Nile flowed northward to the Mediterranean Sea, its seven branches created a complex landscape in Egypt's Delta, and raised the alluvial plain about a meter every 1,000 years by depositing silt. It's important evidence of the floodwaters' annual reliability, both flushing and fertilizing the land.[15] Ancient settlements clustered around the channels, for this farmland, access to trade routes, and local and regional transportation.

If the Nile failed to flood at the right levels, the smaller settlements along the Nile branches could wither and die like appendages starved of blood.[16]

o o o

The floods failed. And failed again. Just as the governor's stonemasons built another impressive chamber for his tomb, Father cut a grave for Teti.

He dug as neatly as he could, but now so many other pits ate into the rock-hard ground, stretching out from the old cemetery. Outside the town walls, around the huts of the refugees' alleys, the vultures and wild dogs circled.

"That will not happen to him," he said through gritted teeth, sharpening a broken pick-head. Nothing he had could be bartered for a better one; there was no copper.

By sunset, Mother lowered a bundle tightly wrapped in her own linen into the ground. He weighed nothing, for a boy of 13.

They were sealing the dusty infill stone by stone when a figure strode up the hill with a squadron of soldiers.

"Hotep, my draftsman told me. Which of them . . . ?" The governor looked behind him, at the emptiness in Seneb's expression, the fragile bones prominent in his sister's cheeks. No taller than an eight-year-old, when her twelfth year had just begun. Her dark eyes were hollow, but she stared right at him, ferocious in her grief.

"My younger son, sir," said Father, rising slowly from a bow. Seneb could not take his eyes from the stones.

"But the extra grain I allotted you . . ."

"We were grateful, my Lord. But after so long, it was no longer enough."

"Gods have mercy. Why did you not ask for more?"

"From whose table would you have taken it?" The governor looked across the town, uncomfortable under Meryt's gaze. "Sir, a priest told me they no longer offer to the snake goddess. There are no snakes in the fields. No mice. They have been eaten." Dry-eyed, her face haggard, Mother put her arm around him.

Meryt watched the governor clench his jaw. He muttered something. The breeze flicked an ostrich feather in one soldier's headband, and she took Mother's hand, remembering the view from the rooftop. The town's generosity had counted for nothing. The governor swallowed.

"We must ask support from my allies; their canals still flow. Take your family south, Hotep, and secure grain for us all. I see you are an honest man."

They left the next day, carrying what little they had. Meryt looked back at the cemetery and promised Teti she would return.

The Old Kingdom's Collapse

As Pepi II's four-generation rule fell into stagnancy, grand royal building projects were a distant memory. Those structures now symbolize for me the fleeting nature of power and glory—rulers in the Old Kingdom had it all, but they spent it. Their successors just had to make do. Only one small pyramid, belonging to a king named Qakare Ibi, is known from Dynasty 8 (2181–2161 BC).[17]

Egypt teetered, then fractured into two ruling polities, as nomarchs built up their own armies. With Dynasty 8 established at Memphis, and Dynasties 9 and 10 (2161–2010 BC) at Herakleopolis,[18] about 100 kilometers south of Cairo, other ruling centers grew at Luxor (Thebes), and farther south at Mo'alla and Edfu.[19] Those regional rulers developed marriage alliances with each other and used their increased wealth to support the development of diverse regional art styles with unusual color schemes and variable quality. The sidelined kings were no longer relevant.

Egypt would never be the same.

The End of an Era

Egyptologists debate fiercely how and why the Old Kingdom ended.[20] We can see social, political, and economic factors at play, but the situation was without doubt complicated.[21] Some have suggested that the drying climate provided an additional push.

Repeated low floods may have caused the abandonment of sites in the eastern Delta that our settlement survey revealed. The archaeological and textual evidence from Egypt and farther afield suggests the river played a far larger role than previously assumed.[22] To see the effect of a consistent lack of water, not just one or two years of low Nile floods, we have to turn to later descriptions.

Unhelpfully, no priest set their Nilometer readings in stone, but Islamic Period hydrologists were more generous to modern-day researchers. Between 1053 and 1090 AD, 28 out of 40 floods were low, causing inflation, starvation, cannibalism, and plague. Egypt's population dropped from 2.4 million to 1.5 million in one century. An eyewitness report from 1068 AD describes a starving woman offering her jewels in exchange for a small measure of wheat.[23]

Blame the 4.2 ka BP Event

At the close of the Old Kingdom, it's not just Egypt in trouble, but everyone across the ancient Near East and Mediterranean. Meet the catchiest moniker in science: the "4.2 thousand years Before Present event," or "4.2 ka BP event," to friends. Culminating around 2200 BC, something very big and very bad happened. It encompassed changes in monsoon patterns and Mediterranean westerlies, leading to droughts and cooling periods across Africa and Asia.[24] But what evidence can we see for a potential drought in Egypt, and at Lakes Turkana and Tana in Kenya and Ethiopia?

Some of the best evidence for the 4.2 ka BP event in Egypt comes from records of Ethiopian highland precipitation. Environmental coring at Lake Turkana, and at Lakes Abhe and Zway-Shala in the Ethiopian highlands, show lower water levels around 2200 BC, which reflect a downturn in the Indian monsoons.[25] We also see low base flow and discharge levels from the White Nile[26] as the rain clouds that filled it moved south. Conversely, when the rain clouds shifted north again, Egypt's floodwaters increased.[27]

Across the Delta, a series of deep core samples revealed a lens of iron hydroxides, mineral residues left by intense dryness in floodplain soils. Plants absorb iron to grow, but in a period of drought, the struggling vegetation cannot absorb nutrients, and the iron remains in the soil.[28] The dates of the soil samples with the iron hydroxides fall neatly between 2200 and 2050 BC—right across the end of the Old Kingdom.[29]

Feeble vegetation cannot hold the land in place. Any rainfall or wind erodes soil by the ton: Buto, a site in the Delta,[30] has a 1-meter-thick sterile deposit with no sherds or any material culture whatsoever, which may be connected to the late Old Kingdom.[31] Nothing flourished but the deserts. At Memphis[32] and Dashur,[33] sands swamped the monuments, a process of desertification connected to climate change that can be seen today with the growth of the Sahara in northern Africa.[34] Evidence for the 4.2 ka BP event stacks up with core analysis throughout the Mediterranean and Near East—and beyond.

In India, oxygen isotope analysis of river plankton indicates weak monsoons in that period, the potential root of the problem. Cave deposits from Israel show a drop-off in rainfall, while lake deposits in Turkey are full of arid, wind-blown silt and sand, with little tree pollen. That's also when the Akkadian Empire tumbled in modern-day Syria and Iraq, while agricultural lands in northern Mesopotamia were abandoned, and refugees reportedly fled to southern Mesopotamia. Total chaos. Nearly 20 different records connected to vital weather patterns suggest a global climate event that lasted for years.[35]

This was no misfortune explicable to the Egyptians through meteorology. For them, the rise of the star Sopdet—our Sirius—announced the floods around the summer solstice, but only the gods' favor filled the riverbed. One of the king's main duties as interlocutor with the gods was to maintain *ma'at*, or divine balance. Low floods were a sign of *ma'at* being badly disrupted, seen as an indication that the king was not doing his job—leaving the people defenseless.

There is great irony in all this, to our modern eyes. Egyptians famously worshipped the sun god Re, one of their most important deities, and, as it turns out, the sun was a likely culprit in the widespread upheaval. Climate experts believe that the 4.2 ka BP event may have been caused by fluctuations in solar radiation, which could have had an impact on regional temperatures and thus the normal monsoon patterns.[36] In light of that, perhaps it *was* Re's displeasure that caused the Old Kingdom's demise.

o   o   o

From the weaving workshop near the city's temple, the fields were so far away, they were a green haze to Meryt. The water was such an expanse here in the south that at first it terrified her.

"How could this great river betray us?" she muttered, helping Mother while Father petitioned the governor for grain. "I'll go down there and throw a stone at it!" Mother smiled. But she no longer laughed so readily.

Father's negotiations took time. There were so many soldiers and citizens to feed here, and the king—who had already lived forever—had finally gone into the West. The governor here could rely on only himself.

From her seat by the window, Meryt watched Nubian delegations disembark, tall and proud, and dressed in colorful leather, with gold and ebony earrings. She stared, wide-eyed, at one representative leading a cheetah. They could not be sent away empty-handed.

"Meryt. Watch how you draw your shuttle or that linen won't fit a doll, let alone a priest." Meryt laughed.

They barely saw Seneb. A letter from the governor at home in the north had granted him scribal training in the House of Life. Father had been speechless for hours at the honor. Now Seneb sat up late by the oil lamp, practicing complex calligraphy; he drew Meryt all the signs that featured cows.

A month after they arrived, she went to wave Father off with the first grain shipment, bound for home.

"The gods will look after you here, my love," he said, but Meryt looked down at the sandbanks near the water's surface and shivered.

The river sucked years away. From his travels, Father brought news that their town hung on, though only the cemetery was growing. One afternoon, Meryt wound between granaries fringing the temple like termite mounds to deliver linens to the House of Life. At the door, chatting to a soldier with a bow almost taller than Meryt, Seneb waved.

"Little sister, join us. Intef, my friend, this is Meryt." Puzzled, she looked up at the young Nubian.

"Intef? But . . ." She stammered, not knowing how to phrase it. "That's an Egyptian name." His smile was bright, with a gap between his smooth front teeth.

"My nickname. The governor says I remind him of his son, Intef. We train together."

"Don't you miss your home . . . ?"

Bustling out, a bald old priest took the bundled linen from her arms.

"Now, Seneb, those priests' rotas won't copy themselves."

"Of course, teacher, I was just about . . ." Chuckling, the priest drew him inside, a hand on the young man's shoulder.

"Once a snare is nicely set, my son, you leave it to do its work." Seneb smiled and looked back. Laughing at something Intef said, Meryt tucked her dark hair over her ear.

In time, she told him of her childhood on the cattle estates, and when they married, Intef gave her a beautiful bowl engraved with cattle, burnished to a shine, glossy and fat.

"My people also cherish their herds, Meryt. We will not forget, even though our home is here, now."

Sopdet came and went, and sometimes the river rose well and sometimes poorly. The governor, and then his son, fought to keep something in the granaries.

Intef and Seneb built onto Mother's house and eventually the old lady took care of all their children while hers were working. Meryt was grateful, trading her finest linen for ducks, medicines, and a celebratory turquoise ring the day Seneb admitted his oldest nephew Teti into the House of Life.

Meryt set out lunch while Father rested beneath the date palm in their courtyard, watching Mother scoop up a little girl with Intef's perfect, gap-toothed smile. Laugh lines around Mother's eyes ran deeper than the irrigation ditches. Meryt sighed. Had her friends from the fields lived to enjoy something like this?

The summer that Meryt's youngest daughter married, her son Teti helped Seneb paint the texts onto Mother's coffin and, only months later, Father's. With his sons, Intef carried it down into the rock-cut tomb in the western cliffs.

Meryt brushed dust from his tight curls, peppered gray now.

"Thank you, my love," she murmured. "Such a burial, after everything they suffered . . ." He squeezed her shoulders, his dark eyes steady.

"Our family is strong. Together, we afford it." Then Intef smiled. "And Seneb's priestly connections were not unhelpful." She laughed, wiping away tears. "Go, love. I'll wait for you."

She carried wooden boats commissioned years ago down into a chamber lit with a single oil lamp. Her parents' things were stacked together, tidily, carefully, more dishes than Mother ever had at home. Enough food offerings for eternity. Side by side, the coffins gleamed.

But while Seneb's sons read the prayers for sealing the door, shaven-headed and austere in their priestly robes, Meryt looked north. Downstream to where her brother Teti lay, alone.

The Real Story of Tell Ibrahim Awad

Tell Ibrahim Awad was a major settlement and seemed to survive the drought while other towns were abandoned. Maybe, like cities during crises today, Tell Ibrahim Awad was a haven to which struggling populations moved. Nearby Mendes was doubtless affected by the lower levels of the Mendesian and Sebennytic Nile branches,[37] but its importance as the regional center of the eastern Delta perhaps made it a potential refuge, able to command resources even when they were scarce elsewhere. This may have drip-fed to its neighbors.

It may not be so surprising that people scraped by there. When cultures experience environmental distress, some archaeologists believe people leave the affected cities and lead simpler lives, more widely dispersed—a sort of early survivalism, if you will, with less competition for resources. This left fewer mouths to feed in these large Delta settlements.[38]

Surviving was still a struggle, though. Potential evidence has emerged for widespread death through starvation or disease at Tell Ibrahim Awad, where Meryt once lived and eventually died. She was one of 74 individuals excavated from a cemetery in use through the Old Kingdom, the First Intermediate Period (or FIP), and the Middle Kingdom.

Among them, the average age at death dropped from 45 years at the end of the Old Kingdom to 36 in the later FIP, mainly due to poor nutrition.[39] Also, among adults from the early Middle Kingdom, a higher percentage of teeth showed enamel hypoplasia, a sign of health stress while the teeth were being formed, perhaps reflecting the dire hunger of their childhoods at the end of the FIP. It's visible in the mouth as striping or pitting on the teeth. Growing up through the Old Kingdom collapse, Meryt and her mother would have shown their difficult start every time they smiled, for life.

The subsequent upturn in fortune was just as visible. Archaeologists noted that 31 to 32 percent of the individuals were buried with grave goods in the FIP. That percentage doubled in the early Middle Kingdom, reflecting a trend of recovery seen across Egypt among the wealthier lower classes.[40]

Though affected by the drought at the end of the Old Kingdom, Upper Egypt didn't seem to suffer so badly. The broad main branch of the Nile held countless billions of gallons more water than the river's subdivided channels in the Delta. Cities such as Edfu, located about 90 kilometers south of Luxor, appear to have thrived in the FIP, and some Nile Valley towns even show population expansion. In fact, settlements in Upper Egypt acted as regional centers following their growth in power and influence as the Old Kingdom waned.

Even so, various inscriptions give a clear sense of hard times of desperate scarcity, instability, and a land in crisis, and the texts are some of the most dramatic of all the writing we have from Egypt. At least seven inscriptions make direct reference to drought or a "time of sandbanks," when the Nile was so low its bed broke the surface. Nomarchs record providing food for displaced persons,[41] and governors from one part of Egypt could well have reached out for help from another.

○ ○ ○

"Mother, you are too old to make the journey."

Tall and with his father's lustrous tight curls, Teti frowned, hands on his hips. His belly was growing rounder. His younger son nodded behind him, willowy in his lector priest's kilt, no matter how Meryt tried to stuff him with roast duck. She thanked the gods daily for their generosity.

"I am not as old as that," she said, packing the beautiful cow bowl into a nest of linen. At the kitchen door, a powerfully built young man shifted the bow on his shoulder.

"Grandmother, no. Not with the strife between Herakleopolis and Memphis . . . My unit will be deployed before Sopdet rises."

Meryt smiled. "Then perhaps I can accompany you north?" He bit his lip. Hadn't Grandfather always said an argument with her was so much wasted breath? Teti sighed.

"Surely Father wanted you to stay with him?" he said. Meryt put bread and cooked beef into pottery cups and set a beer jar ready.

"My love, he did not ask."

As her hair had turned to gray and then to white, Intef had brushed it back to look into her face so often, and still, he had not asked. She smoothed the pale line where she had worn her turquoise ring. It rested with him now.

With her offerings in a woven bag, she walked through the bustle of the city, past the temple. When she used to weave in this neighborhood, the streets were not so crowded. But now, after ever more people fled the drought's cruelty, the close-packed houses formed self-contained villages, homes from home. The tales those new arrivals told still drove Meryt from her sleep, calling out for her family.

A ferryman rowed her across to the west bank. The stela that stood next to her parents' tomb was not so far up the hillside.

"Intef, my beloved," she said, pouring the beer for him, and her parents. "Seneb's sons will lead your cult. And our children will come to you, in their time."

She knew the offering prayers by heart. The chamber beneath her was crammed, painted vividly with motifs from his home and the south. Running her fingers over the stela's inscribed words, she did not know which was Intef's name. The desert wind whisked through the sand and rocks.

"I will find you again in the Field of Rushes." Slowly, stiffly, she got to her feet and walked down the hill. She did not look back.

So soon, Meryt stood aboard a ship, ready to meet the gods with a heart that would not weigh heavy against Ma'at's feather. Nor did her bags: a few fresh-mined amethysts to barter for a simple burial, with letters of commendation to a grandson of the fair-minded governor she remembered. The south wind pushed at her back. By her feet was the bowl that held all her memories and a box of shabtis inscribed with the name of Teti, son of Hotep.

She would go to the canal to pick reeds for him. Perhaps she had not forgotten how to make a boat.

The End of an Era

We know beyond a shadow of a doubt that the Old Kingdom state collapsed. The evidence suggests that climate change played an essential role in the state-level collapse—and in Meryt's imagined life. Tombs left by the nomarchs[42] show how they filled the power vacuum created by the absence of centralized government, and that their rise in power continued into the First Intermediate Period. Certainly, regional prosperity such as Upper Egypt's was insufficient to support international expeditions for quarrying, mining, and trade. Without them, and with an undernourished workforce, pyramid construction was impossible. Perhaps a strong, rich central government might have held off the drought's effects for a few years, but we can only imagine whether the Old Kingdom would have survived even then.

Egyptologists generally view the First Intermediate Period just as its name implies: significant confusion and instability between two periods of greatness. Although at great cost, the Old Kingdom's end paved the way for a time of innovation and experimentation, almost as if the court had stifled the people's creativity—central administration had to break down for the rest of Egypt to break free of long-held traditions.

Poorer people became better off in the provinces, reflected in larger tombs and better quality of grave goods. People began to aspire to immortality without the help of the king, and as religion became privatized, the sacred Pyramid Texts and Coffin Texts once reserved for royalty appear in tombs and coffins of anyone who could afford the draftsmanship. We also see new types of amulets that displayed different styles and functions, and more elaborate shabti figurines in burials, offered as magical servants in the afterlife. Material culture expressed a swell in regional diversity, with changes to object design, form, and quality. Regional painting styles became just as vibrant, with images depicting daily life.

The king could no longer guarantee *ma'at*, the balance of the universe. Perhaps, unable to count on him, people dug deep for greater self-reliance, leading to increased confidence and the recognition of their own abilities. That, in turn, brought more social mobility, as in the case of Meryt's family; the widespread increase in grave goods certainly supports that. But we'll likely never know for sure.

We do know that the First Intermediate Period nomarch Ankhtifi created an alliance of three Upper Egyptian nomes, and his son, Intef, expanded further to create a Theban kingdom based around Luxor. War raged between the Thebans and another regional group, the Herakleopolitans, for control of Egypt,[43] and people's fortunes changed dramatically. The self-designated Theban "royalty" took over the Herakleopolitans' stronghold at Asyut, and then their capital at Herakleopolis, thus reuniting Egypt around 2040 BC and bringing a renaissance for the country, the Middle Kingdom. Quite something, for a Game of Nomes.

To understand the consequences of such devastating turmoil and climate change for us today, we cannot dismiss these so-called collapse events as merely political or economic in nature, nor indeed identify climate change as the sole cause. All of these factors intertwined at the end of the Old Kingdom, creating the perfect storm that affected the life of one woman of Tell Ibrahim Awad, among tens of thousands of others. Unearthing the root causes of change requires digging through the evidence. In this instance, getting the bigger picture from space was only the first step.

You're probably still on that veranda at the Mena House, contemplating dinner as the pyramids' shadows lengthen across the sand. The enormity of those monuments is only made more significant by understanding the period in which the Egyptians built them. They are a testament to the very formation of the Egyptian state, and all that was lost and gained when that state fell. Egypt would rebound in a new beginning complete with pyramids and ancient power plays that seem more fiction than fact to us today. When the world turns upside down, empires may fall, but people rise, in the most unexpected ways.

8

A Capital Discovery

For ancient Egypt, we have the advantage of hindsight. The Old Kingdom had to end to make way for the creative explosion in the Middle Kingdom.[1] What this resilience means for us today—how past cultures have often shown grit when facing insurmountable odds—is an idea we need to study more closely if we are to survive and thrive in future.

Things today do seem dire. Rising oceans, shifting climates, and loss of wildlife habitats rightly concern us. But out of great adversity can come great creativity. By studying such pivotal moments in the historic expression of our humanity, we can see how closely innovation and cultural growth relate to severe societal stress. All will not be lost if modern civilization suffers dramatic setbacks; in fact, much may be gained in the future as we adapt and change.

The Splendor of the "Lost City" of Itj-Tawy

Understanding how and why major periods like the Old Kingdom ended forms the foundation for analyzing how and why societies might rise again. In chapter 7, we left Egypt at the close of the First Intermediate Period. At that time, a king named Mentuhotep II waged war against the Herakleopolitans, defeating them in 2040 BC and earning the name "Subduer at the head of the two lands."[2]

After reuniting the country, Mentuhotep II brought its regions

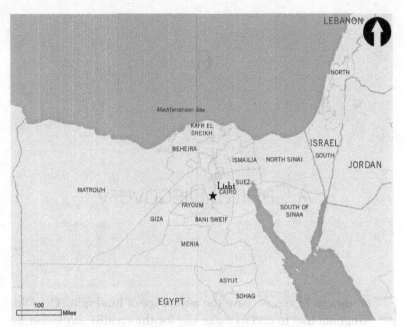

Location of Lisht, Egypt [MAP COURTESY CHASE CHILDS]

back under his control. As things stabilized, he visited northern Nubia for gold, sent missions to quarries and south to the rich lands of Punt, and reopened turquoise mines and quarries in Sinai. Building thus resumed at temples across Egypt.[3] The wealth and stability that had declined during the Old Kingdom began to resurge.

Nonetheless, Dynasty 12 had a rocky start marked by civil strife. Its new king, Amenemhet I (1991–1962 BC), rose to power after serving as a vizier under Mentuhotep's grandson.[4] He moved the capital to a place he called Amenemhet-Itj-Tawy, "Amenemhet, Seizer of the Two Lands." Hail seizer?

In the desert overlooking Itj-Tawy, for short, near today's town of El-Lisht,[5] Amenemhet built his pyramid in the style of Old Kingdom funerary monuments, re-creating the glorious past to broadcast his power.[6] Anyone who had boosted him on his rise received royal favors like funerary monuments, especially those in charge of regional centers in Middle and Upper Egypt and who helped to create flood basins for water redistribution.[7]

For the first time in Egyptian history, the king appointed his son,

Senwosret I (1971–1926 BC), to be his co-ruler.[8] These were tumultuous times, and any shot at stability must have seemed worth taking. Senwosret led military and mining expeditions on behalf of the king and gained sole control of the country after Amenemhet's possible assassination in the thirtieth year of his rule.[9] We don't know who was responsible: Senwosret was conveniently away on campaign in Libya when his father was killed, if the Middle Kingdom *Tale of Sinuhe* has any truth in it.[10] It's an adventure that's well worth a read.

Senwosret I built or enlarged temples at 35 locations, also constructing a pyramid in south Lisht.[11] The art and architecture from his reign are just exquisite, funded by Egypt's burgeoning wealth, the rise of the middle and upper-middle classes,[12] and expeditions sent abroad. Sculptors created lifelike statues of the king, and painters covered tomb walls from Dynasty 12 with realistic scenes of Nilotic birds, the colors of their feathers painted in subtle gradation.[13]

Amid this artistic explosion, we see increasing numbers of bureaucrats, all potential consumers for artisans' work. Literature blossomed, too: any student of Egyptology today starts by learning Middle Egyptian, the lingua franca of this time.[14] Fantastic stories like *Sinuhe*, teaching tracts, dialogues, new religious texts, and even a gynecological prescription survive.[15] This golden era lasted another 200 years until 1750 BC, allowing the royal court at Itj-Tawy[16] to flourish and prosper.

Thriving along the Nile, the city bustled with tens of thousands of people. Exotic traders would have rubbed shoulders with local merchants, musicians, artisans, writers, and embalmers, and you can bet the mummy business roared.[17] The city had a cemetery containing thousands of burials.[18] Out in the desert above the city, behind the limestone hill, or *gebel*, the king's innovatively designed pyramid clambered up out of mud-brick construction ramps that still survive.[19]

Laden barges brought to high-class sculptors pink Aswan granite or dark gray basalt for fine statues and offering tables.[20] Other artisans' workshops specialized in jewelry, alabaster vessels, and wooden models of boats, farming, bread-making, and other household activities, and even miniature soldiers—these little dioramas are an inventive characteristic of Middle Kingdom art and craftsmanship. Just like shabtis, they served as magical attendants for the afterlife.

I first learned about the lost capital at university. My professor discussed the Middle Kingdom and said Itj-Tawy was located somewhere in the floodplain near the pyramid complexes, buried by nearly 4,000 years of Nile silt, and would be hard to find. Sounded like a challenge to me.

The Search for Itj-Tawy

In fact, some of the city might still be visible. One of the previous expedition leaders at Lisht, Metropolitan Museum of Art curator Dieter Arnold, noted extensive Middle Kingdom traces along a canal east of Amenemhet I's pyramid, including pottery, limestone fragments, and column bases.[21] A granite altar from the time of Senwosret I also came out of this canal,[22] suggesting the potential location of a nearby temple. Nothing ever disappears forever, it seems, except socks.

Where there were some indicative remains, I knew that there had to be more. On the space shuttle *Endeavor*, in 1994, NASA flew a sensor system to record the entirety of the Earth's elevation at a resolution of 30 meters. This Shuttle Radar Topography Mission (SRTM) allowed scientists to create, for free, digital elevation models of any place on Earth. Each image is a collection of thousands of elevation points that appears as a shaded image, with darker points marking higher elevations. You can manipulate the data to exaggerate the higher areas, but you cannot see any details of surface features.

Still, free data is free data. In the spring of 2010, I downloaded the Lisht area and built a 3-D model of the site and the floodplain. I then took Landsat data and using ER Mapper, my standard imagery-processing program, draped it over the 3-D model, giving me a 3-D image of the 4-kilometer-wide floodplain to the east of Lisht.

A nifty aspect of SRTM 3-D models is that you can exaggerate subtle changes in the landscape, so when a dip next to the village of Bamha caught my eye, I maxed out the exaggeration scale in the software. An ancient channel of the Nile appeared clearly, starting at Bamha and running southwest toward the Lisht cemetery. We know the Nile once flowed by the city of Itj-Tawy, but Egyptologists had never put the river close to the site in their maps.

A small raised area also appeared in the fields between Lisht and a modern road. There was only one way to know for sure if it was indeed the remnant of a buried ancient archaeological mound.

Coring near Lisht [PHOTO BY THE AUTHOR]

The Gems in the Core

That fall, alongside Cairo University's Department of Geology, we went to the site and took deep core samples in key locations. Powered by several very strong local men who helped get through the dense mud and silt, the 10-centimeter-wide core bit down 7 meters.

Elsayed Abbas Zaghloul, a gentleman scholar from Egypt's National Authority for Remote Sensing & Space Sciences, led the collaboration. We also had two brilliant Egyptological colleagues on the team: Bettina Bader from the Austrian Academy of Sciences, an expert in the pottery of the Middle Kingdom, and Judith Bunbury from the University of Cambridge, a specialist in ancient Egyptian landscapes.

The chances of success would have been small for anyone. You're looking for a city lost millennia ago where the Nile River has shifted 3 kilometers to the east, possibly destroying any trace of it. Working from the merest hint appearing in the NASA data, you then try to pinpoint any urban evidence, but based on the various locations of other Egyptian capitals, the lost city could be anywhere inside a 20-square-kilometer landscape. And you're supposed to find it by drilling a 10-centimeter core. That doesn't even account for the possibility of GPS error, undulations in the landscape, and sheer bad luck.

Even facing ridiculous odds, we drilled. It was like tackling miniature excavation units: our team logged details about soil type, color, density, and inclusions such as stone. We could easily see the earth as it changed over time from silt to clay or sand, and we drew each layer as part of a running plan. I have never in my life seen anyone as excited about dirt as Professor Zaghloul—every time a new core emerged, he would nearly jump for joy at the alternating soil densities. He quickly teased out the history of the land in all its movements; watching him work was like watching a great conductor unravel the wonder of a symphony.

Afterward, we processed each core in water through a series of sieves ranging from 1-centimeter-wide mesh on top to 5-millimeter-wide mesh on the bottom, with gradations in between. Bit by bit, the core gets squelched into the top with water running through into a bucket. It's mucky but satisfying work, as the sediment sorts itself out based on particle size. Large particles like stones get caught first, and the fine silt runs into the bottom of the bucket under the sieves. Totting up the mass of larger particles versus smaller in each core tells environmental stories, about the energy of the river flow depositing it and how silt deposits change over time, and also gives clues as to how the Nile meanders. Sometimes, if you are lucky, you might even find evidence of past human occupation.

After drilling down 4–5 meters, we hit our metaphorical pot of gold. Well, the pot, at least: the core started to bring up ceramics. Bettina worked her cheerful magic, spreading out the finds and examining each piece. As a pottery guru and world expert in the Middle Kingdom, she can look at a tiny fragment from a 4,000-year-old vessel and come close to telling you its serial number. Bettina seemed quite happy when she was done and called me over: all the pottery dated to the Twelfth and Thirteenth Dynasties. There was a lot of it, and it included some beautiful higher-end ceramic fragments—the fine china your grandmother brings out for family holidays.

Meanwhile, Judith—a sensible geologist with a twinkle in her eye—was hard at work on other items she had whisked away. Beaming, she showed me three stones retrieved from the core: amethyst, agate, and one piece of bright orange polished carnelian, covered in tiny holes from ancient drilling attempts. This was the first time that worked semiprecious stones had been recovered from a coring effort in Egypt, and it's rare enough to find them in a full excavation.

The Once and Future City

A single core does not a city make, even with results this tantalizing. And if the artifacts did not come from Itj-Tawy itself, I suspected we'd come down on an artisans' suburb, a district where workshops were so concentrated that our wild stab-in-the-dark drilling stood a chance. The thriving Middle Kingdom court and capital fueled demand, and semiprecious stones were fashionable: just look at the Twelfth Dynasty tomb of Princess Sithathoryunet from Lahun, 30 kilometers to the south, where the royal jewelry includes carnelian, lapis lazuli, amethyst, and turquoise, all set in gold.[23] Keeping these rare and beautiful resources flooding into the capital was so important that high officials at court commemorated their expeditions to obtain them in stelae and inscriptions.[24] It's a very far cry from the impoverished end of the Old Kingdom.

No wonder, though, that the area has kept its secrets hidden—5 meters is a lot of silt. As we saw at Tebilla, the Nile shifts over time, silting up once free-flowing channels, and indeed whole occupation areas. That 4-to-5-meter keyhole to the Middle Kingdom burrowed through the silt that the wandering Nile had left in its wake.[25] What we do not yet know is when the ancient Egyptians abandoned the capital, or when it disappeared beneath the mud.

The city was perfectly placed, close to the desert for the tombs of the king and his court, and strategically right between the Delta and Upper Egypt. Perhaps built to rival the famed "white walls" surrounding the former capital at Memphis,[26] the city had multistory buildings,[27] whitewashed and well spaced. Dozens of ships crowded the harbor, and limestone and granite blocks weighed them down, arriving to fuel the increase in ambitious architecture. Picture busy activity in the high desert, where gangs of men dragged stone toward the pyramid sites on sledges.[28]

It may be that the higher parts of the city can be found close to the modern field surfaces, and we might even be able to excavate the

Looted tombs at Lisht, Egypt [PHOTO BY THE AUTHOR]

parts of the site closer to the surface. Patience is the hardest part of archaeology, but if the city has waited for 3,800 years to be investigated, it can hopefully wait a few more.

Excavation Begins

In all honesty, I did not expect to continue my preliminary work at Lisht, much as I wanted to get back for more coring to see if anything in the ancient city was within reach of excavation. The year after our foray into the floodplain in 2010, the Arab Spring broke out, and given the wide-scale looting south of Giza, the Egyptian Ministry of Antiquities did not permit any new applications because they felt it was too dangerous.

But I was drawn to the site, especially because I saw looting there in high-resolution satellite imagery after early 2011—more than 800 pits appeared.[29] I did not know at the time if these represented looted tombs or just small holes in the ground left after looting attempts.

In the spring of 2015, I traveled to Egypt. Since things had calmed down in the Lisht region, I asked the ministry for a one-day permit to visit and take photographs. The intensity of the damage was shocking; worse still, the looters had targeted many apparently intact tombs. Looting has been taking place since antiquity, but it is painful to see modern evidence firsthand.

I discussed a collaborative project with the then-director of the Dashur and Lisht regions, Mohammed Youssef Ali, to conduct a small survey in the southern part of Lisht and work at a looted tomb. We did not expect to find much left intact.

In December 2015, we broke ground. As the crow flies, the site is 45 kilometers south of the Giza pyramids. It means a two-to-three-hour drive, morning and evening, depending on traffic—a picturesque, if laborious, commute hugging the old course of the Nile along the West Bank. To our right, the pyramids of Abusir, Saqqara, and then Dashur guard the entrance to the chaos of the ancient Egyptian *deshret*, or desert. To our left, we get a disco-ball sunrise, flashing pink, orange, and yellow through the haze that hangs over the date palms and tilled fields of alfalfa.

The journey gets slightly perilous as we turn into Lisht, slowing down to avoid scraping the tightly packed modern houses. The most colorful homes feature paintings of airplanes, buses, and the Kaaba, the shrine at the heart of the Great Mosque in Mecca, if the householders have made the pilgrimage to Islam's sacred city.

Beyond the village fields, where white ibises and orange-crested hoopoes dart about the vegetation, the Nile floodplain gives way abruptly to chert-scattered sand running to hills that rise into the vast Western Desert. The cemetery is just there, on the desert edge, facing us. The site is serene, a place where history asks you to take a deep breath and waits for you to exhale.

In antiquity, it looked just like an overcrowded cemetery today, full of family mausoleums stretching in every direction in painted or limestone-lined mud brick. Unlike most in the United States, though, Egyptian cemeteries were quite lively, as relatives came to give offerings and even share meals in the tomb forecourts,[30] like a never-ending Mexican Day of the Dead. Up above the cemeteries, the pyramids of Senwosret I and Amenemhet I are mountains of sandy rubble today, with some stone casing still intact at the lowest levels. Next to each pyramid are smaller pyramids belonging to the relatives of the king, and a series of deep-shaft tombs created for the highest echelons of society during the Twelfth Dynasty. For the elite citizens who lived and worked in the city of Itj-Tawy, the closer they could be buried to the kings and their pyramids, the more prestigious the spot: desert penthouses for the afterlife.[31]

Mohammed Youssef brought us to the tomb that looters had attacked, just to the east of Senwosret I's pyramid. We saw hints of a T-shaped outline set against the sandy *gebel* where fragmented bedrock peeked through. And we were definitely in a high-priced neighborhood: princes' and viziers' burials might have abutted the pyramid itself, but other prime locations could be found near the pyramid causeways. That's what we had—a tomb overlooking the causeway of Senwosret I's pyramid.

Our mission was to clear enough of the tomb to affix strong metal doors and keep the looters firmly out. The trouble was, the more we cleared, the bigger the tomb got. Several hundred tons of sand in, the place had grown to a warren: we'd need to go large to clear the complex, rock-cut doorways and shafts for lockdown.

Between us and our Egyptian colleagues, the core team was small. We hired about 50 local villagers to do the heavy digging, supervised by six men from the village of Quft, just north of Luxor. Quftis have worked alongside foreign missions since the 1880s, and many have more field experience than Western archaeologists could dream of. They are not only foremen supervising the general workforce, but they also help do fine digging and are skilled practical engineers in the tradition of their ancient Egyptian ancestors. They can move any large stone or shore up any wall. Greg has worked with Quftis for nearly 30 years, and they have essentially adopted him. He happily debates in Arabic with them about the exact sequence of a wall's destruction.

Every excavation in Egypt has a *reis*, a chief workman. Ours, Omer Farouk, has worked beside me since my PhD research in 2005. One day at Amarna, we discovered we are twins—born on the exact same day, six hours apart. His family is now my family and vice versa, and my son calls him Uncle Omer. On our dig, Omer is effectively the Reis of Reises, as the other Quftis working on our team all supervise digs elsewhere. With a gap in his front teeth, a mustache to make a Viennese gentleman envious, and a quick laugh, Omer is straight out of central casting. He also has eyes in the back of his head, and he can smell when a member of our workforce isn't doing what they are supposed to—me included!

If you've seen pictures of the grand old excavations of the early 20th century, you've got a good idea of how that first Lisht season played out. The large workforce arrayed against the desert and our World War II–style camp with white canvas tents had more than a touch of glamour about it. The outhouse, less so.

As Molly Haight, our former student, and Chase Childs got under way mapping the looted tombs, the excavation units went deeper into the tomb's hall. Time seemed to have been particularly ruthless with the site, and it was not because the person who commissioned it cheaped out on design.

Upmarket Afterlife Property

Like other Middle Kingdom tombs that aimed high—even higher than the nomarchs of the Old Kingdom—this tomb had, when new, sought to imitate a pyramid's front driveway. The wish list for the wealthy began with a mud-brick causeway marching up from the Nile floodwaters to the tomb.[32] Brilliant white with paint or limestone, a chapel might await offerings outside the plastered entryway, before a wooden door presented the visitor with the image and name of the illustrious tomb owner.

Inside, a dim hall might be cut into the *gebel*, where six columns held up the roof, and the tomb owner frowned out of the shadowed wall decoration. Tomb shafts might open into the floor of the hall or the forecourt. At the back, three niches sank even further into the rock, housing statues of the deceased, surrounded by his carved biography. All this, so that his body, possessions, name, and achievements live forever. And this tomb owner had ordered everything in the ancient tomb catalogue.

But time doesn't care too much for the aspirations of the wealthy. Only the door's stone hinge socket remained, and the hall was open to the sky. Seemingly because of quarrying and earthquakes, the roof had collapsed. Nature, it seemed, had stripped the tomb owner's name from the walls: maybe a natural catastrophe in antiquity explained the incredible destruction we realized we were seeing. Barely a hieroglyph of the rich decoration abutted another.

But modern sand filled the three niches, the hallway, and the causeway, strewn throughout with 21st-century rubbish. It seemed modern looters had also played their role in its damage.

Our Egyptian colleagues reported that they had recently chased some away and recovered inscribed limestone blocks. We suddenly had hope of some sort of identification . . . And then our colleagues showed us the photographs. The blocks provided the names of the tomb owner's five sons, but not him—or her.

Excavated stone fragments we found had circular-saw marks, showing where the reliefs that would have given us answers had been stolen, and the meters of debris spoke of the ministry's desperate backfilling to stop the thieves. We dug down, to sift facts from the chaos, and the biography of the tomb, if not the owner, took clearer shape.

At the back of the hall, the *gebel* had thwarted the architects' grand plans: the builders had completed the center and right niches but apparently stopped work on the left when they ran into the same weak limestone that eventually brought down the roof. Then, on a wall of the central niche, where the tomb owner would have walked into the world of the living, we found that his image had been hacked out by hundreds of pick strokes, the shape of his kilt and legs a hatched scar in the artwork's smooth surface. Earthquakes cause destruction, but not with a pick, and it is not a modern looter's habit to ruin what can be sold.

In every shovelful we cleared, the beauty of what had been destroyed shone brighter. Gorgeous painted limestone fragments surfaced, in a vibrant palette of lichen green, red, ocher, yellow, black, and precious Egyptian blue.[33] Paintings of fruit, cakes and loaves, flowers, oxen and birds, and countless offering-bearers bringing the feast were smashed into pieces. One little face of an official peered from a fragment, his eye and nose as fresh as if the artisans had completed them yesterday.[34]

Beneath the paint, the sunk relief was finely carved, rendering the detailed contours of each hieroglyph and figure. Some of the inscribed fragments were monumental in scale, rivaling royal or temple inscriptions. And that was just the polychrome niche. The right-hand niche, where the looters had ripped out the blocks recovered by the ministry, had the subtlest unpainted carving. As tombs went, there was no expense spared, and this one must have been a lucrative long-term project for high-level artisans living in the city nearby.

But the tomb owner's anonymity still hung over the site.

A Name for Eternity

"T'alla mudira!" The shout echoed across the hillside one morning, midseason, while I was sorting equipment in camp. *Hurry here, boss-lady!*

I ran to see. The corner of a block stuck out of the ground. One clear inscribed face showed the hieroglyphs *in-t-f*: Intef. We finally had a name. And from the elaboration of the block—the corner of a pillar—it was *his* name. Everyone buzzed in to take a look and in-situ photos before we turned the block. A second inscribed face contained a title, "Hereditary Noble." His wealth was already obvious, but now we knew he was a very high-ranking official.

That broke the dam. More titles followed on other limestone fragments: "Great Overseer of the Army" and "The Royal Seal-Bearer,"[35] meaning the deceased had been a combined secretary of defense and secretary of the treasury. Intef was a military man in a military man's court, a powerful and influential part of Senwosret I's administration, judging by how close he'd parked his tomb to Senwosret's causeway.

Outside the unpainted niche, another relief block appeared showing his sons, or at least their feet, bearing offerings, beside the last words of columns of text. Again and again, Intef describes himself as "Born of Ipi." A stunning in-situ black granite block appeared, on which both their names were inscribed. While it was not unusual for sons to honor their mothers like this in Middle Kingdom tombs, we clearly had a mummy's boy on our hands . . . if no mummy, just yet. The rock-cut structure was still getting more complicated, and voids gaped through the cleared niche walls into later, intrusive shafts. And that's when we hit the find of the season.

Inside the right-hand niche, facedown in the sand and modern debris, we found a 2-meter-tall limestone block covered in inscriptions. It was a false door, a portal between this world and the next, where offerings were made to be consumed by the deceased. Above, in the chamber's characteristic subtle, sunk relief, Intef sat in front of a laden offering table, while below, six text columns outlined his biography.

Smashed. Obliterated. Call it what you want. Great lumps had been pounded off, the text and offering scene scraped and chipped by some form of wide-bladed chisel. Intef's face was gone. Who knows

False door of Intef
[PHOTO BY THE AUTHOR]

who did it, or when. The missing top-left corner was almost certainly the work of modern looters attempting to get to the more portable—and salable—relief blocks lining the room. The rampant chisel marks seemed to suggest less materialistic motives.

Was this monumental sour grapes? Or modern thieves destroying what they could not steal? Something about that doesn't ring true, but then again, looting can be illogical. Maybe this was an older violation, or even punishment.

Either way, fortunately for us, false doors are reasonably formulaic and symmetrical. From the partial glyphs that remain on either side, we could again decipher Intef's key titles, and his insistence that he is born of Ipi. But we still did not know who she was, or why her son was so keen to highlight his maternal lineage. As the season ended, we were left with only questions.

Common though the name Intef is in the Middle Kingdom, we are still wondering how long this Intef served in his positions, since he is not mentioned elsewhere in any previous inscriptions. His title "Great Overseer of the Army"[36] corroborates that he lived in the late Eleventh or early Twelfth Dynasty, backing up his possible position under Senwosret I. Perhaps he stepped on one too many toes, leading to the eventual desecration of his tomb. Or perhaps the sheer scale of his tomb was too arrogant, too conspicuous a challenge to the royal monuments looming over it. Or maybe it was simply nature's comeback for choosing bad rock.

The Mystery Deepens

We went back to Lisht in December 2016 and December 2017, accompanied by additional team members to handle the larger scale of the dig. To get to the bottom of Intef's funerary hall, we had to excavate the 12 meters that remained of the causeway and the tomb's main entrance. In the loving and diligent hands of Rexine Hummel and Bettina Bader, potsherds from increasingly good context gave Middle Kingdom dates and a solid range of wares connected to funerary offerings.

Layers of sand contained mud-brick debris and hundreds of limestone relief pieces ranging from tiny to massive. Despite the overwhelming wave of finds, our dig artist, Shakira Christodoulou, was delighted to have such beautiful things to draw. On-site, Kira sat at a desk up above the main dig crew, humming opera arias while creating perfect watercolor reconstructions of the relief fragments. From a high-end London art shop, she had even managed to get her hands on a paint called, appropriately, "Egyptian Blue."

We had a glimpse, infuriatingly partial, of Intef himself. Only a quarter of his portrait remained, showing the back of a man's wig similar to those seen of Senwosret I elsewhere, and revealing his shoulder, chest, and waist. And our man was taking his soldiering seriously. Where other wealthy courtiers might have themselves portrayed as prosperous and well-fed, Intef could have fronted the cover of a muscle magazine. Perhaps it stood to reason, given how frequently he mentioned his military title, written with a pictogram of a kneeling archer.

As the 2016 season wound up, there were still no other clues about Intef's role or family connections; and amid the madness of the last week of digging, we also had a TV crew filming us. On the day they arrived, just as we dug down into the entryway of the hall, we had a find so spectacular that whispers went around the site that we must have planted it.

As if you could plant a relief block the size of a child's sled and three times as thick.

Image of Ipi, Intef's mother
[PHOTO BY THE AUTHOR]

At first glance, we took it for a seated figure of Intef—the image only extended up to the waist.[37] When the film crew had gotten enough footage, Shakira could finally look.

"Hey, guys . . . how do I put this?" she shouted up to the rest of the registration team. "Dude looks like a lady?" And that's why you still have a dig artist in the age of photography.

The seated man was a woman. Lifesize, down to her delicate feet, she wore a sheath dress with goffered streamers running down her back.[38] In her bangled hand, she held a flail. Royal regalia. This lady was a wielder of power in her own right. We're sure she is Intef's mother, Ipi: no wonder he was so keen to make the point.[39]

Down to the Tomb Floor

Over the course of the 2017 dig, we realized the excavation of Intef's tomb could easily be a lifetime's work. Greg was meters down in the end of the tomb's entrance causeway, peeling back layers where mud-brick walls sealed, crossed, and intersected rock-cut shafts. He was in his bliss, figuring out what layer happened when, and did not want to be disturbed by anyone, especially his wife. He even put up a skull-and-crossbones "do not enter" sign, and if any unfortunate soul walked across his perfectly delineated mud brick, he let it be known that the tomb shafts were already there, waiting . . .

Scattered throughout it all were fragments of one or maybe two red granite offering tables, finely inscribed to Intef's memory. What would have been a fabulously expensive and prestigious object had been burned and truly smashed to smithereens. Increasingly, we got the impression that someone didn't want Intef enjoying his afterlife.

Even the bones of the family were unusually fragmentary, according to our resident bone genius, bioarchaeologist Christine Lee. Christine is one of the best in the world at picking through the welfare of past populations, their diseases and diets, and she had found the remains of male and female adults, and a few children, all of whom were sturdy and mostly healthy. Also, no apparent nutritional deficiencies appeared, showing that the people represented had access to good protein and other wholesome foods—what you'd expect from a prosperous population in a capital city. The bones were likely disturbed by the long-term looting at the tomb, but the breaks were not fresh. So, it happened long ago, and perhaps the bones were smashed at the same time as the tomb. As yet, it is impossible to say.

Finally, as we neared the floor of the tombs' main hall, we began to find mummy wrappings and grave goods among the fragments of painted relief. Despite the extensive looting across millennia, there were pieces of fine alabaster vessels,[40] statuary fittings and amulets made of faience, a gorgeous glazed blue ceramic material,[41] including a broken Sekhmet and little cats only as big as a pinky fingernail.[42]

The gemcutters of Itj-Tawy, whose workshops we happened upon while coring in 2010, had clearly met enthusiastic consumers in Intef's family. Sharp-eyed workmen spotted beads of lapis lazuli, amethyst, agate, and turquoise. In one spellbinding find, an eye inlay stared up out of the sand beside a skull: white marble tinted in lifelike pink at the corners, the onyx pupil polished to a mirror finish. When inset in its original position on the coffin, the effect must have been mesmerizing.

These finds illustrate the great shift in fortunes experienced by many in the Middle Kingdom. We know Intef is a southern Egyptian name, which means his family probably traveled north from Upper Egypt with Amenemhet I. All the art we see in Intef's tomb, the finely carved hieroglyphs, the architecture of the tomb itself, resurged from the dust, starvation, and upheaval of the Pyramid Age's ruins 300 years beforehand.

While the Lisht cemetery had not seen architects and engineers in action for 3,800 years, we had glimpses of Egypt's deep building traditions in action with our Quftis. We occasionally came up against massive limestone pieces the weight of juvenile elephants, and without their removal, we could not excavate deeper. Our Qufti team developed an ingenious system using ropes, intricate knots, ramps, and coordinated manpower to lift them from the 3-meter-deep hall.

With Reis Omer at the helm yelling "As One!" the men would stand six in front, holding ropes, with two at the back pushing, calling "Heyaaaa-HUP," every few seconds. As one indeed, they converted the sum of their power into something greater than the parts. We all watched, amazed. These could have easily been the 150th great-grandchildren of the original Lisht tomb builders.

Near the end of the 2017 season, as my workmen and I cleared around the column bases in the main hall, a dark hole appeared in the floor. We peered into an entrance four millennia old. Broken into in antiquity, and again in 2011, it was likely Intef's original burial place, its stone blocking still plastered in around its edges. Not far away, three intact offering bowls surfaced. One on the tomb's floor suggested a frozen moment. Just maybe, this bowl was placed by the last person to offer to one of Ipi's descendants. We will return to dig deeper in the future.

From Space to Place

For the 2017 season, in addition to continuing excavation, we had the even more pressing and ambitious goal of mapping the southern half of the site, including the looting pits.

Using a total station, a mapping and surveying tool that allows you to take points for exact x, y, and z coordinates, our survey engineer, Ahmed Ibrahim Ahmed, helped us to create a detailed 3-D map of south Lisht. Meanwhile, another team used differential GPS to record looting pits we had mapped on the satellite imagery. A keen young inspector from the Ministry of Antiquities, Mahmoud Allam, and Reda Esmat el-Arafy, a geologist from Egypt's Nuclear Materials Authority and a former PhD student of mine with a curiosity for everything and an infectious laugh, made short and productive work of the recording. We had to see if the imagery had picked up random digging, actual tombs, or natural landscape features.

In just a few weeks, they processed 802 tombs, all previously unknown to Egyptologists. These include a full range of tomb types and will help us to understand burial practices in the region. We're working on a searchable tomb database that covers type, building material, size, location, stone quality, and approximate date of looting. Most of these shaft tombs contain between two and eight additional burials of family units, so together, the tombs probably held the burials of more than 4,000 individuals or families, all of whom lived and died in Itj-Tawy.

We still have over 1,000 potential tombs to map in the northern part of Lisht, representing another 5,000 or more individuals, and those are just the ones that looters have exposed. It is sobering to consider the scale of what remains to be discovered at this one site, and what new light it may shed on the Middle Kingdom.

On the last day of our season, I went to the hilltop overlooking the tomb. The exposed hall and the causeway mined by intrusive later burials were breathtaking. Over every shaft tomb and each chapel niche, we have built heavy-duty brick caps with locked iron doors. Up on top of the *gebel* sits a new guard hut, which our project pays to man, and which beams floodlights across the ancient cemetery. The satellite imagery already indicates that new looting has decreased since we established it.

In the future, we hope to restore Intef's tomb and piece together the shattered reliefs. Though we may never know what brought about their destruction, our work at his tomb and the associated security measures have protected the last remains of the community among whom his family lived and lay at rest for so long. One day, we may find out more about them; Intef's tomb may be one of the many unsolved cases of the past, but given what we've found so far, I remain hopeful.

A Hope Machine for Humanity

In the last two chapters, we've taken quite a journey, from learning how Egypt's great Pyramid Age ended, to seeing it rise again to cultural florescence in the Middle Kingdom. The term "collapse," as used by so many of my colleagues for the end of the Old Kingdom, implies full destruction. I see these time periods more like balloons that deflate and reinflate depending on external forces. From the great disarray Egypt experienced in the First Intermediate Period, we see the Middle Kingdom launch—call it Ancient Egypt 2.0, not better, but different.

Our society today may also need to deflate in order to reform itself and evolve. The lesson from ancient history is that we never stop pushing or testing new boundaries, whether we are individuals trying to learn from our past, or groups of people changing entire power structures. We never have. We never will. One great age ending does not guarantee a new age will emerge, but it might. That's the foresight that the past can give us.

The archaeological site of El-Lisht is restricted to a cemetery today. The city of Itj-Tawy still beckons, beneath the modern, living Lisht, which might contain the descendants of the people in the desert cemetery. We may not know Intef's or Ipi's stories yet, but we have brought them back from oblivion, fulfilling every ancient Egyptian's deepest wish:[43] to be remembered.

Archaeology is a hope machine for humanity, as I see it. My wish is that you will, too, after reading about the rise and fall and rise again of these ancient Egyptian ages, and that you'll see these stories are not only in Egypt. They are everywhere beneath our feet. They are worth digging for, and worth protecting.

9

The Future of the Past

THE SCENE: AN ARCHAEOLOGICAL MOUND, SOMEWHERE IN THE MIDDLE EAST. THE YEAR: 2119 . . .

Robbie marched across a fallow field, scouting the mound rising in front of him. Around 500 square meters, with parts of the wall system visible along the edges of the site, it had not appeared previously in any ground-based archaeological survey. But hundred-year-old satellite imagery showed it clearly. Why had archaeologists never bothered to survey these sites properly? Working under primitive conditions, he supposed. Frankly, it was a wonder they managed to recover any data at all.

With only an hour allotted to complete his work, Robbie wasted no time. He took off his silver metal backpack and popped open the top. Inside, nested among foam-walled compartments, he found dozens of round figures, each the width of a soda can—red, green, blue, and yellow. Robbie laid them out on the ground.

He tapped each once, activating its "survey" mode, and took out a small box containing tiny multicolored machines the size of paper clips, a silver rod, and a frisbee-sized disk. Attaching the disk to the rod, he extended it to the ground and shook out the paper clip machines.

"Wait," Robbie said. They all started buzzing and lined up in a row. "Red go."

Red figures released their propellers and took off: half flew in rows across the site, half in set patterns in a 5-kilometer radius surrounding it. The timer started a 10-minute red-bot countdown. One eye on the clock, Robbie sat down cross-legged and brought up a holo-map on his visor screen. Already, it populated itself with the survey data while each red bot—equipped with LIDAR, thermal infrared, and hyperspectral sensing systems—detected subsurface architecture with near-complete accuracy. The third of the site covered with low vegetation was just as visible as the bare-naked rest.

As 3-D images appeared on the holo-map, relic river courses and canals unfurled, with hypothesized timescales for their movement. Robbie nodded in satisfaction when most of the site's near-surface architecture popped out, with hot spots for the mortuary, administrative, residential, and workshop areas. One of the buildings looked palatial.

There were 40 minutes left till pickup. "Green go," he said. The green bots whirred away. A few inches above the ground, flying through and around the vegetation, they transected the site in routes a few inches apart. On Robbie's screen, the subsurface architecture emerged more clearly in 3-D. The whole site's plan spread down, and down, to 8 meters below the surface. On-screen color gradations indicated early and later phases of construction, comparing buildings to an internal database of thousands of examples. Several dozen glowed brightly. Just 35 minutes left; barely enough time to squeeze in everything on the to-do list.

"Blue go!" The blue bots flew over the highlighted buildings in groups of nine. Hovering a meter apart, the drones drilled holes with powerful lasers and fired pencil-wide probes 7 meters into the ground. Robbie waited while they sent out ultrasonic waves to take readings, and then moved over for the next unit.

The probes sensed something, all focusing at once, and Robbie sat up. Structures appeared, modeled complete with all the objects and burials inside their walls; 90 percent of the rooms glowed brighter.

"That's a lot of hot spots," he muttered. He eyed the countdown, chewing his lip. Only 25 minutes left. "Probes retract. Go yellow, go digbots."

The buzzing row of tiny machines shot over to the exact locations of the hot spots and started digging. Yellow drones followed closely behind, hovering just above the entry points. Digbots burrowed down, scanned each burial, and took a series of samples. When a bot returned to the surface, it delivered ground bone to the yellow drones' onboard spectrometers for DNA sequencing.

Matching. Matching. Their chitter was constant, fevered, as they connected each deceased individual to local and regional family trees, each object to production sites here or hundreds of miles away, each pottery vessel and sherd to a database of thousands.

Robbie watched the data bubble across his screen.

"Fifteen until pickup," purred the auto-remind on his countdown, but a flashing indicator grabbed his attention. He peered closer. A series of scrolls. And was that charring around some of them? He made a waving motion. Five specialist scanbots homed in on the buried archive to record the ancient words. As though Robbie's screen had sucked them from the ground, the scrolls appeared, unrolling, revealing complete texts. Some had even been reused by scribes in antiquity, their ghostly layers spread hovering over the palimpsest.

"Pickup imminent."

The icon for Robbie's centralized database blinked green: mapping and scanning data complete. A few more minutes, and searchable patterns would emerge from the rendered data.

"Bots home," Robbie yelled across the site, switching each off when it flew in, to return it carefully to his backpack. A haunting alert-call made him look up: a primitive recording nearly two centuries old of Tutankhamun's silver trumpet.[1] "Great, right on time. Report."

"Scanning of regional and national site databases complete. 15 separate site-history hypotheses computing, iterations *beginning*. Histories 1–10 eliminated, percent likelihood less than 90. Of remaining 5, 4 agree with site histories up to abandonment in 1177. Abandonment model likelihoods are less than 94 percent likely, leaving one occupation model greater than 95 percent." Robbie nodded, flicking through graphs.

"Give me that one, then."

"Site occupation begins in 3225 BC, settlement with approximately 200 people, expands to small city of 2,000 in 2478 BC. Expansion due to shifting river course, with increased access to international trade goods and evidence of a very wealthy ruling class. In 2310 BC, a regional governor moves to set up an independent army—"

"And seizes control?"

"Correct. More than 50 cities in a 40-kilometer radius. He declares himself king, ruling for 20 years before his chief priest deposes him. Priest loses a major battle in 2290 BC. With 1 meter+ of silt accumulation, there is no ceramic debris, and no evidence of site occupation after that time for a 100-year period."

"Sounds like drought."

"Correct. A drought event 4,300 years ago causes large-scale site abandonment in the region. A 500-person town reappears ca. 1800 BC, with a local ruler, followed by periods of famine, disease, and burning ca. 1177 BC. With the construction of a major toll road, the site has 2,000+ inhabitants during the Roman Period. War causes slaughter of the younger to middle-aged men around 146 AD, disproportionately small evidence for remains of women and girls, all likely captured as slaves."

"Cheerful."

"I have not interpreted affective value. Would you like me to do this?" Robbie jumped.

"No, no, thank you." His midair swipe cleared the query box from the screen. "Finish up."

"A tiny settlement appears during the Umayyad period between 661 and 750 AD that continues to be occupied today."

Visualizations of the site and surrounding landscape appeared, evolving through the time periods to reflect the changes seen by the digbots, with regional maps showing trade hubs and natural resources, home countries of the invading armies, and the relic river courses.

"Site history complete. Percent likelihood of error +/-2 percent."

Robbie cursed. Not the 1 percent he needed.

"When will I learn to deploy the newest probe models?"

"Unknown."

"Oh, quit it—session over."

A complete publication appeared, with sections on regional river systems, architectural phases, site pottery, skeletal remains and DNA, site development, growth, collapse, abandonment, and resettlement. Plans, maps, and reconstructions flashed across the screen. Among them, scanned sherds flew into place piece by piece, rebuilding a beautiful unguent jar.

"And the best bit . . ." Robbie said, smiling. A complete breakdown of foodways across five millennia. It had been a long day, and his stomach grumbled.

"Warning! Warning! Pickup overdue."

He stifled a curse, hitting ACCEPT: FINAL REPORT. "The boss is going to hate that 2 percent." But right now, beer was more important.

Robbie headed back to the landing spot. Sand blurred around him as the thrums of the unmanned aerial vehicle grew louder. He folded his robot avatar into a compact square around his backpack, and the vehicle's magnetic extension picked him up.

A second later, at ArchaeoVisiön HQ, Robbie took off his virtual-reality visor, shaking his head. Those references, in the final report, to a 2010 archaeological survey. Even an excavation report from a nearby site. So much data overlooked!

And, all that dirt . . . The bacteria, the flies, months spent away from the comfort of his pod. Who would ever want to do that?

He wrinkled his nose, blinking at the revolving unguent jar on-screen. Such a waste of time, removing objects from the ground. Every day, he patted the forehead of King Tut's mask in the foyer as he walked in. Well, a perfect replica, 3-D printed. It'd even fool the experts. In gold, too, since the off-world mining really got going. Gold, lapis lazuli: it was all cheap as chips.

"Real potatoes," he murmured. "Now you're talking." He glanced at the hologram clock digits hanging in the air: just on time, for the fifth site completion of the day. Lunch wouldn't interfere with the rest of the day's site pickup schedule, but beer would have to wait. "Quotas, quotas," he said, getting up.

Over his canteen tray, he thought about that error rating. It shouldn't dull his assessments. But what about his ranking? Third overall. He stabbed a cube with his fork and swallowed it a little too fast.

"She'll make me change out the bots for new ones," he said to the dispenser unit. "The boss. But that's fine, right? They've served their term."

But had he? A wall-to-wall screen behind the counter showed a ship's construction site in real time. Rising through a spinning galaxy of automated movement, the explorer vessel grew like that jar. In a matter of months, the ship would launch to the Earth-size exoplanet, Ross 128 b.[2] His own face rolled past on the screen—"Top-rated Archaeotech": his chances were still good to be on that team.

The top 10 ArchaeoVisiön employees would get to go to space. If ArchaeoVisiön could map a hundred large ancient sites a day in their entirety with 20 techs like him, then mapping ruins on other planets was within their reach. During the United Nations Exoplanet Mission prototype contract, they had already logged 10,000 sites.

"And we've got another month to go," he said, scraping up the last few fragments of cube.

"Incorrect," said the dispenser unit. "Canteen service closes in ten minutes."

He stared blankly at it, then looked up at the screen. Humans had survived and thrived and failed in ancient Egypt, Syria, Iraq, and so many other places, yet now Robbie awaited orders to head to the stars.

And what would any of the people he'd recorded have thought about that?

"Whoa, there, Robbie," he said, feeding his tray back into the machine. "You're not some wacko old-school archaeologist." Like the screen said, "Archaeotech." And the tech was what had drawn him in. All the latest toys. Good pay, a chance of a life off-world . . .

Other worlds held the real mysteries. Nearly every site on Earth was mapped.

"It's all just more of the same." He sighed.

His on-screen face rolled back around. Smiling, confident. Restless. Not like the perfectly rendered naivety of his ancient university lecturers, beamed in hologram from his watch. Outside class, he and his friends had laughed about that generation.

Back in 2060, the last of the old-timers, digging in the dirt like creaky bots. Hanging up the last trowels. All about a hundred years old when they recorded their classes.

That look on their faces, though, when they talked about finding something, about the camaraderie in the field or the first extraterrestrial radio waves recorded in the 2070s. Yeah, he'd laughed. He stared up at that vessel rising from the construction site and imagined finding traces of ancient civilizations in space, not knowing how much like those professors he looked.

The truth wasn't in the ground anymore. It was out there.

Welcome Back to the Present!

This sounds completely fantastical, like the story from someone who has, as my kindergarten teacher once said, "more interest in science fiction than science." Not much has changed, clearly. During my

1980s childhood, *Star Wars* cross-fertilized *Indiana Jones,* and planted seeds deep in my head that grew into a real research interest. I've spent nearly all of this book talking about the Earth as seen from space, and even more about where we've been archaeologically, but not yet told you where we might go.

It seems to me, after 20 years of study and research, that archaeologists spend far more time imagining the past than dreaming about the future of the field. Perhaps we become too bogged down in the details or fearful of taking a risk where we might be proven wrong—the horror!

Dreaming Big Dreams

But if we allow ourselves to dream of the future of archaeology, however briefly, we can see that archaeologists, scientists, doctors, and roboticists already use every form of technology I described above. The technologies might not be miniaturized, or as mobile, or have that number of sensors attached, but thinking through how much and how rapidly the technologies we utilize today have evolved, I can feel that world of 2119 approaching.

In tech evolution, 30 years is not very long. Remember that before the early 1990s, almost no one had heard of the internet. A century ago, the telephone had just started to appear in very wealthy people's homes, and now, some 2.53 billion people own smartphones.[3]

Believe it or not, inventors pore over science fiction novels hoping to glean insights into the next big thing that can make them billions.[4] Employing science fiction to envision the future of archaeological exploration could be equally rewarding.

For example, the idea of mapping and excavating an entire site in an hour—or at least the parts of a site that fit together well enough to extrapolate the whole puzzle—is at present the craziest idea of all. A single archaeological team might work at a site for more than 40 years, perhaps the director's entire career, and they would barely scratch the surface.

Let's do some math, because math is fun. A 500-by-500-meter mound, 8 meters in height—not considering what's below the current ground surface—leaves us with a general site volume of 2 million cubic meters. In a single season, an archaeologist and his or her local dig crew could excavate a 10-by-10-meter unit, going down

3.5 meters over the course of two months. This gives us a volume of 350 cubic meters.

Four units that size might be excavated at one site in a season, so 1,400 cubic meters. Over 40 years, assuming a standard dig rate, we would see 56,000 cubic meters excavated, or just under 3 percent of the site. This would produce yearly excavation reports, hundreds of articles, several dozen doctorates, and academic books aplenty.

So, to get to 100 percent, we multiply 40 years by 33. Which gives us 1,320 years of excavation, per site, to understand them fully. Even with year-round excavation, we then need to take into account intensive lab work, analysis, and publication preparation, which easily amount to four to eight additional months for each month in the field.

Now, multiply that times x number of sites in a region.

Despite all the advancements of our golden age of archaeology, it's impossible. And here's another blast of reality: archaeologists may not have the chance to work on a site for more than a few seasons. Funding and permitting issues that we've discussed aside, career changes inevitably cause directors to leave for other sites. Staying site-monogamous takes devotion, mainly for reasons of time commitment. I am going steady with Lisht, my favorite site in Egypt, but I keep finding other sites to map. I don't know what that says about me, and maybe it's better if I never find out.

Where We Are Now

Understanding a site in an hour is obviously closer to fantasy, let alone sci-fi. But looking at the status quo, with the magic toy box the fictional Robbie has at his disposal in 2119, may tell us how close we are to self-driving miniature drones for mapping, surveying, and 3-D reconstruction.

Already, remote-sensing tools are hosted on anything we can get off the ground, from satellites to helicopters and drones—also known as unmanned aerial vehicles, or UAVs. Typical drones used for archaeology measure about 50 centimeters in diameter, but the technology is getting smaller and smaller. You can now buy a palm-size drone as a toy and a novelty mini-drone the diameter of a soda can.[5] Some even carry cameras.[6]

Prior to 2015, the heavier the remote-sensing payload, the larger the drone, and sometimes you had to rely on an airplane or helicopter. Now a standard drone can easily lift a LIDAR system and a thermal infrared or hyperspectral camera, not unlike Robbie's red bots that he used for his initial survey.[7] All of these technologies have miniaturized drastically in the past decade: a good-quality thermal infrared camera is now the same size as a smartphone. Having fully miniaturized versions on palm-size drones a hundred years from now suddenly seems less fantastical.

Each system could theoretically map subsurface features, site activity areas, topography, and relic river courses by 2119.

Hyperspectral Imaging

Something called hyperspectral imaging is an exciting new frontier for archaeological remote sensing. Instead of the standard four to eight bands of visible and near-infrared data that I've spent a lot of this book discussing, hyperspectral imagery can provide hundreds of bands of data, giving clues about the chemical composition of the terrain.[8] It's like going from 8 colors on your computer screen to 256: you'd be able to see far more details and subtleties in your photos.

A handheld spectrometer,[9] a machine the size of a standard high school microscope, can measure the spectral signature of any material based on its chemical makeup. Geologists use them to detect tiny differences in geological strata,[10] but they are fairly new to archaeologists, and we have not yet fully exploited their capabilities. The first step would be to build up signature databases of archaeological sites and zones for comparative purposes.

We already know that everything on the Earth's surface has its own distinct chemical signature. As buried features on sites degrade, they release tiny pieces of building materials that slowly mix with the strata above. While this may not be visible to the naked eye, we can map these changes—enhanced by rainfall—using infrared data. That allows us to locate outlines of mud-brick buildings or settlement foundations.[11] In the case of buried stone features, we can use mid-infrared data to make them more apparent.

Hyperspectral data can also allow archaeologists to identify distinct activity areas on archaeological sites. Ceramic or metal production, for instance, requires burning at high temperatures and leaves clear chemical residues that indicate an industrial zone. The high bone content of cemeteries may change the mineral content of the soil, and produces fragments that can often be observed on top of sites, creating distinct signatures. Each of these different areas would register as clear spikes across the light spectrum and may be far more visible in some bands than others.

Thermal infrared imaging also offers an exciting new avenue of research for archaeologists. In any city during the hottest parts of the summer, the concrete absorbs heat during the day, and at night, when the temperature is cooler, the heat radiates outward. Urban temperatures during summer nights can be 3 to 4 degrees warmer than areas that have more trees to shade them, which can make cities literally glow on satellite imagery at night.[12] Buried archaeological features respond in similar ways, although the temperature differences are far more subtle.

Archaeologists have already used thermal infrared cameras to detect underground ritual chambers known as kivas at Chaco Canyon in New Mexico.[13] That makes it entirely possible that the same kind of imaging could be used to identify buried tombs in other desert environments—perhaps even in Egypt's Valley of the Kings, where archaeologists have spent years searching for hidden burials. You just need to make sure you get the imagery from the right time of day, and from the right time of year, to capture the maximum temperature differences.

Putting multiple sensors on the same drone is something we'll see in the next few years, simply because efficiency cries out for it. And efficiency equals money saved, essential in ever-more-squeezed research budgets. Inevitably, more sensors will better target subsurface survey and excavation. Researchers already fly LIDAR systems and hyperspectral cameras on airplanes at the same time,[14] and as more technology is miniaturized, a standard rig can include even more.

Scanning Above and Below

Let's talk about Robbie's green bots, which can scan each site into its surrounding landscape. Sites do not exist in a vacuum. We've seen how essential it's become to know the availability of raw materials and the shifts of rivers or lakes, for understanding the rise and fall of communities. For that reason, we survey around ancient sites to locate relic watercourses or sources[15] and places where natural resources could have been mined or quarried.

Today's key tools are magnetometry, resistivity, and ground-penetrating radar. And these physical tools themselves are honking great bits of kit, involving backbreaking deployment as crews walk hundreds of miles in a standard survey season. But as these technologies improve, the mapping systems, like other tech, will get smaller and the parts lighter. We can hope—and what footsore, stooped magnetometry specialist wouldn't—that systems could one day be loaded onto self-driving drones just like Robbie's.

Today, researchers wait until the end of work to download their device's data into computers and to process it with software similar to remote-sensing programs. Already, data from these devices can be wirelessly transmitted to computers,[16] but it is not widespread practice yet. Assuming subsurface-sensing and transmission technologies continue to be developed, we can probably expect automatic wireless upload, and easily imagine populating data instantly onto 3-D models of the sites to show fully rendered architecture as far beneath the surface as 5 to 8 meters. Just 50 years ago, we had no subsurface remote-sensing machines at all. In a hundred years, the ground that now hides secrets could well be wide open for us, with no digging involved.

The spectacular 3-D reconstructions delivered by Robbie's blue bots are also already in their infancy. You've seen ultrasonic waves reconstructing the environment in 3-D, but you might not have been aware of it. Bats and dolphins do it naturally, and we've finally cottoned on. Driverless cars send out waves to detect objects in their path, with tentative identifications on which they then act accordingly, such as, person=stop, car=accelerate to avoid a collision.[17] Scientists have mounted this technology on groups of drones,[18] discovering many potential mapping applications. As sensors grow smaller and more sensitive, it's feasible that they could be delivered underground, via a probe.

Although our sci-fi scene is asking even more of in-situ scanning with regard to the discovery of the scrolls, major advances in the scanning and revelation of ancient art and writing are already taking shape. Scientists now use lasers to clear soot from tomb walls and reveal stunning paintings.[19] Ancient manuscripts can be viewed in infrared light to find which ones are palimpsests—those with layers of words that have been sanded off and written over and are now hidden to the human eye.[20]

And phase-contrast X-ray imaging can even peer into the burnt scrolls from the Italian site of Herculaneum, the less famous but even more fascinating cousin of Pompeii, destroyed by the same volcanic eruption of Mount Vesuvius in 79 AD. The tight rolls are too fragile to unwrap and read, but this technology is able to pick out words and letters hidden among the charred papyrus sheets. While the work only represents proof of concept so far, experts are confident that they will soon be able to read entire texts.[21]

Machine Learning—a Cutting-Edge Frontier

So the beginnings of extraordinarily advanced imaging technologies are ready for future development. But we are also getting closer to the connectivity of information that Robbie has at his fingertips, and everything it could contribute to targeting further investigation of a site with pinpoint precision. It's called machine learning.

Machine learning, or computer vision, forms an essential part of most computer science programs today. It is the driving force behind things like facial recognition programs. The computer has access to thousands of examples and compares the pixels it receives for a new feature against those examples via neural networks.

This kind of software drives many of the apps on your phone—the ones you use to find out what song is playing in your favorite café, or what bird you just photographed.[22] Machine learning represents, in some form, a type of augmented reality, in which we use computers to help us sort out signal from noise in our increasingly data-crowded lives.

Satellite imagery represents the perfect type of data to use for machine learning. Looking at large satellite data sets, it took our team of three nearly six months to map all of Egypt's looting pits. Imagine how much faster we could have worked if we had been able to train a machine to detect potential areas of pits by comparing with known examples, and our job had involved confirming those pits rather than searching across hundreds of thousands of square kilometers ourselves. We probably could have finished Egypt in a week.

The possibilities for using machine learning to detect previously unknown archaeological sites in satellite data represent the most cutting-edge frontier in my field right now. If we could eliminate featureless areas automatically, we could zoom in on areas of interest that we might otherwise miss with tired eyes. Data scientists have already developed machine-learning algorithms to perform tasks such as searching satellite images of Greece to detect swimming pools that wealthy homeowners have hidden to avoid paying taxes.[23]

My whole field is based on using the exact same iterative process on sites across the globe today, comparing similar features elsewhere in the results of surveys and remote sensing to identify the most promising hot spots for excavation in our own sites—we just do it the long way round. Machine learning could speed this up enormously, to better target coring and seismic survey. We can but hope.

Other applications could give us a similar virtual hand postexcavation. At the conclusion of a season, what consumes the bulk of all archaeologists' time is pinning down other, already-explored sites that corroborate or explain their own findings, with other occurrences of the same features and objects. It would be nice to have a machine do that for you.

Search engines like the Google Ngram Viewer[24] can already hunt through databases of millions of books to find the first instance of words or patterns of usage. A plagiarism software program using similar search protocols helped an amateur Shakespeare scholar find a book from which the Bard drew major inspiration for his plays.[25]

Those same software principles could apply to finding any "like" things, from city plans, buildings, and walls to fragments of mystery artifacts. If the machine knew the material, shape, size, and technology, it could easily find parallels among objects in a database. Such faster-than-thought comparisons would also help generate complete 3-D reconstructions of the site or object, based on more fully excavated examples elsewhere.

Next Year, I Want a Digbot for My Birthday . . .

But for the actual digging . . . we seem to be light-years from tiny digbots that might someday be capable of the excavation and 3-D scanning described in Robbie's story. Robots and sensors, however, have already become an everyday part of our lives, and advances in robotics are now turning what was once imagination into reality.

A Massachusetts Institute of Technology spinoff company called

Boston Dynamics, for example, has created a series of viral videos of animal-like robots opening doors, walking up stairs, and doing backflips. It's got to be said, the videos bring the words "I'll be back" to everyone's minds, and the robots themselves provoked widespread fear at TED in 2017, when I saw them in action.[26]

We might not need to run from our robot overlords just yet. Another viral video of Roomba the housework robot spreading dog poop liberally across an entire house floor[27] suggests some gadgets have not quite delivered on their promise. But they soon will.

If DARPA, the US Defense Advanced Research Projects Agency, can develop tiny robots that zoom through buildings, mimicking insects,[28] and robots can explore looting pits in Egypt, like the heavily looted site of El Hibeh in Middle Egypt,[29] I can see tiny bots in the future not only doing the actual digging, but also scanning features below the surface in a way that does not disturb the ancient remains. If that seems like a bit of a leap, 3-D high-resolution scans of objects and skeletons are now becoming commonplace in museums and on archaeological sites. And since the digbots are down there, then of course it would make sense for them to take samples for chemical testing and DNA.

DNA analysis is another revolutionary tool in archaeology that is already developing at a rapid pace. Some of you may have gotten your DNA sampled via 23andMe, Ancestry.com, or National Geographic's Genographic Project. These efforts have analyzed the DNA of tens of thousands of individuals, and you can even use your results to track the paths your family took out of Africa into a bigger world.[30] I found out that I am 3.7 percent Neanderthal and 0.9 percent Denisovan. That means I have Neanderthals as great-to-the-nth-factor grandparents, if you think about it. Maybe that accounts for my thick eyebrows.

On a shorter, more recent timescale, DNA from long-dead tissues can assist with the reconstruction of complex family trees, as archaeologists discovered comparing the DNA of the royal mummies in Cairo's Egyptian Museum.[31] In the future, as more DNA tests are conducted on ancient and modern people, perhaps by robots like Robbie's yellow bots, I have no doubt that this will create lineages potentially going back hundreds of thousands of years. We are all cousins, after all. Facilitating ever-larger sample sizes on skeletons at archaeological sites will help tie those populations to location, and to regional and international data sets.

DNA testing in archaeology has already become so advanced that specific diseases are isolated by sampling ancient people's dental plaque.[32] Recent discoveries also include the skin color of a person whose only remains are a 10,000-year-old skeleton.[33] As the field of medicine leaps forward, so, too, will the potential for determining ancient people's appearances and physical histories.

The Future Is Here

In our story, Robbie finishes by reading over an analysis of the site from the computer, which suggests its full history with a high degree of confidence. This might be the part you find the most difficult to accept. Archaeologists need to spend decades honing their archaeological and interpretive skills in order to arrive at middle age, when we can finally make grand, sweeping pronouncements. (I'm just kidding. We start making those in grad school.) A dig director today may write a book about a site after working there for 30 or 40 years, only to see most of her theories disproved by her students 10 years later. Which is all as it should be.

But if you have all the data Robbie's bots collected, representing hundreds of years of standard archaeological work, with the equivalent scientific lab work, then I do not see why it would be impossible to synthesize immediate results, too. We already input data into computers for statistical purposes, to show us how, for example, certain objects became popular and then fell out of use. With large data sets from a single site, we need major computation power these days to analyze it all fully, but this won't be an issue in five years, much less one hundred. If you can input all the data from a site and instantly compare every major building, object, skeleton, and technology with every other similar site, painting its complete picture is within reach.

I, Archaeologist

At the end of our glimpse into the future, we learn that Robbie is a mere tech, operating virtually, via his robot avatar and haptic technology, operated by a touch or gesture. That's probably not so far away from where technology is right now. Virtual avatars are positively old hat in computer games, and we already use drone-mounted cameras to see places and things too difficult or dangerous to access, while controlling them with our tablets or computers. Think about how your TV video game system captures your movements.

I've had a chance to test the next step, haptic technology in a futuristic driverless car where gentle movements to the left or right allowed me to change TV stations.[34] This technology allows sensors to detect your movements and interprets them for computers or other machines. Movie effects of users swiping images off screens or through the air from feet away to design or research something, as in the *Iron Man* films and, years earlier, *Minority Report*, are now pretty much reality. Microsoft's Kinect works in a similar way, allowing surgeons to manipulate MRIs and other images by body movements rather than touching a computer, thus keeping the operating room sterile,[35] and simulated training now allows surgeons to practice operations before doing them.[36] Remote surgeries—and archaeological excavations—may be right around the corner.

Instead of an archaeological team of 20, plus a large local workforce and years of work, an army of robots controlled virtually by 20 technicians could fully explore 100 sites or more in a single day. Physical exploration, as wonderful and fun as it is, could be done far more effectively by our robot avatars. Current developments with robotic technology suggest we may get there in less than a hundred years.

We have begun to see this shift already, as the practice of archaeology increasingly integrates with other scientific fields. From site recording to photography to analyzing our finds, archaeologists now see the importance of collaborating with our colleagues in computer science and engineering. In the future, I think it's very likely that all archaeologists will develop an additional primary expertise within the sciences. Given the opportunity, students are already starting to make those kinds of course choices, and graduate students with strong scientific and interdisciplinary backgrounds have a far greater chance of employment. The nature and sustainability of current academic departmental models is well beyond the scope of this book, but we have to ask ourselves whether archaeology will become a subfocus within the sciences.

Robbie looks down his nose at the "old ways" of archaeology—people taking objects out of the ground and collecting them. Today, the 3-D scanning of objects and fossils has created global databases from which anyone can print versions in various media.[37] Archaeologists now use 3-D-printed objects more often in the classroom, giving students across the globe a feel for precious items that are usually stored away in research labs, like skulls of early human ancestors.[38]

The detail improves constantly. Scientists at the Massachusetts Institute of Technology are experimenting with reproducing colors and textures of materials[39] and have already shown that their printers can work 10 times faster than standard 3-D devices.[40] Perhaps this will be the true end of site looting, when collectors can get any ancient object they want in the original materials, distinguishable from the real thing only under powerful microscopes.

Is There Anybody Out There?

The great science fiction writer Arthur C. Clarke once said, "Two possibilities exist: Either we are alone in the Universe or we are not. Both are equally terrifying."[41] That brings us to what may be a big surprise: all this research may have little to do with archaeology on our own home hurtling through space, and everything to do with competing for the business of exploring potential civilizations on other planets. We already know about thousands of exoplanets thanks to powerful telescopes and advances in computer technologies. As I write this, two of those planets appear to be "Earthlike," although this will take decades to confirm.[42]

Just imagine the possibilities.

The Drake Equation, created by astronomer Frank Drake in 1961,[43] is the formula for the likelihood of there being intelligent life on other planets that's advanced enough for us to detect via electromagnetic waves. As technology advances, the chances of that kind of detection increase. In the future, we will no doubt find more and more Earthlike planets and a potentially infinite number of exoplanets. We may someday get the radio waves that the Search for Extra-Terrestrial Intelligence, or SETI, seeks,[44] or some other sign of life. And it will spur us to explore farther than we ever have.

Aside from the question of how we define life, or indeed, material culture, we must ask how we can even begin to study things about which we will truly know nothing. Assuming we find a planet with life, and assuming we can even recognize its "settlements," we will have no database of known artifacts with which to compare them. Whether it's satellites or probes that find these worlds, we're still relying on hitting the right time window when the settlement sites have not disappeared into dust. Astronauts and NASA engineers probably think they might be best equipped to study them, but archaeologists represent the only field fully equipped to explore and analyze an unknown material culture and its creators. They have my vote.

The irony here does not escape me. For years, archaeologists have had to contend with inane alien theories, including claims that extraterrestrials built the pyramids or are responsible for basically anything anywhere that looks like innovative cultural development.[45] These sentiments are actually racist and bigoted, and unfortunately they still hold wide appeal for those who cannot accept that people of a different skin color created monuments lasting millennia.

Having fought for years against these theories, in outer space, archaeologists will become the aliens, using all our skills to grapple with the complete unknown. Archaeologists also know the history of Earth's exploration and other cultural "first contacts" well, and can draw on thousands of years of what went terribly wrong. With luck, future archaeologists, or those employed at firms like ArchaeoVisiön, will use this sensitivity to avoid the pitfalls and horrors of past journeys. Or perhaps we will just invent new ones for future generations to condemn.

A Window into Our Past

I used to worry that NASA's astronaut program excluded anyone without a bachelor of science degree—with my first degree a bachelor of arts, I can never be an astronaut, even with a specialization in remote sensing. But based on Elon Musk's success with his Falcon Heavy launch in February 2018,[46] I think our future astronauts may in fact come from the private sector. (Though, if anyone at NASA happens to be reading this, I'm still available!)

My major concern is the one I presented with Robbie himself. As we move away from the dirt, the very thing that connects us with the past—the thing that gets beneath our fingernails and contains the real DNA of its past occupants[47]—will be lost. That great sense of anticipation while in the field, of not knowing everything, is what calls us back to the Earth and keeps us humble. You might get lucky in each and every season throughout your lifetime, or you might never make a major discovery. Or you might be wrong. Without that hazard and mystery, the possibility of failure, the archaeological wonder simply vanishes.

Most archaeologists I know have great stories to tell of the discovery that got away—whether it lay just out of reach because they ran out of time or they were beaten to it by a colleague. Sometimes, it's the great secret they know awaits their next season, if only the government would start issuing permits again. Archaeology is always a crapshoot. That's why we keep rolling the dice. When computers do everything for archaeologists, we become the automatons pressing buttons at set times, and the computers become the explorers. It's no longer fun when we cannot come up with a satisfying conclusion ourselves, or at least one that makes sense based on everything we know.

Our techniques might be considered primitive by future explorers, and our behavior barbaric. I firmly believe certain antiquities collectors deserve to be judged in such terms. But as archaeology evolves, I do worry about the loss of that wonder, the sensation I have in front of the Pyramids of Giza even after dozens of visits. When tourists of the future put on their augmented reality glasses to experience a sped-up version of the pyramids' construction, with virtual ancient Egyptian scribes giving them tours, will the experience be the same? Or will it be a futuristic theme park?

Worse still, the idea that in the future archaeology could be perverted into a gigantic corporate moneymaking scheme, on a far bigger level than standard contracts in archaeology today, feels like ashes in my mouth. Today, we already fight for every penny from government sponsors, private donors, and more, and we know our resources are limited. Some would say any additional funding would be good funding, and we must accept that everything will not be roses in the future of exploration. We should think of all the good ways archaeology will advance as a field, and all the bad, to have the discussions needed now to take alternate paths.

Childhood Dreams

We've traveled from science fiction to science in this chapter. I've studied the field of archaeological surveying long enough to be able to sense my own shelf life, and the thought scares me. I am obsolescence in action, and all my colleagues who work in technology have that same fear.

But there are occasions, in spite of it, when we get lucky and have a moment of discovery to carry us through even the darkest days. Sometimes it is the stuff that childhood dreams—and future visions—are made of. Our greatest treasure after all, is not Tutankhamun's mask, but a window into the past, to light our way ahead.

10

The Challenge

I f you look at its history, archaeology has an entry fee of wealth, whiteness, and maleness. The "greats" in the field, the names you study in introductory archaeology classes, fit that ticket—from Jean-François Champollion, the decipherer of Egyptian hieroglyphs on the Rosetta Stone in 1822,[1] to Frederick Catherwood, the early explorer of Maya ruins in Central America in the 1840s,[2] and Hiram Bingham, the so-called discoverer of Machu Picchu in Peru in 1911.[3] The Y chromosome is dominant. But X does mark the spot, after all.

Women in the Field

Women have participated in archaeological exploration from the beginning. Saint Helena (250–330 AD), the mother of Roman emperor Constantine, purportedly collected pieces of the true cross along with other holy relics, making her the first known female archaeologist and the Christian patron saint of archaeologists.[4] Gertrude Bell, the subject of the film *Queen of the Desert*, is called the "Mother of Mesopotamian Archaeology," and the National Museum of Iraq in Baghdad owes its foundation to her. Fluent in Arabic, she shared invaluable diplomatic information about Iraqi politics during World War I that numerous British officers could otherwise not obtain.[5]

Kathleen Kenyon, excavator of Jericho, the first major city of the ancient Near East, is considered one of the greatest archaeologists of the 20th century.[6] She trained Donald Redford, an eminent Egyptologist, under whom I learned excavation on my first dig at Mendes—I like to think of her as my archaeological grandmother.

It's even possible, in fact, for a famous woman to be a clandestine archaeologist, and the evidence is right under your nose, much like a guilty murderer on a train. Yes, that train, and that author.

Agatha Christie married Mesopotamian archaeologist Max Mallowan and accompanied him on digs to Iraq, which she loved.[7] She wrote *Death on the Nile* while wintering in Aswan at the Old Cataract Hotel, an establishment you must visit before you die, to witness its ageless oriental splendor. Agatha loved marking pottery with tiny numbers, a job well suited to those who can patiently add detail to intricate mystery plots. In 1946, she published one of the greatest archaeological poems of all time, "A-sitting on a Tell," part of which I share here:

> *I'll tell you everything I can*
> *if you will listen well:*
> *I met an erudite young man*
> *a-sitting on a Tell.*
> *"Who are you, sir?" to him I said.*
> *"For what is it you look?"*
> *His answer trickled through my head*
> *like bloodstains in a book.*
> *He said: "I look for aged pots*
> *of prehistoric days*
> *and then I measure them in lots*
> *and lots of different ways.*
> *And then (like you) I start to write,*
> *my words are twice as long*
> *as yours, and far more erudite.*
> *They prove my colleagues wrong!"*
> *But I was thinking of a plan*
> *to kill a millionaire*
> *and hide the body in a van*
> *or some large Frigidaire.*

So, having no reply to give,
and feeling rather shy,
I cried: "Come, tell me how you live!
And when, and where, and why?"[8]

Simply glorious. The poem in its entirety speaks with gentle mockery and so much affection of what archaeologists do. Not much has changed in the decades since then, in terms of lifestyle, although Agatha certainly never had to worry about Wi-Fi connection issues on-site.

Excavation photos from the 1940s do not look very different from those we take today. If you look closely, few people of the countries where the work took place appear as professional staff members. Fortunately, that is now changing, but not quickly enough. I addressed the American Schools of Oriental Research annual conference in November 2016, and it shocked me to see the sea of white. I'm lucky to teach at one of the most diverse college campuses in the country in Birmingham, Alabama, but Egyptology and the archaeology of the ancient Near East as a whole have a long way to go.

We must increase outreach to middle- and high-school students, have active recruitment to increase student and faculty diversity, include more graduate student support and postdoctoral opportunities, have junior faculty mentoring . . . and on and on. The wonderful quote, "If you can see it, you can be it," resonates deeply with me. We have to create experiences that not only invite everyone to participate in discovery but allow participants to see people from backgrounds they can relate to, so they can imagine their own future in a field they can shape.

Across the board, we need to do better. More diversity in archaeology means a diversity of perspectives, approaches, and ideas—all so welcome. When more women started entering the field in the 1970s, gender archaeology began to take its rightful place. Now, with more acknowledgment of the contribution of LGBTQ+ scholars, we have a better understanding of the nuances of sexuality in the ancient world. Most archaeology graduate programs now report a greater percentage of women than men, but even so, I have seen too many female students turn away from academic careers because of family issues, harassment, and being passed over for funding or jobs.

Things will change, and they must.

Up to the 1960s, many women finished their archaeology and ancient-world doctorates before most colleges would hire women. The road ahead looked bleak. The best success story I know from that era is that of the great writer and storyteller Barbara Mertz, who wrote under the pen name Elizabeth Peters.[9] Some of you may be fans of her work; I certainly am. She spun stories of the fictitious Amelia Peabody, Egyptologist and murder-mystery-solver extraordinaire.

Barbara once told me that after finishing her PhD in 1947 at the University of Chicago, she could not find a job. Male Egyptologists told her she had wasted her time. At that point, she had always wanted to write, so write she did. Instead of scholarly articles, she started writing fiction, basing the world of Ms. Peabody on the heyday of Egyptology in the late 1800s. And, for good measure, she created characters based on those misogynist Egyptologists, and she killed them off in ways that each deserved. She died in 2013, a beloved Egyptology figure, a millionaire, and not caring one bit. I aspire . . .

Admittedly, we have issues with the diversity of people doing archaeology in North America and Europe. But it is far worse in Central and South America, Asia, the Middle East, and Africa. When I sit down with archaeological and cultural heritage ministries overseas, women represent only 5 to 10 percent of the archaeologists I meet. This is a subject recognized by women in these countries, and it appears to be changing, with occasional news stories featuring up-and-coming women in archaeology.[10] Let's hope they become more frequent.

Knowledge Is Not as Free as It Should Be

Male or female, if you do not come from an upper-middle-class or a wealthy family, then your chances decrease for having an education, books, and internet access, let alone a successful career. If you're lucky enough to have all these, plus the right connections, only then might you get the training you need to be an archaeologist. But as you begin your graduate work, you hit a literal wall. You'll hit many of them: paywalls.

Access to academic research represents one of the greatest hurdles to budding scientists across the world, when a single article from an online journal can cost $25 to download, which is easily a week's wages for many government workers outside most Western countries. Journal subscriptions, bundled by corporate publishing superpowers such as Elsevier, can cost thousands of dollars, far beyond what any poorly funded ministry or university can afford. Academic publishing as an industry will hopefully be pushed to change by new open-access journals, where many of my colleagues and I now prefer to publish.

This data accessibility does not stop with journal articles. For many archaeological sites in the past, excavation directors died before they got around to publishing their excavations. To dig without publishing is irresponsible and unacceptable, but these bars were only recently set, after archaeology's 200-year run-up. Writing up requires years of painstaking research and careful collation of field notes. Not fun, and often not funded. To expect people to work that hard for nothing would be unthinkable in the private sector.

This said, old dig records can be gold mines for unpublished archaeological work. Graduate students are now plowing through museum storerooms and university libraries, attempting to reconstruct important but long-forgotten excavations. There's still much more to sort through. I've heard from a friend about mosques and storerooms in Cairo filled floor to ceiling with 100 years of unpublished excavation notes and reports by Egyptian and European archaeologists. We have no idea what great discoveries lurk there—maybe missing tombs, or new dynasties. The wider archaeological world will never know until archivists scan them and translate the original notes from Arabic or French.

More recently, horror stories tell of an entire season's worth of records disappearing in luggage on the trip back. Or 20 years' worth of unpublished records vanishing in a house move. Nowadays, we are so fortunate to be able to photograph site-book pages on a phone or tablet to create a pdf for each excavation unit to upload to the cloud. Also, on our dig at Lisht, our resident mapping genius Chase Childs recently developed systems to record registration on tablets using a customized data-entry program. Photographs, with GPS location data, upload automatically and can connect to our project's geographic information system. Easy, if you live and work in 2018, in a country with access to great technology and financial resources. We take all this for granted.

Money Talks

But what happens if you're a student archaeologist with no recourse to funding whatsoever? Going on a dig as a field-school participant is far too expensive for most undergraduates.

Many students must spend the summer working to afford to go to school, period. In addition to sacrificing summer wages, to go on a US university-led excavation, they must pay for their plane ticket, visas, luggage, supplies and gear, room and board, and any tuition if the field school is for academic credit. A student can easily spend $5,000–$8,000 for a single excavation, which would "cost" more than $10,000 if you factor in lost wages. You cannot dig abroad as an undergraduate from the United States without scholarships or a wealthy family.

In my case, without 100 percent coverage from these scholarships, I could never have afforded to go on any digs, which would have greatly disadvantaged my career. On a personal level, I would never have met my husband.

Even if you can pay for the travel, most digs assume you are able-bodied. Living in difficult conditions, doing intense physical labor, and walking a long distance to and from sites across unstable terrain is impossible if you use a wheelchair or have other physical issues or illnesses. Fortunately, many excavations in the United States and Europe benefit from roads and clear paths for access, but some places present major challenges.

One of our ceramic specialists, the bubbly, funny, kindly Rexine Hummel, had difficulty walking to and from the van to the site at Lisht every day. At 82 years of age, Rexine has reached goddess status in Egyptology, and has been a personal friend of our dig for many years. The Quftis on-site had the idea to build her a wooden palanquin, so my husband designed one to carry her in style. Everyone spontaneously sang and clapped during her arrival and departure, turning the beginnings and the ends of our workdays into parades and making joy out of something painful.

Getting out to the field to dig may simply not be possible for everyone, though some excavations offer the public the chance to feel involved remotely. A British web platform, DigVentures, offers opportunities to excavate in person and to follow archaeologists online as they conduct their research.[11] It also raises funds for excavations via donations and the online sale of branded items like T-shirts and chocolate replicas of an Anglo-Saxon grave marker, dubbed the "NomNomNom Stone."[12]

Most people do not realize that even five dollars can make a difference to an archaeological team. If 50 people give a few dollars each, that can feed your team for a few days. This broadens participation and moves away from traditional archaeological funding models that emphasize larger donations.

Rules, and More Rules

Throughout the world, each country sets its own priorities and guidelines concerning who can work there. In some countries such as the United Kingdom, a strong tradition exists for local volunteers on excavations. Everyone from the age of being-able-to-handle-a-trowel-safely (Just kidding! Trowels are safe in no one's hands!) to as-old-as-you-please is welcome to work, as part of community engagement initiatives. During an award-winning project at Lyminge in Kent,[13] volunteers actually took blocks of annual leave from their day jobs to take part. If you live close to an archaeological site, and the dig director welcomes volunteers, please do ask to take part: you'll most likely be of great help to an overworked, understaffed team.

In general, though, the question of who has the right to explore ancient places is complicated, loaded with politics and, in some cases, the historical abuses of other countries' heritages during the colonial era.

Egypt's Ministry of Antiquities grants us the opportunity to dig. The ministry has strict rules and regulations surrounding permits to do archaeological work, and scrutinizes the CVs and background of each team member, as it should. This makes it difficult to get your foot in the door on projects there unless you have a specific skill to offer, like those of a ceramics analyst or survey specialist. Outside of Europe and North America, mounting expeditions to dig abroad is the exception rather than the rule. The majority of archaeologists who are Chinese or Indian, for example, work in China and India, respectively, although this is beginning to change. In 2017, a Chinese team for the first time applied to work at Karnak in Egypt, and I know they will be welcomed with hospitality by their Egyptian co-workers when the project progresses.[14]

One of the most exciting aspects of international archaeology is the opportunity for cultures to share expertise, technologies, and perspectives. However, in Egypt, India, or any country where a foreign archaeologist happens to work, great inequalities may exist in training and resources.

Note, I did not say skill, passion, commitment, or talent. Those working under adverse conditions with minimal resources have a lot to teach us. The Ministry of Antiquities in Egypt regularly makes global headlines announcing tombs, sites, and other findings of its own projects: in 2017 alone, my co-director at Lisht, Adel Okasha, found a new pyramid while directing a mission at Dashur, just north of Lisht.

Negotiating the politics of working at sites around the globe is only the first step in the journey to reach the peoples and cultures that came before us.

Touching the Past

When we visit an ancient ruin, the past is touchable and yet impossible to see. The trauma our parents, grandparents, and ancestors experienced can even affect our own cells profoundly,[15] but comfortingly, perhaps, when our mothers bear us, they carry our cells with them for the rest of their lives.[16] Our bodies are living archaeological sites, connected to the past and future simultaneously.

The bridge to thousands and even hundreds of thousands of years ago is contained in our DNA, which also is connected with the DNA of at least two other species, the Neanderthals and Denisovans.[17] A new discovery of tools from Kenya dating to 320,000 years ago reveals evidence of long-distance trade for obsidian. The team also found ocher, which the researchers suggest may have been mixed with fat for painting.[18] We'll probably never know what was so brightly painted, although it was perhaps people's bodies, clothing, or decorative objects long since turned to dust. This suggests that we have been innovative and creative from our earliest days as *Homo sapiens*, and however this colorful resource was used, the fluctuations in climate and the environment in East Africa at this time caused its availability, and that of food sources, to be variable and unpredictable.[19] These challenges made cooperation with other people a good strategy for survival—something we'd do well to consider today.[20]

Archaeological Sites as Time Machines

Archaeological sites contain our cultural DNA. They are places where we can contemplate, compare, and marvel at human diversity and creativity. I've met many people who've seen the countless heads carved into the Temple of Bayon in Cambodia or the grand mountain vistas beneath the terraced housing of Machu Picchu in Peru. Every single one has had to take a deep breath before describing, not what they saw, but how they felt, witnessing such beauty.

That sensation is the only working time machine I know. It removes us from where we stand and hooks us on a thin, pale, wavering thread connecting us across time to our ancestors. We see in that instant all that we were, and all we can be, and seeing it changes us. Perhaps future people will stare in wonder at our skyscrapers, if they still exist, or our art.

Such archaeological wonders, monumentally transformed by human minds and hands, force us to stop and imagine. If you visit the Pyramids of Giza, you stand in the same place where the Greek historian Herodotus and the French general Napoleon stood, more than 2,200 years apart. What is crazy to consider is that we are closer in time to Cleopatra than she was to the pyramids' construction.

Looking at scenes painted on the walls in the Tombs of the Nobles in Luxor, you see the colors of the floodplain; you see women and men plowing the fields with oxen and harvesting after the crops have ripened. Right outside, those scenes come to life in the modern tilled fields nearby. (Just ignore the farmer on his cell phone.) With all that has changed, the past can still be experienced in unexpected ways—we haven't lost as much as we think.

Diversity Defines Our Species

We are the distillation of all the cultures, languages, art, music, and dance that came before us. We carry this within us at all times, but today that is all too easily forgotten. Diversity *matters*. It mattered for creating who we were and who we have become.

Think about English, formed from French, Greek, Latin, and Germanic languages, among others, with borrowed words and idioms from Persian, Hindi, Urdu, Polynesian, and so many more. Look at the food we eat. In a single meal—let's say a simple stir-fry of vegetables over rice and a glass of beer—we have foods from nearly every inhabited continent: rice from Asia, peppers from South and Central America, tomatoes from South America, onions from Central Asia, eggplants from South Asia, wheat from Africa, hops from Europe,[21] and spices from absolutely everywhere.[22] Your dinner is the result of thousands of years of selective plant cultivation, trading networks, and an interconnected, modern global economy.

We thrive when multiple cultures intertwine and morph into something different, with more layers. We are better and stronger as a species for our diversity. Imagine practicing linguistic exogamy—marrying outside your native language—which is common in the northwest Amazon of Colombia and Brazil.[23] I mean, my husband and I both speak English, but I swear we speak different dialects when he cannot find the mayonnaise in the fridge:

"It is on the middle-left shelf, dear."

"Where?"

"The one on your left. The one you're looking at right now."

"I don't see it."

"You're staring right at it. Your hand is touching it."

"I still don't see it." Frustrating, yes. But somehow those kinds of exchanges bind us together more tightly.

Understanding how and why our diversity is essential to our survival has become that much more important in a fractured world, where more people push against economic immigrants, refugees, and those with different religious or cultural traditions. As a result, everywhere I travel there is a lack of hope, a general sense of heaviness.

But we are in fact all related, maybe twentieth cousins, but cousins nonetheless,[24] an assertion backed by DNA and computational research. When you tell someone that, they are amazed. This understanding of our interrelatedness and interconnectedness can only come by studying the past, however contentious a species we are sometimes.

"Why do we fight, if we are all related?" people ask. They clearly have never been to a family Thanksgiving dinner.

Changing Our Perspective

Our species has lived almost everywhere on the globe and at a scale almost impossible to imagine. We have survived and got on, or not, under the most challenging conditions, through political instability and war and climate change. We can learn how to survive in better ways by looking back and looking within. The clues are all there. We just need to travel 400 miles into space and turn our heads a bit to the side.

In archaeology, perspective is everything. The same feature on an ancient site will appear vastly different depending on what season or even time of day you examine it with your own eyes, on the ground and from space. You've learned in this book how archaeological photographers love early morning light and how perspective applies to seeing ancient sites from space, and you have gotten hints of what we might see in the future.

Now what we need is a radical shift in perspective for the world in general. We need to look down and marvel at all our achievements, but also reflect on everything that went wrong and why. We cannot be so naive as to use the rise and fall of past civilizations to justify our behaviors and the abuse of the Earth today, or to think that if past civilizations survived previous bouts of climate change, we can keep on acting irresponsibly. The smallest fraction of the number of people alive today populated Earth in prehistoric times. Estimates vary from a few million to 10 million. Populations only grew to the hundreds of millions after the rise of agriculturally based societies.[25] Resources were abundant and land far more available around 10,000 years ago.

Those days are gone.

Learning from the Past

In the field of law, attorneys look for precedents. We must do this more when we make decisions that might affect millions of people. World leaders today could benefit from tapping into a database of past civilizations and historic ideas on subjects ranging from climate change and economies to the best forms of construction. If we were to make archaeology more a part of the fabric of our modern world, the past could inform all our choices through innovative studies and the sweeping scale of information hard won by innumerable generations of our ancestors.

The archaeological record shows us how much of the past is still guiding us forward. So many of our modern traditions and practices have been around for many thousands of years. Take recycling: most of us recycle our cans, glass, plastic, and paper, and occasionally items in our homes can be reused. If you think this came from the 1960s green movement, try the ancient world.

We see the reuse of stones from pyramids and temples in cities today. Old Cairo is built from ancient Egyptian ruins. Odd columns, doorjambs repurposed as lintels: it all adds to the quirky beauty of much later architecture. My favorite parts are where the builders accidentally put the stones with hieroglyphic inscriptions faceup instead of facedown, so they can be read today. Even at Lisht, Amenemhet I reused hundreds of inscribed blocks from the pyramid complexes of Old Kingdom rulers.[26] Something borrowed, something blue, something old, something new—it apparently applies to ancient buildings as well as weddings.

The Past Is Ever Present

Sometimes, we see this fusion of past and present in the people we encounter on digs. In the Delta, our workwomen normally remove earth in buckets carried on their heads, just like the ancient lady whose remains we found at Tell Tebilla. They march in tandem to the spoil piles, as graceful as Greek goddesses, with reddish hair and wide, almond-shaped green eyes.

The husbands all know that their village has the best-looking women in all of Egypt—a secret they proudly share. The women wear empire-style gallabiyahs, the traditional nightgown-like dress of Egypt. Greg and I asked a friend if their clothing or appearance might hark back to the 13th-century crusader battle at Mansoura, led by Louis IX of France.[27] "Clothes, yes!" he chuckled. "But for looks, try the Scotsmen garrisoned here during World War II!"

Something happened a few years ago that gave me perspective on the physical changes that we modern Westerners exhibit—a humbling moment for the ages. I was crossing the Nile in Luxor with Greg, on our way to a pleasant day of sightseeing on the river's West Bank. On the ferry, we sat next to a classic little old lady, who weighed maybe 80 pounds sopping wet. Wearing a black dress, she had a weathered face, partly obscured by a headscarf. Next to her was a bamboo cage, double the size of a standard carry-on bag, full of squawking chickens. As the ferry landed and we prepared to disembark, she motioned to the cage and to her head.

Aha! She wanted a strong I-go-to-the-gym-every-day-and-lift-weights Western woman to help her, a feeble, elderly Egyptian lady, pick up the cage and put it on her head. My ego swelled. I had an audience among the ferry passengers. They would all witness my good deed.

With a smile, I bent down, took hold of the cage, and heaved. And heaved again. And really put my back and legs and everything I had into it. The damned thing would not budge. I tried one last time, nearly pulling every muscle in my body. My audience, which had somehow doubled in size, all lost it laughing, and the Arabic I could understand was not complimentary.

The little old lady just looked at me, shook her head, pushed me to the side, and, in one motion, heaved the cage onto her head and walked down the ramp to applause. I deserved the humiliation; I'd made every possible wrong assumption. And in that moment, I realized just how strong people across the world really are when they do intense physical labor daily, and how strong people have been for thousands of years. I bet those folks are still laughing.

Insights for Our Future

Archaeology, just like my experience on the ferry, should inspire us and humble us in equal measure with all the insights it gives us into past cultures. Some populations of humans (modern *Homo sapiens*) moved from East Africa into the rest of the world, beginning, many anthropologists think, over 60,000 years ago. Using our feet and small boats, we dispersed and eventually settled in virtually every habitable corner. In the process, our ancestors adapted to very different conditions from where they first arose—cold, hot, dry, and wet climates. After growing up in Maine, I've lived in the South now for 12 years, and I have come to like the heat. A lot. Also, my biscuits are fabulous. I've evolved, like our ancestors.

The past teaches us that we can adapt quickly, but also that when we do not adapt fast enough, our settlements and even way of life can collapse. Rainforests now cover cities and cultures that never could have envisioned their own demise. Collapse is never simple or caused by one factor but many interacting factors. Archaeology can give us perspective, to see such events in all their complexity, as we've seen in so many instances discussed in this book.

For our survival, there is now a push for the colonization of Mars.[28]

I wish the folks involved would take a long hard look at the history of colonization on Earth: it's not in the top 10 things we got right. Or top 100,000. No archaeologists or anthropologists are currently consulting for any of the various groups planning the Mars voyages. The language being used—the very idea that we "must" leave Earth to survive[29]—is laughable to archaeologists. We've survived here for over 200,000 years, and that's a decent track record.

I'm not saying we shouldn't attempt to travel to Mars. But the wording of the venture matters. Our world is the only one we've ever known, and giving up so irresponsibly on our home is not something our ancestors would have understood. Nature is resilient. Fish stocks can return with well-managed protected areas,[30] and forests can be regrown.[31] There'd be less plastic in the sea if we removed it and stopped producing it.

As you've seen in this book, humans can be resilient, too. Who could have predicted in 1940 that Germany would, some 80 years later, be a beacon for diversity and inclusion, and an upstanding power in Europe, holding things together? Eight decades is not long in the timescale of human history.

From another perspective, our hands have gone from holding stone tools to smartphones in less than 10,000 years, a fraction of our existence as humans. The leaps our species has taken should give us hope for the future. More than that, we have a good chance of thriving, if only we unlock our great human potential.

Archaeologists function as cultural memory hoarders, the khaki-wearing bards singing the songs of cultures long absorbed back into the earth, hoping people pause for a moment and listen. Digging is, for me, a great act of rebellion, against capitalism, the patriarchy, you name it. Because at our core, archaeologists believe that everyone in the past is worth learning about: rich and poor, mighty and weak.

It's not about skin color or whether someone was an immigrant or grew up on the wrong side of the donkey tracks. It's about the human story. By the way, archaeologists are terrible gossips; we take fragments of data and spin them into grand tales of love, power, and political intrigue. Right or wrong, maybe we have added another footnote to the history of humanity.

The main challenge we face is that we are at risk of losing so much, when there is clearly so much left to find and protect.

11

Stolen Heritage

Imagine a beautiful painted pot on display in a museum. Warm golden lights bathe it, bringing out subtle blue and red painted patterns. You cannot help but admire it; you want to know more. You read the label: "Maya ceramic vessel; Central America. Part of the Henry Smith Collection. 9.201.1993." It's unhelpful, to say the least.

The curators might have classified the object as Maya because it looked similar to other vessels on display from excavations. But this object, which came to the museum through a bequest from a collector, has no context, no relationship to its site or connection to the assemblage of other remains that might have been found around it—in fact, no information—because archaeologists did not excavate it. Looters did.

We will never know if it represents a rare vessel type, used only during royal coronations, an ordinary family's most beloved possession, or a sacred item brought out a few times a year for important festivals. The ancient artifact becomes objectified, a beautiful, lifeless thing with no meaning or purpose behind it. Its cultural role in everyday life is lost forever. Getting people to understand the true value of an object is a Herculean task. Perhaps academics are to blame for writing too many arcane articles that exclude a larger audience. Maybe television turns that objectifying eye too readily on the glamorous golden things. But it is terribly hard to get people to recognize the difference between financial and cultural value.

Even humble objects in our own homes can have higher intrinsic value than their price tag. Greg and I have a beautiful painting of a young Armenian girl wearing a white headscarf on our dining room wall. For more than 50 years, it hung in my grandparents' dining room. The figure shared every meal, heard every family discussion, watched small children grow up and have children of their own, and eventually saw one of those children become a parent. The Armenian girl was the only one in the room when my grandmother passed away. The painter never became famous, and the work has no monetary value on the market, but to my family, and to me in particular, it is priceless.

Assessing the value of ancient objects is, admittedly, difficult, and it might be overenthusiastic or, at least, impractical to say every ancient object is priceless. Likewise, even jaded academics are not immune to the allure of beautiful things. King Tutankhamun's death mask is a top item on the list of any visitor to Egypt, and I, too, always make a beeline there to say hello. The precious materials might be an attention grabber, but the object represents so much more than a shimmering mask. It's a symbol of archaeological potential—of everything out there waiting to be found.

But antiquities in private collections bring a different dimension to the concept of "value." Some might be treasured family heirlooms, and some owners might readily offer them for public display in museums or special exhibitions; but some collectors simply covet them. They cannot let go, they must have more, and they do not care who suffers so they can get that fix.

Friends and colleagues who have visited homes filled with antiquities tell me that the owners like nothing more than to show them off and brag about how they got them. Acquiring those things is like killing during a hunt—with overpowered weaponry and minimal skill—and the artifacts are then displayed in the same way such a hunter would pose for ghastly, tacky photos or show off mounted animal trophies. Perhaps the owners know the specific place of origin of the objects, but more often than not they have only the country or region. And they do not care.

Looted tomb near Giza [PHOTO BY THE AUTHOR]

From Ancient Sites to eBay

Today there's a new chapter in the history of collecting antiquities. Thanks to eBay and similar websites, anyone can own a scarab for a few hundred dollars. I just typed in "antiquities," and 55,000 objects appeared. Clicking on "Egyptian antiquities" narrowed that to 5,000. On the first page of fifty objects, half of which dealers market as "real," I would say maybe two or three seemed like sure bets. Some looked to be close copies, as if artisans had created them in the presence of originals but botched some details. An expert could spot the fakes. Most suckers with a credit card wouldn't have a clue.

I have mixed feelings about this after speaking to the eBay team. I asked if they could remove the antiquities from their website, since any real objects probably represent looted goods. They told me, "We can do it, but those guys are the lowest-hanging fruit. You want to find the real bad guys. Go after them first."

Looting has a long history. King Tut's burial party helped themselves to unguents from jars—thick, perfumed skin creams, which, unlike items bearing the king's name, could not be tracked. Howard Carter and his team, the archaeologists who found Tut's tomb, saw hand-scoop imprints in the unguent vessels.[1]

Even so, walking across a heavily looted site breaks my heart. Where the ground is strewn with human remains, mummy wrappings, and recently broken pottery from looters, I know we have lost part of history forever. Each bone, each piece of mummy, comes from a formerly living, breathing, laughing, loving human being, no different from you and me. How would you feel if the final resting places of your loved ones were desecrated like this?

In addition to the obvious, physical destruction that looters leave behind, they may also do irreparable damage to modern societies. In many places today, groups identify with ancient cultures, and even revere them. People may be proud of their associations and celebrate religious and cultural traditions going back thousands of years; looting and site destruction can erase irreplaceable cultural memories. When hundreds of sites are attacked, it is as if vandals have burned entire libraries of books about that culture.

Some of these issues hit very close to home. In the United States, looting in the Southwest is connected to the growing methamphetamine and opioid epidemics. American looters can be highly organized and opportunistic: after the US government shutdown of January 2018, messages appeared on metal-detecting LISTSERVs within hours, essentially saying, "C'mon, boys, no one will be watching. Let's go loot Civil War sites."[2]

Riots in Your Neighborhood

My career found a new focus after the events of the Arab Spring. The images we saw livestreaming from Egypt on Al Jazeera English were almost impossible to process. If there is a hustling, bustling, thrumming, never-stopping center of the universe, Tahrir Square in the middle of Cairo wins that accolade. It always felt like home to us. Around its edges, in clockwise order, sit the Egyptian Museum; a series of cheap and cheerful hotels favored by archaeologists; the American Research Center in Egypt, an archaeological organization of great help to American missions; and the Nile Hilton, now Ritz-Carlton, whose food court used to double as a day-off HQ for Egyptologists.

By January 25, 2011, hundreds of thousands of people had poured into the square, chanting, raising flags, calling for freedom from the corruption of the 30-year-long presidency of Hosni Mubarak. We stayed glued to our computer for days. Then we woke that Saturday to news that the Egyptian Museum had been looted.

I broke down in tears, assuming the worst. I had proposed to my husband in that museum, on February 29, 2004, amid the most beautiful Egyptological treasures on the planet. Unforgettable scenes of Egyptians forming a human chain around their cultural heart flooded the news: "This is no Baghdad!" they shouted, many in tears themselves.

It took hours for the news to arrive that the thugs had left most of the museum untouched. The break-in was a desultory smash and grab, and in the following days, hardworking curators recovered most of the stolen pieces.

Relief. For a brief 24 hours. Then the rumors raced around the internet about large-scale looting at Giza and Saqqara.[3] I joined a global email LISTSERV with several hundred archaeologists, all of whom had a lot of thoughts about the situation in Egypt. Unhelpful emails multiplied, leveling accusations against my Egyptian colleagues for not doing enough to stop the looting during an ongoing revolution. All the while, those same colleagues were risking their lives to fight off looters at sites across Egypt.

I wrote an email telling everyone that the only way to know if looting had affected sites would be to examine before-and-after satellite imagery. Fortunately, that prompted a more welcome message, signed by Chris Johns, then editor-in-chief of *National Geographic Magazine*.

Chris asked if we could, in fact, map looting from space. I said yes. One of my colleagues, Elizabeth Stone at Stony Brook University in New York, had pioneered the use of high-resolution satellite imagery to document looting in southern Iraq following the US invasion in 2003.[4] I told Chris I already had data from 2010 to use as the before imagery.

The National Geographic Society, working with the GeoEye Foundation, helped purchase new data from Saqqara, taken just two weeks after the revolution began. When I pored over the two data sets, the signs were devastating: clear bulldozer tracks, just to the northeast of Djoser's Pyramid complex, evidence of recent, brazen looting. I sent the images back to National Geographic, which was the beginning of a collaborative relationship focused on the archaeology and cultural heritage of Egypt.

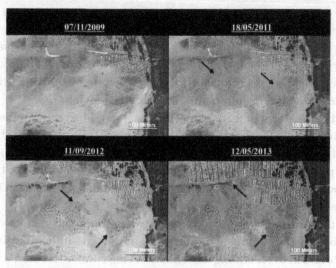

Before and after high-resolution satellite images of looting near Saqqara
[IMAGES COURTESY DIGITALGLOBE]

That May, the Antiquities Coalition invited me to Egypt, to accompany a group of former diplomats and government officials, including one of President George W. Bush's press secretaries. I had prepared a briefing dossier to share with the Egyptian government, updated with new imagery taken a few days before I set out, which showed the increase in looting at important sites like Saqqara and Dashur.

We went to the parliament building for a meeting with Egypt's ministers of tourism, foreign relations, antiquities, and foreign affairs. Walking into the room, I was overwhelmed. The ceiling seemed to rise a hundred feet in the air, with cascading ornate drapery, and the press and the entourage of each minister swarmed beneath it all. I had zero diplomatic experience and assumed I'd be at the kids' table.

We sat down opposite the ministers, all of whom had copies of my dossier. Deborah Lehr, head of the Antiquities Coalition, who was leading our delegation, thanked everyone, set the stage . . . and then turned to me, saying, "Now Sarah will be discussing the results of her satellite research and the implications for cultural heritage in Egypt."

Oh.

I did the only thing I knew how to do: be an Egyptologist.

No one said a thing as I walked them through the stages of looting at some of Egypt's most well-known sites. Frightening images with undeniable meaning. People were grave, concerned, and still in shock from what had happened to their country. They listened, hard.

I was too terrified to properly process the raised eyebrows when I did my best to thank everyone there profusely in Arabic. I wondered if I had violated every rule of international diplomacy. But then there were big smiles and lots of thumbs-up from the ministerial entourages. One lady added, "You sounded like a country bumpkin, but we all understood you." (My Arabic is better now, though I have improved mainly in the areas of dirty jokes and insults.)

Those meetings changed my life. I knew, of course, the role of archaeology and history in global politics, but to experience them firsthand and have a role in shaping them—I had parachuted out of the ivory tower and into a bigger, scarier world.

The Story Grows

National Geographic's support of this project grew into funding for the analysis of looting trends across all of Egypt. I hired a team to help with the data processing. When you're faced with 12 years of data across a country more than 700,000 square kilometers in area, with thousands of archaeological sites, you need your Avengers to assemble. We used mainly Google Earth open-access data for the project, since commercial satellite data would have cost us over $40 million.

In a six-month period, looking at high-resolution imagery from 2002 to 2013, we mapped over 200,000 looting pits.[5] They are easy to detect once you know what to look for: a dark square, surrounded by a doughnut of earth left by the looters in their search for lucrative tomb shafts, which can be as deep as 10 meters. The pits average about a meter in diameter, which means they're easy to detect on the imagery. Among the thousands of sites we examined, we found evidence for looting or site destruction at 279. A heavy pall hung in the air as my team and I worked away on the data and witnessed the ongoing erasure of history.

The most fascinating story emerged from the post-2008 data. Looting during the 2002–2008 period occurred at a constant rate. We expected to see the big jump in 2011. But science has a way of upsetting neat, convenient conclusions. Looting got exponentially worse in 2009, after the global recession. Yes, the looting moved quickly in 2011, but only after the upward trend had already started; it is not who holds the local political reins, but the global economy, that does the driving.

We crunched the numbers to try to determine future trends. Our conclusion is that if nothing is done, by 2040, all of Egypt's sites will be affected by looting.[6]

Our global archaeological heritage has a serious problem, one that cannot be fixed with anything other than a well-planned and thoughtful long game. If archaeologists and other experts do nothing to combat these issues, most ancient sites in the Middle East alone will disappear in the next 20 to 25 years.[7]

Hope or Hopelessness

Prior to this, you have read so many stories about discovery and retelling history. If you care about the value of future discovery, this chapter *hurts* to read, because you now know exactly what is at stake from these losses. Part of me is sorry I set you up for this, but mostly I'm not. Every site my team and I find makes us ask what we missed, and what else might be gone.

Sometimes light appears at the end of the tunnel. My colleagues who map looting have testified before the US Congress and the State Department and shared satellite imagery that shows the ongoing destruction committed by terrorists and international criminals. Katharyn Hanson, a remote-sensing Wonder Woman who works as a Fellow with the Smithsonian Institution's Museum Conservation Institute,[8] contributed her expertise, and as a result, the 2015–16 Congress passed the Protect and Preserve International Cultural Property Act (HR 1493). It advocated for the creation of a cultural property coordination committee and imposed import restrictions on Syrian archaeological materials.

In 2014, six of my colleagues and I testified at the US State Department in support of import restrictions on Egyptian antiquities. I shared my looting data, while others discussed the effects of looting on specific sites. This led, in 2016, to the first bilateral memorandum of understanding on cultural property protection between a country in the Middle East/North Africa and the United States.[9]

In the fall of 2017, an illegal antiquities trafficking case made headlines.[10] The craft store Hobby Lobby, ubiquitous in the United States, makes over $3 billion annually. Driven by their passion for proving the truth of the Bible, the store's owners, the Green family, started collecting antiquities and founded the Museum of the Bible, a $500 million institution in Washington, DC, which displays thousands of Middle Eastern objects.

Several years ago, the Greens met with experts in the illegal trafficking of antiquities, including attorney Patty Gerstenblith of DePaul University, a deity in the field of cultural property and the law, who wrote the standard textbook on the subject.[11] The Greens expressed concern over cylinder seals from Iraq that they had considered purchasing, since they suspected the seals might have left Iraq illegally following the Iraq War. Gerstenblith and her colleagues concurred, advising the Greens not to purchase the objects. The message was crystal clear: buying them was an illegal act and would have serious consequences.

But the Greens bought the objects anyway and imported them into the United States as "roof tiles." The authorities caught them redhanded, throwing into question the legality of much of the Museum of the Bible's collection, and fined them $3 million.[12] While such a penalty is the financial equivalent of a simple rounding error for billionaires, investigators continue their case against the Greens, scrutinizing hundreds of additional objects as of winter 2018.

Preventing future cases like this is anything but easy. One of the biggest challenges facing law enforcement involves the establishment of "probable cause" for antiquities smuggling. This term refers to reasonable grounds for pressing a charge or making an arrest. Once that probable cause exists, the lawyers' jobs are far easier when trying to bring a case to trial, but customs and immigration officials still face huge obstacles gathering evidence. When they suspect an individual of purchasing antiquities illegally, they have to prove, beyond a reasonable doubt, that looters dug it up. They also have to pinpoint when the looting took place.

Looters, We Are Watching You

Technology such as satellite imagery could not only help governments identify objects as looted, but help find the very provenance that gives objects priceless context for archaeologists.[13] I can imagine your raised eyebrows, and I understand your skepticism. I have spent this book discussing all that satellites can—and cannot—do for archaeology. We cannot zoom in from space and see individual objects. Even if we *could*, I would be more likely to win the lottery than to catch the exact moment when looters removed a mummy from the ground. Without any photographic evidence for an object's place of origin (it's not common for looters to pose for selfies), we might not be able to support a determination of probable cause.

Please grant me the benefit of the doubt for a moment more. If we could figure out an object's site of origin, the implications would be enormous. Countries would have a stronger case for repatriation of their cultural heritage, and Indigenous communities might be empowered to ask for those objects to be returned for display in local museums. While the exact archaeological context is still lost, simply knowing an object came from that site advances archaeological knowledge. Finally, it would help prove an object's origin—the first step in proving it was looted—in court cases and prosecutions, sending people to jail for assaulting our global heritage. Believe me, this can move from hypothetical dream to reality.

Operation Mummy's Curse

As part of a *National Geographic* story on looting in Egypt, I gathered information on specific cases.[14] I met the author, my partner in uncovering crime, Tom Mueller, a curly-haired, dashing spitfire, in New York in the winter of 2014. He was familiar with my Egypt looting data, but he wanted to see the industry downstream—what happened to stolen antiquities on the Western end of the market.

At the invitation of US Immigration and Customs Enforcement (ICE), Tom and I received clearance to visit a secretive destination indeed. Somewhere in Brooklyn stands an imposing light-brick building with faux windows and a single back-entrance loading dock. It is a storage facility for confiscated art—things collected by the rich and famous of New York. After we had the once-over from the security desk, we were initiated into the upper floor, where boxes of every imaginable shape and size were stacked floor to ceiling, just like the scene from the end of *Raiders of the Lost Ark*. (And yes, I scanned the stacks for ark-shaped boxes. No luck.)

Our agent contact ushered us downstairs to a brightly lit room where antiquities were laid out, recovered during what they called—and I am not making this up—"Operation Mummy's Curse."[15] In

2009, based on suspicious import documents, ICE had recovered an Egyptian sarcophagus cut in half and sent through the US Postal Service. They made their bust in the New York garage of a well-known collector of Egyptian antiquities, Joseph Lewis III.

Lewis had received the sarcophagus and other goods from a dealer named Mousa "Morris" Khouli. Special Agent Brent Easter had already busted Khouli for a looted statue head from Iraq, but he suspected that was just the first whiff of a very dirty rat. Stalking the website of Khouli's company, Windsor Antiquities, Easter found multiple Egyptian objects that Khouli claimed had come from the United Arab Emirates.[16]

Khouli finally admitted that they came from Egypt, meaning they violated Egypt's National Stolen Property Act,[17] which forbids removing antiquities from the country. Easter made a bust, finding objects worth $2.5 million. Khouli only got six months of house arrest, community service, and a year's probation. Lewis pleaded ignorance of receiving stolen goods, and, after the case was retried in 2014, was made to forfeit several objects seized by Homeland Security and was cleared of all charges.[18]

Tom told me afterward that he wished someone had taken my picture to capture the look on my face as I walked into the room with the recovered antiquities: shock, disgust, and utter amazement. At that moment, this Egyptologist could not speak, for an ancient vision floated before me, weightless, into the vault of memories to be relived on my deathbed. Reds, whites, creams, blacks—a palette of perfection was painted on a 2,400-year-old sarcophagus unlike any I had ever seen. The decoration included a beautiful carved face, perhaps a portrait of the deceased.

Managing to tear my eyes away, I toured the other objects while the *National Geographic* team took photographs for the story. From Middle Kingdom boat models and a wooden sculpture from around 1800 BC, to additional coffins supposedly from the same sarcophagus set, all were recovered by ICE. The agent explained that colleagues of mine had translated the sarcophagus texts,[19] giving it a date between the Late and Ptolemaic Periods, perhaps the same era as Artaxerxes III's attack on Tell Tebilla.

Thanks to those texts, my vision had a name: Lady Shesep-Amun-Tayes-Herit. ICE knew her sarcophagus had entered the United States illegally but had no idea of her point of origin. I suggested that

I use her as a test case, to see if the satellite database we had spent so long compiling might help. That summer, she would be repatriated, so the research was a worthwhile endeavor.

There's No Place Like Home

Maybe, just maybe, the satellite imagery documented this specific looting incident, assuming the lady came from a cemetery and not a rock-cut tomb in the cliffs. Common 2,500 years ago, a cliff burial would have hidden her from satellites, so fingers crossed.

I started narrowing down a database of 279 looted sites, with occupation dates for each based on previous excavation and survey data. Agents brought me radiocarbon dates for the sarcophagus, which confirmed the Late to Ptolemaic Period date range of 664–30 BC. So, step one was to determine which of the 279 looted sites had cemeteries of the right date. This narrowed down the possibilities considerably, to 33.

As I turned my head to the side to look at the lady's face, her eyes caught mine. I saw tiny glints in the corners—grains of sand. Thank goodness the looters did a bad job cleaning up the wood. The sand meant a desert origin, and the great state of preservation also suggested someplace dry.

The second step was to narrow down the sites even more, to a cemetery along the desert edge. We also needed a site near an urban center, as our lady represented the highest form of art, created by a da Vinci–quality workshop. In antiquity, we would expect to find them in a large city.

Only 10 sites now matched the criteria. Fortunately, we had the lady's date of arrival stateside. It can take a year or more from an object's exhumation to its trafficking to foreign markets. The pieces were seized between September and November 2009, and the looting probably occurred between 2005 and early 2009.

Much of the looting documented on the satellite imagery took place from 2009 onward, after the global recession. Only 5 sites out of the 10 had looting before 2009, and only one site, Abusir el Malik, had thousands of looting pits from 2005 to 2009.

In ancient Egypt, names often ran in families, and Shesep-Amun-Tayes-Herit is not a name you see every day. A coffin with the exact same name, from the same period as our lady—now located in the

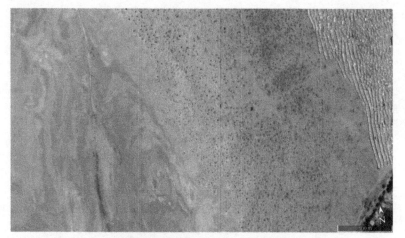

Abusir el Malik, Egypt. Note the thousands of looting pits.
[IMAGE COURTESY GOOGLE EARTH]

Tampa Museum of Art in Florida[20]—gave us a crucial link. That wooden sarcophagus, colorful but not nearly as artful, had a provenance of Abusir el Malik. It seemed too strong a coincidence. I also found a statue of a scribe from "the Saqqara region," the same region as Abusir el Malik, on which the name Shesep-Amun-Tayes-Herit appeared, in this case as the scribe's mother.[21]

With a long history of looting, Abusir el Malik is a cratered moonscape, with tens of thousands of looting pits, old and new, and intense new activity in that crucial range. Human remains lie across the site like leaves beneath a tree in fall. My colleagues who have visited come back visibly shaken. It seemed ever more probable that this was our lady's home.

She was laid to rest in an elite cemetery there 2,500 years ago, in a time when a city flourished there, along the banks of the Nile. From the title recorded on her sarcophagus—Chantress of Amun—she worked in a temple, one of the highest positions a female private citizen could hold. She probably lived in a multistory house, appointed with considerable luxury, and was beloved by her family. They worked to ensure she was buried in a sarcophagus made and painted by the city's elite artisans, and it follows that her tomb was filled with statues, shabtis, jewelry, and all the finery imaginable. The lady's family paid the priests well to make her offerings, probably for several generations. Her name is now remembered; the looters stole her things and destroyed her body, but ironically, they helped preserve her memory and fulfill her dreams of immortality.

A Drop in the Bucket

Finding the likely origin of a single sarcophagus is a first step. Once archaeologists have data on looted sites, they can then create lists of objects likely looted from those sites, and that could help break the chain from looter to market.

But understanding the mechanisms behind the whole dark trade is key. Currency devaluations, unemployment, a drop in tourist numbers, and price inflation all provoke looting. Security is far better now at large archaeological sites, but at remote sites, the looting may get worse before it improves. Innovative solutions are needed to combat this issue, one of the great "hidden" problems of the 21st century. Hidden, but so dangerous.

Some experts have suggested that looting has deep ties to terrorism in places like Libya, Iraq, and Syria, and has funded considerable arms purchases.[22] Anecdotal evidence for this exists in spades. In Syria, ISIL's looting of antiquities was "overseen" by the same branch of the caliphate's government that managed oil profiteering, with a charge of 20 percent "rent" of the total value of items looted by the groups who tear apart ancient sites.[23] Elsewhere, there are potential connections to the drug trade and human trafficking. While more work remains to be done on these illegal networks, they are likely connected.

Profits in the antiquities trade are rumored to be significant, with numbers thrown around ranging from millions to several billion dollars a year. As with any black-market trade, it is impossible to know for sure. Far more work needs to be done to tease apart the networks and to understand how objects move from places like Egypt to Europe, Asia, and the United States. Outraged proclamations from governments and organizations such as UNESCO are too easily ignored. The problem requires a global movement to stop the *collection* of illegally obtained antiquities.

We cannot say that every looter is a terrorist. It is not that simple. We need to understand what classes of people profit from looting and what life is like for the average looter, in order to discern the true nature of the crisis.

In local looting rings in Egypt, village collectives have been known to split the minor proceeds from any objects sold. Local looters—and they are often children—may get a small fee per object or be paid per night of digging, no matter the risk. Tunnels collapse. Open shafts are literal pitfalls in the dark. Sometimes guards discover a looter working deep down a shaft, and even if the guards are unarmed, ample large stones abound. As one guard told me, "He dug his own grave. I just eased his passage." It's an understandable antipathy, considering that site guards, usually mature men and fathers, are regularly shot at and sometimes killed by the more organized looting rings.[24]

It is a desperate crime. Locals may sell to criminal elements, but they loot out of a need to support their families. Even for those for whom looting is a side hustle, as I have heard it described, it may often be for meat to feed a large family, or for money to pay for an operation. Not quite desperation, but neither are these "first world problems." If we can look with empathy at this end of the crisis, we have a chance of coming up with effective solutions.

Wealthier individuals also loot or serve as middlemen, and that's where the real money starts to be made. Professional criminals loot, too, without it being their primary source of income; the antiquities trade, gunrunning, prostitution—it's all the same in the underground networks that both buy and sell for profit.

The big money is made by end sellers, perhaps via large auction houses or private dealers, though we do not know how much the network marks up pieces along the way. The people who really cause that first shovel to be stuck into the sand are the buyers in the West and Far East—ranging from anyone bidding on a $100 scarab online to those paying millions at a high-end auction for a sculpture. They drive the market.

If no demand existed, looting would simply not be at the current level. It's that we must combat first. Similarly, cultural demand for endangered animal parts and exotic pets must be tackled through comprehensive reeducation combined with rigorous punitive measures, or countless wild species will be lost. The blame for both the trade in wild animals and antiquities cannot be shifted down the food chain—it is the top-level consumers who must be sought out. Even, and perhaps especially, if that means looking in our own cultural mirror.

Solutions . . . Maybe.

Satellite imagery only complements ground-based action to protect sites. Local training and educational initiatives are essential and have already had a great impact on site protection, and there are hundreds of such projects globally. They move beyond the "poverty porn" sold by so many NGOs and nonprofits to real programs that help local people find legitimate, sustainable, economic value in their heritage.

Partnering with key stakeholders from communities near archaeological sites and learning what their needs and skills are can be a powerful way to assist with site protection. When those towns and villages see their economic situations improving, they know their future is with the past. Also, engagement with youth is essential. We can show them that they are the true guardians of their cultural treasures and that there are great livelihood opportunities through tourism.

An example of what can be done comes from Jordan, where archaeologist Morag Kersel has worked with the Petra National Trust, for their Petra Junior Rangers and Youth Engagement Petra programs. She helped them to create a module for over 100 girls aged 12 to 17, about the importance of archaeology, museums, and protecting sites from looters. The participants then interviewed tourists and the people running stalls at Petra, asking questions about the sale of antiquities. These types of workshops can empower youth to become stakeholders in protecting their own history.[25] Kersel has also pioneered the use of drones to map looting at sites in Jordan as part of a program she calls "Follow the Pots." She has my vote for one of the coolest women working in the Middle East today.[26]

Where local people are engaged, it makes all the difference in the world. Consider Luxor. Compared to the rest of Egypt, virtually no looting has occurred there that's visible on satellite imagery. Yes, looting does happen, but given the hundreds of sites and the scope of the archaeological landscape, it is minimal. Nearly 100 percent of Luxor's economy has close ties to the tourists who come to see the area's ancient wonders.

With the uncertainties that arose in 2011, many tourists have stayed away, and everyone in Luxor has struggled, from tour guides to hotel staff to the guy on the corner selling tomatoes to his cousin in the hotel kitchen. Even so, the value placed on ancient Egyptian heritage stands strong. Please come to Luxor yourself. You'll find cheap hotels, great food, lovely people, and you'll make a difference in the war against looting.

Not all sites, however, can be turned into tourist attractions. It is costly and time-consuming, and there are not enough tourists to visit the countless places left to be discovered. Only the most die-hard tourists tend to visit small sites or those off the beaten path.

Nonetheless, solutions can be found—new economic and educational opportunities for the people near archaeological sites can be created. These people can be given new skills to make local handicrafts based on ancient styles to sell through cooperatives in big cities or online, or in local bazaars. Archaeologists working on sites can engage the local communities. Many of my colleagues give site tours to local schools and community members during their dig seasons.

Sometimes our work can have unintended positive consequences. At Tell Tebilla, a young villager named Abira worked with us as a basket-woman, removing excavation debris. Her interest was so impressive, and her teenage English put our Arabic to shame. The day her high school exam results came in, her uncle brought a crate of pop for the entire team: she'd passed at the top of her class. We were all proud of her. Abira ended up going to Cairo University to study Egyptology, and later told me seeing women working as Egyptologists on our dig inspired her.

As for site protection, what if a worldwide database of sites existed, fully trackable at all times, with global hot spots appearing when looting, development, or climate change posed a threat? Think of a 21st-century version of the Monuments Men, the brave men and women who helped to save priceless treasures from the Nazis in Europe during World War II. Instead, we could have Monuments People, a force of millions, of all ages, across the globe, mapping high-resolution imagery, finding sites, identifying looting, and sharing that data with governments and archaeologists. Just imagine all it could achieve.

Now, how can we possibly mobilize that force?

12

Space Archaeology
for Everyone

Given the devastating extent of site destruction, the odds seem
stacked against us. Although the dire reality is clear, many
archaeologists have become more optimistic because of the
rapid advances in technology and science. Even with those advances,
however, the harsh truth is that site destruction outpaces our capac-
ity to protect traces of the past.

We need to work faster and smarter, and we need more people.
We need an archaeological revolution to upend traditional approaches
and broaden participation. Not enough of us can work as archaeologists to begin to make a dent in the backlog. So many people have
wanted to be archaeologists since the age of five, and of all times they
should be able to realize that dream now, when we have such a massive workload ahead of us. Turning to the public for help might be
one of the most intriguing new possibilities for archaeology.

We also need to ask who the past is for, and who gets to add to
our shared human story via new archaeological findings. The greatest age of discovery in archaeology may be ahead, not this moment,
even though so many are now using new remote sensing and other
technologies. Nonetheless, it is coming, and it will arrive when everyone can contribute. You probably don't believe me, after reading so
many stories of scientists' discoveries. You think it's impossible. Now
those odds, I like.

The Power of Many

You have probably heard of crowdsourcing. Everyone does it and may not realize it. When you ask on Twitter or Facebook for advice about plumbers or restaurants or the best diapers, you engage the wisdom of the crowd. Some may think the crowd can't be relied upon to help with anything *scientific*, but the answer is a resounding yes, it can.

The first major crowdsourcing effort, called Galaxy Zoo,[1] showed the world just how much the general public could help scientists. Based at Oxford University, the project began when scientists realized they had a million photographs of galaxies from the Sloan Digital Sky Survey but no way to classify all of them. As an experiment, they created an online classification platform that gave participants three choices: spirals, mergers, or ellipticals. The creators thought it would take the crowd years to get through the data, but 150,000 people made 50 million classifications in the project's first year.

With numerous people confirming the same images, the accuracy of the crowd equaled that of scientists. The experiment has now evolved into a website called Zooniverse, which hosts dozens of crowdsourcing projects, from identifying bird plumage to transcribing World War I journals. I had a try at that, finding this description: "Fine night, perfectly calm, troops crowded." Resisting the urge to Google, I hoped that it remained fine and calm for the British 9th Battalion, King's Royal Rifle Corps, fighting on the Continent 100 years ago.

I can hear you saying, well, picking shapes and colors, reading messy writing . . . Welcome to kindergarten! It's hardly brain surgery. Aha! Meet Eyewire,[2] which is under the direction of super-brainy scientist Amy Robinson. Eyewire allows people worldwide to help map the neurons of the brain in 3-D through an online game. Fun, elegantly designed, and easy to use, the game includes competitions among the hundreds of thousands of regular users. Eyewire and Galaxy Zoo opened my eyes to the potential of getting netizens to pitch in on projects, and I'm not the only archaeologist seeing that. Crowdsourcing has taken off big-time in archaeology over recent years.

The Levantine Ceramics Project[3] crowdsources among scholars working across the Mediterranean, to share data on ceramic wares made over a 7,000-year span, from the Neolithic era through the

Ottoman period. In early 2018, the project had some 250 professional contributors, who have uploaded information about more than 6,000 ceramics. That data can be sorted by shape, period, site name, country, and region, making it easy for specialists to find parallels or matches while in the field, and facilitating the interpretation of excavations as they happen. We can now imagine a future when every archaeological object type appears in a similar database, allowing for interpretation of finds within hours of unearthing objects. Heady stuff.

Crowdsourcing that relies on the general public has the great advantage of bringing lots of fresh eyes to a project. My own work with satellite imagery is time-consuming, can be expensive, and takes enormous focus. Before I start a project, I have a pretty good idea of the types and range of things I will find on my screen, and I sometimes dismiss a lot, especially in places I know well, such as Egypt. But as we saw in earlier chapters, assumptions can hurt us in research when we're dealing with the overly familiar.

An Egyptology colleague told me about taking his friend's eight-year-old daughter to the Valley of the Kings, where a complex scene of the underworld in the tomb of Ramses VI had perplexed him for months. The little girl pointed out a tiny detail he had missed, and the whole scene finally made sense to him. I did not appreciate this story until Greg and I brought our then-four-year-old son to Egypt in the summer of 2017. To explain things, we got down on his level, and for the first time looked *up*. We saw things we had never seen before, in our 50 combined years of work in Egypt.

But if the untrained can help archaeologists with their research, it makes you ask why we need to learn to interpret and analyze imagery. There are chunks of academia that require years of intensive training, and gaining that expertise is essential for more nuanced analyses. But here's why I want to include others in the fun: as a girl growing up in Maine, 5,000 miles away from pyramids and camels and everything exotic that I ever dreamed of, I could not have imagined the career I have now. That girl is still there, reminding me that everyone deserves a chance to explore and find amazing things.

For everyone lacking access to the education, resources, or mobility to get into the field, we need a way to bring archaeology *out* of the field. There's a very simple reason why: our race against time is perilous.

Someone with major expertise could search a 100-kilometer-square area in a day, if that area did not require significant imagery processing. But with the entire Earth to explore—some 197 million square miles, minus the oceans—there are still 60 million square miles of surface left to analyze. That would take an imagery-processing specialist 4,566 years to finish. If I had been born in Egypt's Old Kingdom, when Khufu was polishing his electrum-plated pyramidion to crown his tomb at Giza, I'd just be finishing today.

The Story of GlobalXplorer

My own plunge into the world of crowdsourcing began in 2015 when I was unexpectedly nominated for the annual $1 million TED Prize. It's not something for which you can apply, and it's not like the Oscars—it's about what you're *going* to do for the world, not what you've done. I had to invent a wish, one big, inspiring idea that would lead to global change. Easy if you say it quick. Oh, and you're only allowed a 50-word pitch.

I had a lot of help and did a lot of soul-searching while preparing the presentation. My good friend Raghava KK, a brilliant artist from India, told me that if the process didn't nearly destroy me, then I wasn't doing it right. And it nearly did. I got depressed and hopeless— what I wanted to do went against all my ingrained academic notions of archaeological ownership. I almost gave up. But Greg convinced me to stick with it, and so I plowed on . . . and resolved to give away everything I had worked on all my professional life. So here it is:

"I wish for us to discover the millions of unknown archaeological sites across the globe. By building an online citizen-science platform and training a 21st-century army of global explorers, we'll find and protect the world's hidden heritage, which contains clues to humankind's collective resilience and creativity."

We could turn archaeology upside down, empowering everyday people from all walks of life to participate in the process of exploration. It did not matter that I had only a small chance of winning, it was worth it, just for the chance for a world where all the kids who dream of seeing far-off places and making discoveries could do both.

When Chris Anderson, the head of TED, called to let me know I had won, I was utterly unable to respond. A heavy mantle of responsibility settled on my shoulders. I would be championing a far larger vision than I could ever have imagined. I finally got to share this crazy idea at the yearly TED Conference in February 2016 in Vancouver, Canada.

At the beginning of the process, in the fall of 2015, I knew nothing about creating an online platform design and even less about online gaming, aside from playing solitaire. If you had asked me what UX and UI were, I would have told you to go to the hospital to get your rash checked out. (They stand for User Experience and User Interface, in case you didn't know, either.)

Fortunately, I could draw on the expertise of the TED community and crowdsourcing veterans like Amy Robinson, who had gained invaluable insights during the creation of the Eyewire website and could not have been more generous with her time and advice. I slowly built up a team while exploring the Wild West of crowdsourcing. It was—and still is—a great age of experimentation.

We wanted to create an online experience that would bring people back again and again, and engage a broad audience, reward them for their efforts, and, most important, make something that works. We had no idea what we were doing, and we would not know until we launched.

We named the platform GlobalXplorer (GX). From the design stage, GX needed to be sophisticated but simple and easy to use, yet engaging enough to draw in computer-savvy aficionados. It took us six months. We did deep dives into user archetypes—that is, the kinds of people most likely to use GX.

In an ideal world, we would create something that everyone would want to use. But nothing can be everyone's thing. After much debate and narrowing down, we picked four archetypes we thought would bring in the broadest audience possible: a master's degree archaeology student who wants to make a difference in the field; a tech-savvy early thirtysomething who loves gadgets and exploration but does not have a lot of time; a retired professional who loves traveling and has a little more time, but perhaps needs help with technology; and a disabled stay-at-home grandparent who is outright scared of technology, but has hours to dedicate to a new interest.

Our team worked with Mondo Robot, a wonderful platform-design team based in Colorado. We had our dream laundry list of the features we wanted to include, and then we had to pare it back. One point of no compromise was giving our participants an immediate

Discovery image from the globalxplorer.org platform
[IMAGE COURTESY GLOBALXPLORER]

Looting on a satellite image of a site in Peru
[IMAGE COURTESY GLOBALXPLORER AND DIGITALGLOBE]

sense of community on GX, as if they were on an archaeological excavation. Another important focus was creating a game that rewarded participants for their efforts with interesting content about the country where we would start.

After a year of hard work, my team and I launched GX, an online, citizen-science, crowdsourcing, satellite-imagery platform that allows anyone in the world, whether 5 or 105 years old, to help in the process of locating and protecting ancient ruins. We focused on Peru for several reasons: first, Peru is world famous because of Machu Picchu; the archaeological sites are not difficult to spot in satellite imagery, since they mainly comprise stone or mud brick; and the Peruvian government has a strong tradition of supporting innovative archaeological work. A drone-based mapping program is already in place at the Ministry of Culture, streets ahead of other countries.

We launched with a fantastic on-the-ground partner in the Sustainable Preservation Initiative (SPI), a group whose mission includes empowering local women living near ancient sites to become economically independent through selling their handicrafts.

Ultimately, our goal with GlobalXplorer was to empower the world to become archaeologists and see the world as we do. We wanted to give users the tools they need to imagine the past and the people who lived in it, and to make them stakeholders in how history gets written.

Playing the Game

At the outset, users view a short tutorial for the first level: looting detection. That includes examples of what looting looks like in Peru, both close up and farther away, and in different landscapes. On completion of the tutorial, people begin their expedition. Each image is a snippet of a larger satellite image measuring 300 square meters, offered at random like a card dealt from a deck.

When we process satellite imagery, we typically zoom in no more than that, so this is an authentic experience. People have two categories to choose from with a click: "looting" or "no looting," depending on how they assessed the image. And then onward, to another tile.

And no, we do not include any GPS points or map information on the expedition page, before you get concerned that these images potentially give a leg up to looters. Unrecognizable and untraceable, the image could come from anywhere in Peru except the impenetrable rainforest.

After viewing 1,000 images, participants progressed to the next level, identifying illegal construction on archaeological sites. This seemed to confuse people, so we eventually took it down. I've learned that making any platform responsive to user feedback is so important.

The last level, site discovery, proved to be the most difficult level for our citizen scientists. Archaeological sites, as it turns out, are hard to spot from space . . . and now I see what the PhD was for! We show many examples in the discovery-phase tutorial, and people learn that it just takes time and practice to discern what might be an ancient feature: another authentic experience.

To make it all fun, we gamified everything into 10 distinct levels, each with a badge bearing the image of an ancient Peruvian artifact. Users level up as they view more images. They begin as a Pathfinder, advance to Wayfinder, and continue all the way up to level 10, Space Archaeologist. *Quelle surprise!*

Every week during the opening campaign, which officially lasted three months, users unlocked new content about Peru's archaeology and history that was provided by the National Geographic Society. The more levels people completed, the more rewards they unlocked, like Google Hangouts, Facebook Live sessions, and personal messages from our team. The platform is still live on the GlobalXplorer website, and all the National Geographic content is still available—please do have a look, my bet is that you'll enjoy it. As users get better at finding Peru's sites, they learn more, see more known sites, and find even more sites.

On the back end, we set up data delivery to show us pins where users had found features. A minimum of six users had to agree that a feature appeared in an image before the tile came to us to assess. Also, to give users a sense of their performance, everyone received a "consensus score" showing how much they agreed with other users. Everyone started off at only 50 percent, by the way, even me. Fair is fair.

We could not guess what would happen when we opened the platform to the public, on January 30, 2017. It might crash. Users might expect far more than we could do on our budget; a million dollars might sound like a lot, but with complex technical work, it shrinks quickly. The response exceeded our wildest imaginations. Within a week, users had examined more than a million tiles, and we started getting emails from our participant community. The idea that anyone could contribute to finding archaeological features from anywhere, as long as they had a computer or mobile phone, blew people's minds.

As I write this, over a year after the platform's launch, we've had over 80,000 users from more than a hundred countries, including Afghanistan, Yemen, and American Samoa. No Greenland yet, but if you read this and live in Greenland, please give it a try. Our users have examined over 100,000 square kilometers of satellite data—that's over 15 million tiles to date.

Since we wanted to create a global community, we set up a Facebook page, where anyone could share images for commentary. We developed frequently asked questions and had a responsive email team for any inquiries or issues. One of the days when I was supposed to answer questions from our community in a Google Hangouts meeting, we had an internet disaster: the link broke. We had to resort to a group chat, which I thought could go horribly wrong. A group of 50 random strangers on the web. And me. I expected the worst.

And yet . . . archaeology is a great unifying force, and that hour we all spent writing to each other was magical. Excitement about the platform, the discoveries, and the future potential of this project drove the conversation. The group asked wonderful and insightful questions, supported and encouraged each other, and had constructive suggestions for how we could improve the platform. It restored my faith in humanity—even on the internet.

Our user numbers alone do not adequately convey the personal stories we have received from so many of our participants, who truly do range in age from young children to seniors in their 90s. A woman from the Netherlands wrote us to say that GlobalXplorer got her through the tragedy of losing a young family member. Late at night, when she felt despairing, she'd log on and play for a few hours and felt like she was contributing to something worthwhile. She told us GX acted as a lifeline back to a more normal life, and I can't even say how much that moved and humbled us.

Maha, in India, shared with us that he always wanted to be an archaeologist, but his parents had pressured him to go into medicine—a "practical" profession. He obeyed them but always regretted it. Now he was able to play GlobalXplorer with his seven-year-old nephew. Few cases could better sum up what we set out to achieve: he said he did not know if his nephew would be an archaeologist, but he wanted to be the one who showed him that he can pursue his dreams no matter what.

My absolute favorite story—and my new favorite person—is Doris May Jones. Remember our elderly disabled grandparent archetype? Well, Doris is 91 years old and is largely housebound in her wheelchair in Cleveland, Ohio. She has always loved exploration and has a passion for geology. She signed up for GX straightaway, and, of course,

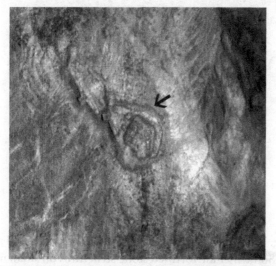

Major settlement feature in Peru from the globalxplorer.org platform
[IMAGE COURTESY GLOBALXPLORER AND DIGITALGLOBE]

she reached the level of Space Archaeologist. She is one of our top superusers. I had the chance to Skype with Doris, and I do not know who was more excited. Hearing her genuine enthusiasm and keenness made me think, you know, we really got something right.

The Proof of the Pudding

Our crowd got such a lot out of GX, and we reached out even further than we had hoped, but we couldn't yet tell whether the platform would actually work—whether users would find real archaeological sites that archaeologists did not know about. Did they get better at site identification, or did they inadvertently mark a bunch of modern farms as ancient features? We've all been there!

In our assessment of the thousands of potential features, the users had about a 90 percent success rate at identifying things of a genuine archaeological nature. They found more than 700 features we called "Rank 1"—larger sites that did not appear in the Peruvian Ministry of Culture's database of more than 14,000 archaeological sites. Result! We sent Rank 1 sites straight to specialists for further review.

And then there's the rest. Sites ranged in size from small animal enclosures to massive hilltop settlements that were a kilometer or

New Nazca lines taken from drone photography
[IMAGE COURTESY LUIS JAIME CASTILLO]

more long. The platform's largest findings have populated a detailed database. Some include fortified stone structures on small mountaintops, and other sites look like large settlements. To begin to classify them, we can compare them to known sites, but of course experts will need to weigh in to tell us what each represents. To date, our users have found over 19,000 previously unrecorded archaeological sites.[4]

Specialists who have previously surveyed the areas covered have begun to look over the results and confirm the platform users' success, especially in inaccessible mountainous regions. Archaeologist Luis Jaime Castillo has taken extensive drone video footage of new sites there, developing innovative techniques to map sites on slopes—normally harder to view in satellite imagery—along the way. Working with Ministry of Culture archaeologist Johny Isla, Luis Jaime located over 50 new Nazca lines near 40 of the sites the crowd mapped. Needless to say, this made headlines.[5]

Archaeologists also plan to survey possible new features near Machu Picchu. While experts know a great deal about the famous royal site's elite housing, they still know very little about the settlements of the people who served the uppermost echelons there: precisely what our crowd may have discovered. It's the stuff of archaeological dreams.

Our collaboration with the Sustainable Preservation Initiative has led to new student training and the development of bike paths around Pachacamac, a major tourist site just outside Lima. These paths allow locals to guide tourists around the site, showing it to them in a new way and bringing more income to communities nearby. GlobalXplorer

*Ancient cuy enclosure at the site
of Canchari*
[IMAGE COURTESY
LARRY COBEN]

is not just about finding ancient sites, but also about using new and old technologies in tandem to connect local communities, tourists, and the digital world to ensure the site's protection for the future.

On the Ground in Peru

Peru's archaeology deserves the best future we can secure for it. I was lucky enough to visit several times to meet with government officials and our partners there. I felt truly upside-down south of the equator, not speaking the language or having any context for the archaeology. Even the food was a surprise. Everyone told me I needed to try guinea pig, a delicacy called *cuy* in Peru. Yes, it grossed me out momentarily. Most meat does, in fact, taste like chicken to me, which this did. But I had no inkling that my dinner would in any way connect to my archaeological work.

To give me a taste of Peruvian archaeology, the head of SPI, Larry Coben, a tall and affable colleague I've known for years, invited me to dig with him for a day at the site of Canchari in the Cañete Valley. To get to his site about two hours outside Lima, we trekked across fields and canals and climbed up the side of a steep hill. And unlike in Egypt, where we have workers to help, in Peru you do most of the manual work yourself.

I dug in, removing the soft silty earth with gusto, next to large mud-brick walls. To be honest, it was exactly like Egypt; almost identical upper-level dirt, similar mud brick, but no pottery. When we had to leave, I made Larry promise he'd update me on our mystery unit. He did just that, emailing to say we'd been working in an ancient *cuy* enclosure. What I eat generally does not predict what I find—otherwise I'd be due the world's largest ancient chocolate factory. Still searching for that one.

First step, Peru; next step, the world! We see so much potential in this platform, but we have a long way to go. What I've described represents a proof of concept, but now we need to scale up. We'll be in the middle of our next country, India, in 2019, after a complete platform rebuild. The crowd told us what worked and what did not, and we are redesigning everything as I write this. For example, a virtual sandbox will guide you when you first use the platform, giving you instantaneous feedback for the first 20 tiles you examine. It will then tell you if you have marked a site or not, and why you might have gotten it wrong.

Home to part of the Indus Valley, one of the world's three great riverine civilizations, India is virtually unexplored by modern archaeologists compared with Egypt and Mesopotamia. There could be tens of thousands of unmapped sites there, perhaps hundreds of thousands. We'll not only be focusing on site discovery, but, through on-the-ground partnerships with key cultural organizations, we hope to reach millions of India's schoolchildren, empowering them to shape their own history.

Wonder Women (and Men, and Children, and Everyone)

I love archaeology because it gives me insights into what it means to be human—real, physical evidence I can touch and ponder. In the future, we hope archaeologists using crowdsourced data will record themselves visiting the sites for the first time. We want to post that footage on our platform, so users will get to experience it as well—the perfect way to reward them for their time and dedication. The crowd has given us the gift of their time, and we want to give them the greatest gift I know as an archaeologist: wonder.

In an age of a thousand distractions, we have to ask what wonder can really do. It could translate into real-world action, such as joining a local museum, visiting a historic site, or attending archaeology lectures. Or maybe encouraging someone not to buy an artifact for sale online. I hope it will cause millions of people to care more about how we all came to be, to take more pride in their cultural identities, and to strive to protect the places we came from.

More than anything else, this project is meant to push the boundaries of archaeological exploration, to reveal our shared history. This was a grand experiment. If a 91-year-old woman from America's heartland can be a quiet archaeological hero, then we have an army of space archaeologists out there waiting to be mobilized.

Our audacious goal is to map the entire world in the next 10 years. With millions of archaeological sites unfound, and tens of thousands of known sites threatened by looting, the first step toward protecting them is to know where they are. Maybe, in the future, automating the search using artificial intelligence and then having the crowd verify the features identified with AI will vastly speed up the process of discovery. Instead of taking four months to survey 100,000 square kilometers, I believe we could complete an entire country in a single week, perhaps even days.

But even when we have maps of all the world's sites that are visible on the surface, and the crowd can identify major areas of looting, there will still be a great deal of work to do.

Each country has its own internal processes and laws concerning site protection, and early detection means those law-enforcement bodies can step in earlier. And with a new detection system in place, we might be able to convince countries to strengthen laws about antiquities sales for potentially looted objects.

With so much new data, we will need to come up with innovative ways for the crowd to get involved. Taking advantage of drones in countries that allow them, we can ask the crowd to image newly discovered sites, providing detailed information that we cannot see from satellite imagery. The mission of platforms like GlobalXplorer could evolve from one of site detection to site categorization, with widgets to draw visible architecture or provide other information. Users could sort through old excavation and survey reports or help find parallels for excavated features. All it would take for anyone to become an explorer is the will to discover, a screen, and a bit of patience.

The View from the Stars

There is something different about finding clues about the past from hundreds of miles in space. Maybe it is that satellite images allow archaeologists to see a world without borders, full of possibility, past, present, and future. Astronauts on the International Space Station talk about how much their experience of orbiting 16 times a day alters their perspective, showing them how truly fragile and wondrous the Earth is.[6] As a result, many have become evangelists for protecting our planet.[7]

I believe that the same thing has happened to me and to everyone who spends enough time staring at Earth from space. I can't tell you exactly how many hours it takes to rediscover the wonder that we all had as children, and then to pair it with a grown-up desire to make things better for our kids. Look long enough and it will happen, I promise.

This all started with my grandfather back in Maine. When I was small, we would stare together at his aerial photos of forests. Maybe looking wasn't what inspired me, but the idea that an elder would care enough to impart his great wisdom to a child. That intergenerational connection and love led me down ancient rabbit holes and into outer space. My work is my personal thread across the bridge of time. Sometimes, when I am working on my computer late at night, I can feel the presence of my grandfather. He has never stopped teaching me about the possibilities of the work I do.

And archaeological work is all about possibilities. We hope to find answers to all our big questions beneath the Earth's surface, but more often, we find more questions pointed back at us. The world now has a chance to take part in telling our shared human story, writing entirely new chapters and filling in the footnotes. We are all the storytellers for tomorrow. Our future depends on our ability to search from above and beneath, so we can look out to the stars and beyond, just like our ancestors did.

Acknowledgments

This book would not have happened if it were not for many extraordinary people and organizations. I am overwhelmed with immense gratitude for the many humans who keep on holding out their hands to me when I need it, or when I don't even know to ask. These acknowledgments are in no way exhaustive. If I have forgotten anyone, I owe you. This was written in a turbulent time for our country, and writing this book gave me much-needed perspective and an outlet. I hope it has given you, the reader, a bit of needed perspective, too.

First, at Abrams Artists Agency: This book never would have gotten off the ground (pun intended) if it weren't for the amazing Mark Turner, who told me, "It is time." He introduced me to Steve Ross, the best agent and friend an author could ask for. Steve, you believed in the potential of this book from the start, and in me, and have been unfailingly encouraging and generous with your advice and time.

At Holt, my editor, Michael Signorelli, helped me in my journey from scientist to proper writer. From the moment we met, this has been a perfect fit. Thank you for your tough love and for reading early drafts containing terrible jokes that needed to be buried in tombs forever. May they never resurface.

Big thanks as well to Madeline Jones, who helped to make this book sing. Thanks as well to publicist Carolyn O'Keefe, and Jessica Weiner and Jason Liebman in marketing. Shout-outs to designer Meryl Levavi, jacket designer Nicolette Seeback, copy editors Jane Haxby and Carol Rutan, production editor Hannah Campbell, managing editor Kenn Russell, editor-in-chief Gillian Blake, and VP of marketing and publicity Maggie Richards.

Shakira Christodoulou, your pen is mightier than a sword. Thank you for your keen editorial eye and for teaching me how to be a better writer, and especially for your help with making the Meryt story come to life.

Ann Williams, your archaeological writing wisdom helped to make everything better. Helen McCreary, thank you for your goddess fact-checking and attention to the most minor of details. Roger Lewin, your next-level editing eye helped more than you'll know.

To the Ministry of Antiquities in Egypt, I am endlessly grateful for your guidance and support of the joint mission at Lisht. Thanks especially to former Minister of Antiquities Zahi Hawass, Minister of Antiquities Khaled el Enany, Moustafa Waziry, Aynman Eshmawy, Alla Shahat, Mahmoud Afifi, Moustafa Amin, Mohammed el Badie, Mohammed Ismail, Hany Abu el Azm, Adel Okasha, Yasser Hassan Abd el-Fattah, and Mohammed Youssef Ali. Magdy Rashidy and the staff of Travel Harmony: you make magic happen every year for us. Ya Omer: I love you and your family. For my Lisht dig family, thank you forever for coming to work with me: Rexine Hummel, Bettina Bader, Reda Esmat, Christine Lee, Kira, Chase, and Greg. To the people of Lisht and Tell Tebilla: we could not work in Egypt without your expert digging.

To my field, generally: All of you continue to astonish me with the amazing discoveries and insights you make on an almost weekly basis. If anyone publishes anything after this goes to press, I promise to include it in my next book. Thank you all for pushing the boundaries of our field, for questioning long-held assumptions, and for being so supportive of my own work. I tell people that remote-sensing specialists are some of the nicest people in archaeology, especially Francisco Estrada-Belli, Damien Evans, David Thompson, and Farouk el Baz. Keep on being great. For the cultural heritage community, especially Donna Yates, Brian Daniels, Cori Wegener, Morag Kersel, Patty Gerstenblith, Laurie Rush, and Richard Kurin: I cannot thank you enough for your support, mentoring, and challenging me to think bigger always.

At GlobalXplorer, I work with the best people on the planet. Chase Childs, Haley Hand, Jennifer Wolfe, Cheyenne Haney, Rebecca Dobrinski, Nick Maloof, and Shreya Srinath, you all blow me away daily with your passion, brilliance, and dedication. Thank you all for being so supportive and kind while I've shown up at work bleary-eyed from late nights of writing and editing. All of you have read assorted drafts of various chapters, and your honest feedback was deeply appreciated.

At National Geographic, where I have been an explorer since 2012, I have another family. While some of you have moved on to other adventures in the last few years, I want to acknowledge you all here: Alex Moen, Gary Knell, Jean Case, Terry Garcia, Matt Piscitelli, Cheryl Zook, Rebecca Martin, Brooke Runnette, Anastasia Cronin, Kasie Coccaro, you all have welcomed me, held me up, and cheered me on nonstop. A lot of work in this book took place because of the generous financial support of National Geographic. I want to give a special thank-you to my very dear friend Chris Thornton. We have been through a lot together the last few years, and you've given me a lot of courage to face my demons. Thank you for always being there.

To my National Geographic explorer family: Lee Berger, Enric Sala, Sylvia Earle, the Leakey family, the 2012 Emerging Explorer Class (represent forever). I love cheering you on when I see you on TV or in my in-flight magazines. Keep on reaching new heights and depths with your adventures. You make me proud.

The Tuesday Agency: a major thank-you to Trinity Ray and team for being so gracious.

For my TED family: I want to give you all endless hugs. Your support of me and my work has been and continues to be extraordinary, and I will be paying it forward for a long time. It all started when I had an unexpected phone call left at my office in the summer of 2011 from Logan McClure inviting me to apply to the TED Fellows program. Tom Rielly and Emeka Okafor interviewed me and the rest was history. Chris Anderson, you changed my life and my field, and I will be forever grateful. Juliet Blake, you have been endlessly kind and encouraging to me, and you throw the best dinner parties in the entire world. Anna Verghese, my dear friend, thank you for being my sounding board, cheerleader, and #1 fan. The TED Prize (now the Audacious Project) team and others: Danielle Thompson, Hasiba Haq, Kate May, Courtney Martin, John Cary—you all have helped to elevate me, encourage me, and shape my vision for my wish. Erin Alweiss, you are the best PR person, fashionista, and supporter an archaeologist could ever want. Another major thank-you to Gina Barnett, who helped me find my voice. A special mention to Tom, my dear friend and sharer of jokes that are for no one else's ears. You helped me be myself.

To my TED Fellow family: I want to thank all of you individually, but it would require an encyclopedia set. The friendships I have formed, the love and support you have given me when I really needed it, and the laughter at my terrible jokes (and especially applauding my onetime stand-up comedy performance) have given me life. You all inspire me to do more and be a better human—and you give me hope for the future. To the TED Fellows team: Tom Rielly, Shoham Arad, Patrick D'Arcy, Renee Friedman, Samantha Kelly . . . just wow. Other thank-yous to Susan Zimmerman, Kelly Stoetzel, Helen Walters, Dave Isay, Raj Panjabi, Jill Tarter, Drew Curtis, Adam Savage, Simon Sinek, Luke Dubois, Juan Enriquez, Diana Enrique Schneider, Monica Lewinsky, Amanda Palmer, and Neil Gaiman for your friendship and love and support.

At UAB, where I teach, my chair, Doug Fry, has been suffering alongside me finishing his own book—thanks for your great solidarity. This book started with the support of our original dean, Tennant McWilliams, and I must thank him for his enduring friendship. Dick Marchase and Gail Andrews, you have been such amazing friends and supporters of me and my family.

In Birmingham, I am blessed with incredible friends and supporters everywhere I go—you are an amazing community of people who hold me up and make me feel good about being here: Matt and Amy Hamilton (and your two adorable kids), our local mom and dad Jim and Liz Reed, Victoria Hollis, Lou and Tina DeNeen, the Ross family (Ami, Kenyon, Jackson, Katie, and Izzy), Dylan Fernany, Austin Senseman (my airplane husband), Rosie O'Beirne and family, Josh Carpenter, Deon Gordon, Sanjay Singh, members of the Birmingham Downtown Rotary Club, Innovation Depot, and the nice people who check us in at the zoo and McWane Science Center every weekend. Our dear friend Dee allows us to get things done. Thank you for treating our family like your own.

I work with amazing people across the globe. In India, Nakul Saran, Shloka Nath, Anica Mann, I cannot thank you enough for your belief in our mission and your extraordinary support. I cannot wait to see what happens. In Peru, special thanks to the Ministry of Culture and the Sustainable Preservation Initiative. Larry Coben and Luis Jaime Castillo, you have been and continue to be wonderful friends and colleagues. Thank you.

Monica Byrne, you have been there every step of this journey. Eric Cline, your encouragement and friendship have been cherished.

GlobalXplorer has had wonderful mission supporters. Brian and Beth Ellyn McClendon, Todd Park, Wallace Mallone, thank you for your generosity and guidance. At DigitalGlobe, where the satellite images you have seen in this book originated, huge thanks to Shay Har-Noy, Nancy Coleman, Jeremy Hale, Caitlin Milton, Ryan Herman, and team, and Luke Barrington. Other major thanks to Lyda Hill—a true champion of women in science—and her team, Nicole Small and Margaret Black. Mondo Robot has been a phenomenal organization with whom to partner for our platform. Thanks especially to Chris Hess. For funding our work, special thanks to the US National Science Foundation and the Social Sciences and Humanities Research Council of Canada.

In the United Kingdom, thanks to my dear friend Dan Snow and his beautiful family. Flora Spiegel and Tony Miller, Curtis, and Ruth, you are our home and family away from home. To the extraordinary Department of Archaeology at Cambridge University, I will forever be grateful to wonderful lecturers who continue to be supportive and kind. To the BBC team: Louise Bray, Harvey Lilley, Dallas Campbell, Liz Bonnin, and Nathan Williams, you helped make so much of this research possible. Also thank you to Rick Barton of the Orkney Research Center for Archaeology, Dr. Val Turner, and the volunteer team from the weekend at Papa Stour.

In Canada and Newfoundland, thank you to the gracious Martha Drake and her team at the Provincial Archaeology Office, Gerald Penny and his team, and especially Blair Temple, from Gerald Penny and Associates. Also thank you to our Newfoundland team members Dr. Karen Milek, Oskar Sveinbjarnarson, and Dr. Davide Zori. Dr. Fred Schwarz, Hockey Gale and his family, and the lovely and welcoming people of Newfoundland, thank you. I miss the Jigg's dinners and the gorgeous music.

Thanks to Jim Bildner, Stephanie Khurana and team at DRK, and the community of Young Global Leaders. I'm lucky to be a part of such amazing organizations with extraordinary people. Major thanks to the Archaeological Institute of America and ASOR for being such leading organizations.

For all my Bangor, Yale, and Cambridge friends: you know who you are. I promise I'll be better about being in touch now that this book is done.

Abigail Washburn and Béla Fleck and Juno and plus one: I love y'all. Watching the eclipse together was the magic spark that lit the writing of this book.

For my close family: Mom, Dad, Aaron, Kate, David, Jeanette, Ben, Emily, Steve, Mike, you've all been there every step of my journey. Your love has sustained me and nurtured me.

Greg, my beloved husband: your patience is a bottomless well, and your good-natured spirit has endured much in the completion of this book. I wouldn't be here without you, and there is no way I would have been able to do much of what I've written about without your wisdom and support. If there is a diamond-encrusted chalice for Husband of the Millennium Award, it is all yours. Gabriel, munchkin, Mommy has not played with you as much as she would have liked while writing this book. I'm going to be making up for it for a long time. By the time this comes out, you will be able to read it, which to me is a testament to your perseverance. I'm so proud of you I cannot stand it. You give your daddy and me life and are the best thing that has ever happened to us. Thank you as well to our little furry beasties, who provided endless needed nuzzles and cuddles.

Finally, this book is dedicated to my aunt, Sue Young, who was a second mother to me and my brother growing up. You have taught me so much about the gift of life, hope, love, overcoming odds, and patience. You have loved us all unconditionally and never forget anything. You make me believe the world can be a better place, someday.

Notes

Introduction

1. For examples of stereoscopes and how to use them, see Thomas R. Lyons and Thomas Eugene Avery, *Remote Sensing: A Handbook for Archeologists and Cultural Resource Managers* (Washington, DC: Cultural Resources Management Division, National Park Service, US Department of the Interior, 1977).
2. Technology, Entertainment and Design, "Ideas Worth Spreading."
3. Jonas Gregorio de Souza et al., "Pre-Columbian Earth-Builders Settled Along the Entire Southern Rim of the Amazon," *Nature Communications*, vol. 9, no. 1125 (2018), https://doi.org/10.1038/s41467-018-03510-7.

Chapter 1

1. There is an ongoing debate over what constitutes an archaeological site, and this will vary by state or by country. I believe a site is any place where human activity took place in the past, from a small lithic scatter to a massive temple.
2. Kareem Shaheen and Ian Black, "Beheaded Syrian Scholar Refused to Lead ISIS to Hidden Syrian Antiquities," *Guardian*, 19 August 2015, https://www.theguardian.com/world/2015/aug/18/isis-beheads-archaeologist-syria, accessed 14 February 2018.
3. Palmyra was inscribed as a World Heritage site in 1980. Ongoing efforts at the site can be seen here: "Site of Palmyra," UNESCO, https://whc.unesco.org/en/list/23, accessed 14 February 2018.
4. *John R. Clarke, Looking at Lovemaking: Constructions of Sexuality in Roman Art, 100 B.C.– A.D. 250* (Berkeley: University of California Press, 1998).
5. Leonard Lesko, ed., *Pharaoh's Workers: The Villagers of Deir el Medina* (Ithaca, NY: Cornell University Press, 1994).
6. Gregorio Oxilia et al., "Earliest Evidence of Dental Caries Manipulation in the Late Upper Palaeolithic," *Nature: Scientific Reports*, vol. 5, no. 12150 (2015), https://doi.org/10.1038/srep12150.
7. Gregory Mumford, "The University of Toronto Tell Tebilla Project (Eastern Delta)," *The American Research Center in Egypt Annual Report, 2001* (Atlanta: Emory University West Campus, 2001), 26–27.
8. Dorothea Arnold, "Statues in Their Settings: Encountering the Divine," *Ancient Egypt Transformed: The Middle Kingdom*, ed. Adela Oppenheim et al. (New York: Metropolitan Museum of Art, 2015), 19.
9. Adel Allam et al., "Computed Tomographic Assessment of Atherosclerosis in Ancient Egyptian Mummies," *Journal of the American Medical Association*, vol. 302, no. 19 (2009): 2091–94, https://doi.org/10.1001/jama.2009.1641.
10. "The Two Brothers: Together in Life and Death," Manchester Museum: Collections: Gallery Picks, http://www.thestudymcr.com/collections/pick/the-two-brothers/, accessed 15 February 2018.

11. Konstantina Drosou et al., "The Kinship of Two 12th Dynasty Mummies Revealed by Ancient DNA Sequencing," *Journal of Archaeological Science: Reports*, vol. 17 (2018): 793–97, https://doi.org/10.1016/j.jasrep.2017.12.025.

12. Robert Ascher, "Experimental Archeology," *American Anthropologist*, vol. 63, no. 4 (1961): 793–816, https://doi.org/10.1525/aa.1961.63.4.02a00070. For an example of a forward-thinking approach to experimental archaeology, see Michael Brian Schiffer et al., "New Perspectives on Experimental Archaeology: Surface Treatments and Thermal Response of the Clay Cooking Pot," *American Antiquity*, vol. 59, no. 2 (1994): 197–217, https://doi.org/10.2307/281927.

13. Neil Peterson, "Kicking Ash, Viking Glass Bead Making," *Experimental Archaeology* (April 2017), https://exarc.net/issue-2017-4/ea/kicking-ash, accessed 17 February 2017.

14. Kumar Akhilesh and Shanti Pappu, "Bits and Pieces: Lithic Waste Products as Indicators of Acheulean Behaviour at Attirampakkam, India," *Journal of Archaeological Science: Reports*, vol.4 (December 2015): 226–41, https://doi.org/10.1016/j.jasrep.2015.08.045.

15. Wendy Marston, "Making a Modern Mummy," *Discover Magazine*, March 2000, http://discovermagazine.com/2000/mar/featmaking, accessed 17 February 2017.

16. Nicholas David and Carol Kramer, *Ethnoarchaeology in Action* (Cambridge: Cambridge University Press, 2001), https://doi.org/10.1017/CBO9781316036488.

17. Colin Hope, *Egyptian Pottery*, Shire Egyptology (London: Bloomsbury, 2008).

18. For a fascinating application of cognitive archaeology, see Nathan Schlanger, "Understanding Levallois: Lithic Technology and Cognitive Archaeology," *Cambridge Archaeological Journal*, vol. 6. no. 2 (1996): 231–54, https://doi.org/10.1017/S0959774300001724.

19. P. Oxy, "Letter of Heras to Theon and Sarapous," *The Oxyrhynchus Papyri* (London: Egypt Exploration Society, 2011), 76; Bernard Pyne Grenfell and Arthur Surridge Hunt, *Oxyrhynchus Papyri I* (London: Egypt Exploration Fund, 1898), 185–86.

20. David Kennedy, "'Gates': A New Archaeological Site Type in Saudi Arabia," *Arabian Archaeology and Epigraphy*, vol. 28, no. 2 (2017): 153–74, https://doi.org/10.1111/aae.12100.

21. Gregory Mumford, "A Late Period Riverine and Maritime Port Town and Cult Center at Tell Tebilla (Ro-nefer)," *Journal of Ancient Egyptian Interconnections*, vol. 5, no. 1 (2013): 38–67, https://doi.org/10.2458/azu_jaei_v05i1_mumford.

22. Mohammed Effendi Chaban, "Monuments recueillis pendant mes inspections," *Annales du Service des Antiquités de l'Egypte*, vol. 1 (1910): 28–30.

23. Gregory Mumford, "Concerning the 2001 Season at Tell Tebilla (Mendesian Nome)," *The Akhenaten Temple Project Newsletter*, 2002, 1–4.

24. John Taylor, "The Third Intermediate Period (1069–664 BC)," *The Oxford History of Ancient Egypt*, ed. Ian Shaw (Oxford: Oxford University Press, 2004), 330–68.

25. Aidan Dodson, *Afterglow of Empire: Egypt from the Fall of the New Kingdom to the Saite Renaissance* (Cairo: American University in Cairo Press, 2012), 167–73.

26. Alan B. Lloyd, "The Late Period (664–332 BC)," in Shaw, *Oxford History of Ancient Egypt*, 369–94.

27. Lloyd, "The Late Period (664–332 BC)," in Shaw, *Oxford History of Ancient Egypt*, 383–85.

28. Stephen Ruzicka, *Trouble in the West: Egypt and the Persian Empire, 525–332 BCE*, Oxford Studies in Early Empire (Oxford: Oxford University Press, 2012).

29. Ruzicka, *Trouble in the West*, 182–84.

30. Sarah Parcak et al., "Using Open Access Satellite Data Alongside Ground Based Remote Sensing: An Assessment, with Case Studies from Egypt's Delta," *Geosciences*, vol. 7, no. 4 (2017), https://doi.org/10.3390/geosciences7040094.

31. Larry A. Pavlish, "Archaeometry at Mendes: 1990–2002," *Egypt, Israel, and the Ancient Mediterranean World: Studies in Honor of Donald B. Redford*, ed. Gary N. Knoppers and Antoine Hirsch (Leiden: Brill, 2004), 61–112.

32. Karl W. Butzer, *Early Hydraulic Civilization in Egypt: A Study in Cultural Ecology*, Prehistoric Archeology and Ecology (Chicago: University of Chicago Press, 1976).

Chapter 2

1. Donald B. Redford, "Mendes," *The Oxford Encyclopedia of Ancient Egypt*, ed. Donald B. Redford, vol. 2 (Oxford: Oxford University Press, 2001), 376–77.

2. Donald B. Redford, *City of the Ram-Man: The Story of Ancient Mendes* (Princeton, NJ: Princeton University Press, 2010).

3. Redford, *City of the Ram-Man*.

4. Matthew J. Adams, "An Interim Report on the Naqada III—First Intermediate Period Stratification at Mendes," *Delta Reports (Research in Lower Egypt)*, ed. Donald Redford, vol. 1 (Oxford and Oakville: Pennsylvania State University, 2009), 121–206.

5. Ann Macy Roth, "Funerary Ritual," *The Oxford Encyclopedia of Ancient Egypt*, ed. Donald B. Redford, vol. 1 (Oxford: Oxford University Press, 2001), 575–80.

6. Anthony J. Spalinger, "Festivals," in Redford, *Oxford Encyclopedia of Ancient Egypt*, vol. 1, 521–25.

7. Donald B. Redford, "Mendes," in Redford, *Oxford Encyclopedia of Ancient Egypt*, vol. 2, 376–77.

8. Jennifer Houser Wegner, "Shu," in Redford, *Oxford Encyclopedia of Ancient Egypt*, vol. 3, 285–86.

9. "Catacombs of Kom Ash Shuqqafa," *Lonely Planet: Egypt* (2017), https://www.lonelyplanet .com/egypt/alexandria/attractions/catacombs-of-kom-ash-shuqqafa/a/poi-sig/437604 /355232, accessed 4 February 2018; "Catacombs of Kom El-Shouqafa," Egyptian Tourism Authority, http://www.egypt.travel/attractions/catacombs-of-kom-el-shouqafa/, accessed 4 February 2018.

10. *Reference Guide to the International Space Station: Utilization Edition* (Houston: National Aeronautics and Space Administration, 2015), https://www.nasa.gov/sites/default/files /atoms/files/np-2015-05-022-jsc-iss-guide-2015-update-111015-508c.pdf, accessed 4 February 2018.

11. Marco J. Giardino, "A History of NASA Remote Sensing Contributions to Archaeology," *Journal of Archaeological Science*, vol. 38, no. 9 (2011): 2003–9, https://doi.org/10.1016/j .jas.2010.09.017.

12. See Section 3 in Thomas R. Lyons and Thomas Eugene Avery, *Remote Sensing: A Handbook for Archeologists and Cultural Resource Managers* (Washington, DC: Cultural Resources Management Division, National Park Service, US Department of the Interior, 1977).

13. Marco Giardino and Bryan S. Haley, "Airborne Remote Sensing and Geospatial Analysis," *Remote Sensing in Archaeology*, ed. Jay K. Johnson (Tuscaloosa: University of Alabama Press, 2006), 47–77.

14. Markus Immitzer et al., "Tree Species Classification with Random Forest Using Very High Spatial Resolution 8-Band Worldview-2 Satellite Data," *Remote Sensing*, vol. 4, no. 9 (2012): 2661–93, https://doi.org/10.3390/rs4092661.

15. Alok Tripathi, *Remote Sensing and Archaeology* (New Delhi: Sundeep Prakashan, 2005); Charles F. Withington, "Erts-1 Mss False-Color Composites," *Erts-1: A New Window on Our Planet*, Geological Survey Professional Paper 929, ed. Richard S. Williams Jr. and William Douglas Carter (Washington, DC: U.S. Government Printing Office, 1976), 3–11.

16. Thomas Martin Lillesand et al., *Remote Sensing and Image Interpretation*, 7th ed. (New York: John Wiley and Sons, 2015).

17. "UCS Satellite Database," Union of Concerned Scientists, 2017, www.ucsusa.org/nuclear -weapons/space-weapons/satellite-database#WnyaZpOFhHR, accessed 8 February 2018; David Yanofsky and Tim Fernholz, "This Is Every Active Satellite Orbiting Earth," *Quartz*, 2015, qz.com/296941/interactive-graphic-every-active-satellite-orbiting-earth/, accessed 8 February 2018.

18. Giardino, "A History of NASA Remote Sensing Contributions to Archaeology."

19. Arlen F. Chase et al., "The Use of LiDAR in Understanding the Ancient Maya Landscape: Caracol and Western Belize," *Advances in Archaeological Practice*, vol. 2, no. 3 (2014): 208–21, https://doi.org/10.7183/2326-3768.2.3.208.

20. Arlen F. Chase and Diane Z. Chase, *Investigations at the Classic Maya City of Caracol, Belize: 1985–1987*, Monograph 3 (San Francisco: Pre-Columbian Art Research Institute, 1987).

21. John Weishampel, personal communication, 2008.
22. Arlen F. Chase et al., "Ancient Maya Regional Settlement and Inter-Site Analysis: The 2013 West-Central Belize LiDAR Survey," *Remote Sensing*, vol. 6, no. 9 (2014): 8671–95, https://doi.org/10.3390/rs6098671; Chase et al., "The Use of LiDAR in Understanding the Ancient Maya Landscape"; Chase et al., "Geospatial Revolution and Remote Sensing LiDAR in Mesoamerican Archaeology," *Proceedings of the National Academy of Sciences*, vol. 109, no. 32 (2012): 12916–21, https://doi.org/10.1073/pnas.1205198109; Arlen F. Chase et al., "Airborne LiDAR, Archaeology, and the Ancient Maya Landscape at Caracol, Belize," *Journal of Archaeological Science*, vol. 38, no. 2 (2011): 387–98, https://doi.org/10.1016/j.jas.2010.09.018.
23. D. R. Wilson, ed., *Aerial Reconnaissance for Archaeology*, Research Report No. 12 (London: Council for British Archaeology, 1975).
24. Timothy Darvill et al., "Stonehenge Remodelled," *Antiquity*, vol. 86, no. 334 (2012): 1021–40, https://doi.org/10.1017/S0003598X00048225; "History of Stonehenge," English Heritage, 2017, www.english-heritage.org.uk/visit/places/stonehenge/history/, accessed 2 February 2018.
25. J. E. Capper, "XXIII.—Photographs of Stonehenge, as Seen from a War Balloon," *Archaeologia*, vol. 60, no. 2 (1907): 571, https://doi.org/10.1017/S0261340900005208.
26. Steven Cable, "Aerial Photography and the First World War," *National Archives* (blog), National Archives, UK, 2015, https://blog.nationalarchives.gov.uk/blog/aerial-photography-first-world-war/, accessed 4 February 2018.
27. Birger Stichelbaut et al., eds., *Images of Conflict: Military Aerial Photography and Archaeology* (Newcastle upon Tyne, Cambridge Scholars Publishing, 2009); "First World War Aerial Photographs Collection," Imperial War Museum, https://www.iwm.org.uk/collections/, accessed 5 February 2018.
28. Antoine Poidebard, "La trace de Rome dans le désert de Syrie," *Syria*, vol. 15, no. 4 (Paris: Paul Guenther, 1934); Giuseppe Ceraudo, "Aerial Photography in Archaeology," *Good Practice in Archaeological Diagnostics: Non-Invasive Survey of Complex Archaeological Sites*, ed. Cristina Corsi et al., Natural Science in Archaeology (Switzerland: Springer International Publishing, 2013), 11–30.
29. O. G. S. Crawford, "A Century of Air-Photography," *Antiquity*, vol. 28, no. 112 (1954): 206–10, https://doi.org/10.1017/S0003598X0002161X.
30. Kitty Hauser, *Shadow Sites: Photography, Archaeology, and the British Landscape 1927–1955*, Oxford Historical Monographs (New York: Oxford University Press, 2007).
31. O. G. S. Crawford, *Man and His Past* (London: Oxford University Press, 1921); Kitty Hauser, *Bloody Old Britain: O. G. S. Crawford and the Archaeology of Modern Life* (London: Granta Books, 2008).
32. Hauser, *Bloody Old Britain*.
33. O. G. S. Crawford and Alexander Keiller, *Wessex from the Air* (Oxford: Clarendon Press, 1928); O. G. S. Crawford, "Durrington Walls," *Antiquity*, vol. 3, no. 9 (1929): 49–59, https://doi.org/10.1017/S0003598X00002970; O. G. S. Crawford, "Woodbury. Two Marvellous Air-Photographs," *Antiquity*, vol. 3, no. 12 (1929): 452–55, https://doi.org/10.1017/S0003598X00003793; "Britain from Above," Historic Environment Scotland, Archives and Research, https://www.historicenvironment.scot/archives-and-research/archives-and-collections/britain-from-above/, accessed 4 February 2018.
34. Anonymous, "Crawford, Osbert Guy Stanhope (1886–1957), Archaeologist," National Archives, UK, https://discovery.nationalarchives.gov.uk/details/c/F40530, accessed 4 February 2018.
35. D. R. Wilson, *Air Photo Interpretation for Archaeologists*, 2nd ed. (Stroud, Gloucestershire, UK: Tempus, 2000).
36. Geert Julien Verhoeven, "Near-Infrared Aerial Crop Mark Archaeology: From Its Historical Use to Current Digital Implementations," *Journal of Archaeological Method and Theory*, vol. 19, no. 1 (2012): 132–60, https://doi.org/10.1007/s10816-011-9104-5.
37. Crawford and Keiller, *Wessex from the Air*.
38. "Internet Maps Reveal Roman Villa," BBC News, 21 September 2005, http://news.bbc.co.uk/1/hi/world/europe/4267238.stm, accessed 8 February 2018.

39. Harold E. Young, "Photogrammetry in Forestry," *Maine Forester, Annual Edition*, ed. Steve Orach (Orono, Forestry Club, University of Maine, 1950), 49–51.

40. "The 7 Best 3D Scanning Apps for Smartphones in 2018," ANIWAA, http://www.aniwaa .com/best-3d-scanning-apps-smartphones/, accessed 6 February 2018; Izak Van Heerden, "4 Ways to Turn Your Cell Phone into a Thermal Camera: FLIR vs Seek vs Therm-App vs CAT," TectoGizmo, 2017, https://tectogizmo.com/4-ways-to-turn-your-cell-phone-into-a -thermal-camera/, accessed 6 February 2018.

41. "St Joseph, (John) Kenneth Sinclair (1912–1994), Geologist, Archaeologist, and Aerial Photographer," *Oxford Dictionary of National Biography*, http://oxfordindex.oup.com/view /10.1093/oi/authority.20110803100533580, accessed 10 November 2018.

42. Irwin Scollar, "International Colloquium on Air Archaeology," *Antiquity*, vol. 37, no. 148 (1963): 296–97, https://doi.org/10.1017/S0003598X00105356.

43. J. K. S. St. Joseph, ed., *The Uses of Air Photography: Nature and Man in a New Perspective* (London: John Baker, 1966); Nicholas Thomas, "The Uses of Air Photography, Review," *Proceedings of the Prehistoric Society*, vol. 35 (1970): 376–77, https://doi.org/10.1017/S007949 7X00013682.

44. Kevin C. Ruffner, ed., *Corona: America's First Satellite Program*, CIA Cold War Records Series (Washington, DC: Center for the Study of Intelligence, Central Intelligence Agency, 1995).

45. "Corona," National Reconnaissance Office, www.nro.gov/history/csnr/corona/index .html, accessed 7 February 2018.

46. "EarthExplorer," US Geological Survey, https://earthexplorer.usgs.gov/, accessed 7 February 2018.

47. Tony J. Wilkinson et al., "The Geoarchaeology of Route Systems in Northern Syria," *Geoarchaeology*, vol. 25, no. 6 (2010): 745–71, https://doi.org/10.1002/gea.2033.

48. "Tiros 1," NASA Space Science Data Coordinated Archive, https://nssdc.gsfc.nasa.gov /nmc/spacecraftDisplay.do?id=1960-002B, accessed 7 February 2018.

49. "Tiros," NASA Science, 2016, https://science.nasa.gov/missions/tiros/, accessed 7 February 2018.

50. Williams and Carter, eds., *Erts-1: A New Window on Our Planet*.

51. "Landsat Looks and Sees," NASA, 19 July 2012, https://www.nasa.gov/mission_pages /landsat/news/landsat-history.html, accessed 10 November 2018.

52. J. C. Fletcher, "ERTS-1—Toward Global Monitoring," *Astronautics and Aeronautics*, vol. 11 (1973): 32–35, https://ntrs.nasa.gov/search.jsp?R=19730056718, accessed 30 January 2018; "Landsat Missions," US Geological Survey, https://landsat.usgs.gov/, accessed 7 February 2018.

53. Williams and Carter, eds., *Erts-1: A New Window on Our Planet*.

54. Williams and Carter, eds., *Erts-1: A New Window on Our Planet*.

55. "EarthExplorer," US Geological Survey, https://earthexplorer.usgs.gov/, accessed 6 February 2018.

56. Charles F. Withington, "Erts-1 Mss False-Color Composites," in Williams and Carter, *Erts-1: A New Window on Our Planet*, 3–11.

57. Williams and Carter, eds., *Erts-1: A New Window on Our Planet*.

58. Laura Rocchio, "Landsat 1," NASA, https://landsat.gsfc.nasa.gov/landsat-1/, accessed 7 February 2018.

59. Rocchio, "Landsat 1."

60. Rocchio, "Landsat 1."

61. Samuel N. Goward et al., eds., *Landsat's Enduring Legacy: Pioneering Global Land Observations from Space* (Bethesda, MD: American Society for Photogrammetry and Remote Sensing, 2017).

62. Mary Marguerite Scalera, *Aerial Archaeology in the Space Age*, unpublished NASA report, 1970.

63. Giardino, "A History of NASA Remote Sensing Contributions to Archaeology."

64. Richard E. W. Adams, "Ancient Maya Canals: Grids and Lattices in the Maya Jungle," *Archaeology*, vol. 35, no. 6 (1982): 28–35; R. E. Adams et al., "Radar Mapping, Archeology, and Ancient Maya Land Use," *Science*, vol. 213, no. 4515 (1981): 1457–68, https://doi .org/10.1126/science.213.4515.1457.

65. John Noble Wilford, "Spacecraft Detects Sahara's Buried Past," *New York Times*, 26 November 1982, https://www.nytimes.com/1982/11/26/us/spacecraft-detects-sahara-s-buried -past.html, accessed 7 February 2018.

66. J. F. McCauley et al., "Subsurface Valleys and Geoarcheology of the Eastern Sahara Revealed by Shuttle Radar," *Science*, vol. 218, no. 4576 (1982): 1004–20.

67. Boyce Rensberger, "Did Stone Age Hunters Know a Wet Sahara?" *Washington Post*, 30 April 1988, https://www.washingtonpost.com/archive/politics/1988/04/30/did-stone -age-hunters-know-a-wet-sahara/7904219b-96e6-413f-8872-a8e40475f6d7/?utm_term= .9cbfeb978ab7, accessed 10 November 2018.

68. Thomas L. Sever, *Feasibility Study to Determine the Utility of Advanced Remote Sensing Technology in Archeological Investigations*, Report No. 227 (Mississippi: NASA, 1983); Giardino, "A History of NASA Remote Sensing Contributions to Archaeology."

69. Thomas L. Sever and James Wiseman, *Conference on Remote Sensing: Potential for the Future* (Mississippi: NASA, 1985); Giardino, "A History of NASA Remote Sensing Contributions to Archaeology."

70. Sever and Wiseman, *Conference on Remote Sensing*.

71. Thomas L. Sever and David W. Wagner, "Analysis of Prehistoric Roadways in Chaco Canyon Using Remotely Sensed Digital Data," *Ancient Road Networks and Settlement Hierarchies in the New World*, ed. Charles D. Trombold (Cambridge: Cambridge University Press, 1991), 42–52.

72. Payson D. Sheets and Brian R. McKee, eds., *Archaeology, Volcanism, and Remote Sensing in the Arenal Region, Costa Rica* (Austin: University of Texas Press, 1994).

73. Pamela Sands Showalter, "A Thematic Mapper Analysis of the Prehistoric Hohokam Canal System, Phoenix, Arizona," *Journal of Field Archaeology*, vol. 20, no. 1 (1993): 77–90, https://doi.org/10.2307/530355.

74. "Spot," CNES Projects Library, Centre national d'études spatiales, https://spot.cnes.fr /en/SPOT/index.htm, accessed 7 February 2018.

75. Thomas L. Sever and Daniel E. Irwin, "Landscape Archaeology: Remote-Sensing Investigation of the Ancient Maya in the Peten Rainforest of Northern Guatemala," *Ancient Mesoamerica*, vol. 14, no. 1 (2003): 113–22, https://doi.org/10.1017/S0956536103141041.

76. "Declassified Satellite Imagery-1," US Geological Survey, https://lta.cr.usgs.gov/declass _1, accessed 7 February 2018.

77. Ronald G. Blom et al., "Southern Arabian Desert Trade Routes, Frankincense, Myrrh, and the Ubar Legend," *Remote Sensing in Archaeology*, Interdisciplinary Contributions to Archaeology, ed. James Wiseman and Farouk El-Baz (New York: Springer, 2007), 71–88; Thomas H. Maugh II, "Ubar, Fabled Lost City, Found by L.A. Team; Archeology: NASA Aided in Finding the Ancient Arab Town, Once the Center of Frankincense Trade," *Los Angeles Times*, 5 February 1992, http://articles.latimes.com/1992-02-05/news/mn-1192_1 _lost-city, accessed 7 February 2018.

78. Payson Sheets and Thomas L. Sever, "Creating and Perpetuating Social Memory Across the Ancient Costa Rican Landscape," in Wiseman and El-Baz, *Remote Sensing in Archaeology*, 161–84.

79. Kasper Hanus and Damian Evans, "Imaging the Waters of Angkor: A Method for Semi-Automated Pond Extraction from LiDAR Data," *Archaeological Prospection*, vol. 23, no. 2 (2016): 87–94, https://doi.org/10.1002/arp.1530.

80. Damian H. Evans et al., "Uncovering Archaeological Landscapes at Angkor Using LiDAR," *Proceedings of the National Academy of Sciences*, vol. 110, no. 31 (2013): 12595–600, https://doi.org/10.1073/pnas.1306539110.

81. Damian Evans et al., "A Comprehensive Archaeological Map of the World's Largest Preindustrial Settlement Complex at Angkor, Cambodia," *Proceedings of the National Academy of Sciences*, vol. 104, no. 36 (2007): 14277–82, https://doi.org/10.1073/pnas .0702525104.

82. Niamh McIntyre, "Lost City in Iraq Founded by Alexander the Great Discovered by Archaeologists," *Independent*, 25 September 2017, http://www.independent.co.uk/news /world/asia/lost-city-iraq-alexander-great-founded-discover-archaeologists-qalatga -darband-a7965651.html, accessed 7 February 2018; "The Darband-I Rania Archaeologi-

cal Project," British Museum, http://www.britishmuseum.org/about_us/museum_acti vity/middle_east/iraq_scheme/darband-i_rania_project.aspx, accessed 5 February 2018.

83. Jack Malvern, "Lost City of Alexander the Great Found in Iraq," *Times*, 25 September 2017, https://www.thetimes.co.uk/article/lost-city-of-alexander-the-great-found-in-iraq -pw6g2dtvj, accessed 5 February 2018.

84. Jayphen Simpson, "Here's a Map with Up-to-Date Drone Laws for Every Country," Peta-pixel, 20 September 2017, https://petapixel.com/2017/09/20/heres-map-date-drone -laws-every-country/, accessed 5 February 2018.

Chapter 3

1. Stephen Ruzicka, *Trouble in the West: Egypt and the Persian Empire, 525–332 BCE*, Oxford Studies in Early Empires (New York: Oxford University Press, 2012).

2. Giovanni Di Bernardo et al., "Ancient DNA and Family Relationships in a Pompeian House," *Annals of Human Genetics*, vol. 73, no. 4 (2009): 429–37, https://doi.org/10.1111 /j.1469-1809.2009.00520.x; Jim Shelton, "Creating a Malaria Test for Ancient Human Remains," YaleNews, 17 March 2015, https://news.yale.edu/2015/03/17/creating-malaria -test-ancient-human-remains, accessed 25 March 2018.

3. Julie Dunne et al., "Organic Residue Analysis and Archaeology: Guidance for Good Prac-tice," Historic England, 2017, https://content.historicengland.org.uk/images-books /publications/organic-residue-analysis-and-archaeology/heag058a-organic-residue -analysis-and-archaeology-guidance.pdf/, accessed 5 March 2018.

4. "Scientific Dating," Historic England, 2018, https://historicengland.org.uk/advice /technical-advice/archaeological-science/scientific-dating/, accessed 2 March 2018.

5. Eric H. Cline, *1177 B.C.: The Year Civilization Collapsed*, Turning Points in Ancient History (Princeton, NJ: Princeton University Press, 2014).

6. "Magical Figure," Metropolitan Museum of Art, https://www.metmuseum.org/art /collection/search/546350?sortBy=Relevance&ft=lisht&offset=0&rpp =100&pos=56, accessed 15 January 2018.

7. Timothy Darvill, *Concise Oxford Dictionary of Archaeology*, 2nd ed. (New York: Oxford Uni-versity Press, 2008); "Archaeology 101," Lesson Plans, Archaeological Institute of Amer-ica Education Department, https://www.archaeological.org/pdfs/education/Arch101.2 .pdf, accessed 3 March 2018; "Introduction to Archaeology: Glossary," Archaeological Institute of America, 2018, https://www.archaeological.org/education/glossary, accessed 2 March 2018.

8. An excellent TV program that showcases archaeological efforts is *Time Team*, shown in the United States (PBS) and United Kingdom (Channel 4). One of the best episodes is set here—"The Real Vikings: A Time Team Special," Tim Taylor, creator and series pro-ducer, and Philip Clarke, executive producer (2010).

9. Anna Wodzińska, *A Manual of Egyptian Pottery. Naqada III—Middle Kingdom* (Boston: Ancient Egypt Research Associates, 2010), http://www.aeraweb.org/wp-content/uploads /2010/02/egyptian-pottery-v2.pdf, accessed 30 January 2018.

10. Ralph Blumenthal, "NASA Adds to Evidence of Mysterious Ancient Earthworks," *New York Times*, 30 October 2015, https://www.nytimes.com/2015/11/03/science/nasa-adds-to -evidence-of-mysterious-ancient-earthworks.html, accessed 30 January 2018.

11. Orri Vésteinsson and Thomas H. McGovern, "The Peopling of Iceland," *Norwegian Archaeological Review*, vol. 45, no. 2 (2012): 206–18, https://doi.org/10.1080/00293652 .2012.721792.

12. Vésteinsson and McGovern, "The Peopling of Iceland."

13. Thomas Ellwood, *The Book of the Settlement of Iceland: Translated from the Original Icelandic of Ari the Learned* (Kendal, Cumbria, UK: T. Wilson, 1898); Orri Vésteinsson et al., "The Settlement Exhibition—the Settlement of Iceland," Reykjavik City Museum, http:// reykjavik871.is/, accessed 8 March 2018; John Steinberg et al., "The Viking Age Settle-ment Pattern of Langholt, North Iceland: Results of the Skagafjörður Archaeological Settlement Survey," *Journal of Field Archaeology*, vol. 41, no. 4 (2016): 389–412, https://doi .org/10.1080/00934690.2016.1203210.

14. See "English Summary," https://www.islendingabok.is/English.jsp, accessed 7 March 2018.

15. "Kissing Cousins? Icelandic App Warns If Your Date Is a Relative," Associated Press, 18 April 2013, www.cbc.ca/news/business/kissing-cousins-icelandic-app-warns-if-your -date-is-a-relative-1.1390256, accessed 5 March 2018.

16. Rose Eveleth, "Icelanders Protest a Road That Would Disturb Fairies," *Smithsonian Smart-News*, 15 January 2014, www.smithsonianmag.com/smart-news/icelanders-protest-road -would-disturb-fairies-180949359/, accessed 5 March 2018.

17. "The Vikings Uncovered," executive producers Eamon Hardy and Cameron Balbirnie, BBC One (UK) and PBS America (US), 2016.

18. Brian N. Damiata et al., "Subsurface Imaging a Viking-Age Churchyard Using GPR with TDR: Direct Comparison to the Archaeological Record from an Excavated Site in Northern Iceland," *Journal of Archaeological Science: Reports*, vol. 12 (2017): 244–56, https://doi .org/10.1016/j.jasrep.2017.01.004.

19. Sveinbjörn Þórðarson, "The Icelandic Saga Database," http://sagadb.org/, accessed 5 March 2018.

20. "The Settlement Exhibition," Reykjavik City Museum, http://borgarsogusafn.is/en/the -settlement-exhibition/about, accessed 4 March 2018.

21. Grassland replaced birch around AD 900 during a major environmental shift. See Orri Vésteinsson and Thomas H. McGovern, "The Peopling of Iceland," *Norwegian Archaeological Review*, vol. 45, no. 2 (2012): 206–18, https://doi.org/10.1080/00293652.2012 .721792.

22. Orri Vésteinsson et al., "The Settlement Exhibition—Aðalstræti: The Longhouse," Reykjavik City Museum, http://reykjavik871.is/, accessed 8 March 2018.

23. Steinberg et al., "Viking Age Settlement Pattern of Langholt, North Iceland."

24. Iceland's in-country archaeological database is called *ísleif*.

25. Steinberg et al., "Viking Age Settlement Pattern of Langholt, North Iceland."

26. Jeroen De Reu et al., "From Low Cost UAV Survey to High Resolution Topographic Data: Developing Our Understanding of a Medieval Outport of Bruges," *Archaeological Prospection*, vol. 23, no. 4 (2016): 335–46, https://doi.org/10.1002/arp.1547.

27. Called relief displacement. See Thomas R. Lyons and Thomas Eugene Avery, *Remote Sensing: A Handbook for Archeologists and Cultural Resource Managers* (Washington, DC: Cultural Resources Management Division, National Park Service, US Department of the Interior, 1977).

28. Barbara E. Crawford and Beverley Ballin Smith, *The Biggings, Papa Stour, Shetland: The History and Excavation of a Royal Norwegian Farm*, Monograph Series, ed. Alexandra Shepard (Edinburgh: Society of Antiquaries of Scotland and Det Norske Videnskaps-Akademi, 1999).

29. Anna Ritchie, "Great Sites: Jarlshof," *British Archaeology*, vol. 69 (2003); "Jarlshof Prehistoric and Norse Settlement: History," Historic Environment Scotland (2018), www .historicenvironment.scot/visit-a-place/places/jarlshof-prehistoric-and-norse -settlement/history/, accessed 10 March 2018.

30. Athos Agapiou et al., "Optimum Temporal and Spectral Window for Monitoring Crop Marks over Archaeological Remains in the Mediterranean Region," *Journal of Archaeological Science*, vol. 40, no. 3 (2013): 1479–92, https://doi.org/10.1016/j.jas.2012.10.036.

31. Christina Petty, *Warp Weighted Looms: Then and Now—Anglo-Saxon and Viking Archaeological Evidence and Modern Practitioners* (PhD diss., University of Manchester, 2014).

32. Barbara Crawford, *A Progress Report of the First Season's Excavation at "Da Biggins,"* Papa Stour, Shetland (Edinburgh: Scottish Society for Northern Studies, 1978).

33. Paul Nicholson and Ian Shaw, *Ancient Egyptian Materials and Technology* (Cambridge: Cambridge University Press, 2009).

34. Anna Linderholm et al., "Diet and Status in Birka: Stable Isotopes and Grave Goods Compared," *Antiquity*, vol. 82, no. 316 (2008): 446–61, https://doi.org/10.1017/S0003598X 00096939.

35. Crawford, *Progress Report of the First Season's Excavation at "Da Biggins"*; Barbara Crawford, *A Progress Report on Excavations at "Da Biggins," Papa Stour, Shetland, 1978* (Edinburgh:

Scottish Society for Northern Studies, 1979); Jon A. Hjaltalin and Gilbert Goudie, *The Orkneyinga Saga: Translated from the Icelandic* (Edinburgh: Edmonston and Douglas, 1873). A translation of the document can be seen in Crawford and Smith, *The Biggings*, 48.

36. Crawford, *Progress Report on Excavations at "Da Biggins."*

37. Simon Keay et al., "The Canal System and Tiber Delta at Portus. Assessing the Nature of Man-Made Waterways and Their Relationship with the Natural Environment," *Water History*, vol. 6, no.1 (2014): 11–30, https://doi.org/10.1007/s12685-013-0094-y.

38. Keay, "Canal System and Tiber Delta at Portus."

39. Simon Keay et al., *Portus: An Archaeological Survey of the Port of Imperial Rome*, Archaeological Monographs of the British School at Rome (London: British School at Rome, 2006).

40. Simon Keay et al., "Archaeological Fieldwork Reports: The Portus Project," *Papers of the British School at Rome*, vol. 76 (2008), 331–32, https://doi.org/10.1017/S0068246200003767; "Portus Project," University of Southampton, http://www.portusproject.org/, accessed 11 March 2018; Simon Keay et al., "The Role of Integrated Geophysical Survey Methods in the Assessment of Archaeological Landscapes: The Case of Portus," *Archaeological Prospection*, vol. 16, no. 3 (2009): 154–66, https://doi.org/10.1002/arp.358.

41. Shen-En Qian, "Enhancing Space-Based Signal-to-Noise Ratios Without Redesigning the Satellite," SPIE Newsroom, 2011, http://spie.org/newsroom/3421-enhancing-space-based-signal-to-noise-ratios-without-redesigning-the-satellite?SSO=1, accessed 3 March 2018.

42. According to the weather history at www.timeanddate.com/weather/italy/rome/historic?month=9&year=2011, it didn't rain once in August or September in Rome.

43. Rosa Lasaponara and Nicola Masini, "Detection of Archaeological Crop Marks by Using Satellite QuickBird Multispectral Imagery," *Journal of Archaeological Science*, vol. 34, no. 2 (2007): 214–21, https://doi.org/10.1016/j.jas.2006.04.014.

44. Simon Keay et al., "High Resolution Space and Ground-Based Remote Sensing and Implications for Landscape Archaeology: The Case from Portus, Italy," *Journal of Archaeological Science*, vol. 52 (2014): 277–92, https://doi.org/10.1016/j.jas.2014.08.010.

45. Keay, "High Resolution Space and Ground-Based Remote Sensing."

Chapter 4

1. Kent V. Flannery, "The Golden Marshalltown: A Parable for the Archaeology of the 1980s," *American Anthropologist*, n.s., vol. 84, no. 2 (1982): 265–78.

2. Kenneth L. Feder, *Frauds, Myths, and Mysteries: Science and Pseudoscience in Archaeology* (New York: Oxford University Press, 2017).

3. Steven L. Cox, "A Norse Penny from Maine," *Vikings: The North Atlantic Saga*, ed. William W. Fitzhugh and Elisabeth I. Ward (Washington, DC: Smithsonian Institution Press, 2000), 206–7; Erik Wahlgren, *The Vikings and America* (London: Thames and Hudson, 1986), 146.

4. William Fitzhugh, "Vikings in America: Runestone, Relics, and Revisionism," *Minerva: The International Magazine of Art and Archaeology*, vol. 11 (July/August 2000): 8–12.

5. Jesse L. Byock, *Viking Age Iceland* (New York: Penguin, 2001).

6. "Eirik the Red's Saga," trans. Keneva Kunz, *The Sagas of Icelanders*, ed. Örnólfur Thorsson and Bernard Scudder (New York: Penguin Books, 2001).

7. William Fitzhugh, "Vikings: The North Atlantic Saga," *AnthroNotes: Museum of Natural History Publication for Educators* (Smithsonian Museum of Natural History), vol. 22, no. 1 (2000): 1–9.

8. Wahlgren, *Vikings and America*, 91; Peter Schledermann, "A.D. 1000: East Meets West," in Fitzhugh and Ward, *Vikings: The North Atlantic Saga*, 189; Magnus Rafnsson, "Archaeological Excavations at Qassiarsuk, 2005–2006 (field report)," NV nr, 03–07: Náttúrustofa Vestfjarða, NABO, Grønlands Nationalmuseum & Arkiv. 2007, https://doi.org/10.6067/XCV86H4FRS.

9. Wahlgren, *Vikings and America*, 26, n. 21.

10. Eli Kintisch, "Why Did Greenland's Vikings Disappear?" *Science*, 10 November 2016, http://www.sciencemag.org/news/2016/11/why-did-greenland-s-vikings-disappear, accessed 10 March 2018.

11. Robert Kellogg, *The Sagas of the Icelanders* (New York: Penguin Books, 2001).

12. Wahlgren, *Vikings and America*, 90–91.

13. Kellogg, *Sagas of the Icelanders*.

14. Birgitta Wallace, "The Norse in Newfoundland: L'Anse aux Meadows and Vinland," *Newfoundland Studies*, vol. 19, no. 1 (2003): 5–43.

15. Wahlgren, *Vikings and America*, 92.

16. Mats G. Larsson, "The Vinland Sagas and the Actual Characteristics of Eastern Canada: Some Comparisons with Special Attention to the Accounts of the Later Explorers," *Vinland Revisited: The Norse World at the Turn of the First Millennium. Selected Papers from the Viking Millennium International Symposium, 15–24 September 2000, Newfoundland and Labrador*, ed. Shannon Lewis-Simpson (St. John's, NL: Historic Sites Association of Newfoundland and Labrador, 2003), 396, fig. 5, and 398.

17. Magnus Magnusson, "Vinland: The Ultimate Outpost," in Lewis-Simpson, *Vinland Revisited*, 94.

18. Anne Stine Ingstad, *The Norse Discovery of America, Volume One: Excavations of a Norse Settlement at l'Anse aux Meadows, Newfoundland 1961–1968*, trans. Elizabeth S. Seeberg (Oslo: Norwegian University Press [via Oxford University Press], 1985); Wahlgren, *Vikings and America*, 93.

19. Ingstad, *Norse Discovery of America, Volume One*.

20. Charles S. Lindsay, "A Preliminary Report on the 1974 Excavations of Norse Buildings D and E at L'Anse aux Meadows" (unpublished report on file, Provincial Archaeology Office, Confederation Building, St. John's, NL, 1975).

21. Helge Ingstad, *The Norse Discovery of America, Volume Two: The Historical Background and the Evidence of the Norse Settlement Discovered in Newfoundland*, trans. Elizabeth S. Seeberg (Oslo: Norwegian University Press [via Oxford University Press], 1985).

22. Janet E. Kay, *Norse in Newfoundland: A Critical Examination of Archaeological Research at the Norse Site at L'Anse aux Meadows, Newfoundland*, British Archaeological Reports International Series 2339 (Oxford: Archaeopress, 2012), 44–45, figs. 3.1–5.

23. Davide Zori, "Nails, Rivets and Clench Bolts: A Case for Typological Clarity," *Archaeologia Islandica*, vol. 6 (2007): 32–47.

24. Kay, *Norse in Newfoundland*, 44–45, figs. 3.1–5; Birgitta L. Wallace, *Westward Vikings: The Saga of l'Anse aux Meadows*, rev. ed. (St. John's, NL: Historic Sites Association of Newfoundland and Labrador, 2012).

25. Kay, *Norse in Newfoundland*, 44–45, figs. 3.1–5.

26. Kay, *Norse in Newfoundland*, 59.

27. Kay, *Norse in Newfoundland*, 45.

28. Wallace, *Westward Vikings*.

29. Birgitta L. Wallace, "The Later Excavations at L'Anse aux Meadows," in Lewis-Simpson, *Vinland Revisited*, 165–80.

30. Donald H. Holly Jr., *History in the Making: The Archaeology of the Eastern Subarctic*, Issues in Eastern Woodlands Archaeology (Lanham, MD: AltaMira Press, 2013), 114; Birgitta L. Wallace, "The Viking Settlement at L'Anse aux Meadows," in Fitzhugh and Ward, *Vikings: The North Atlantic Saga*, 216, fig. 14.21.

31. Holly, *History in the Making*, 113–14 and 115, fig. 5.2; Kay, *Norse in Newfoundland*, 66; Birgitta Wallace, "The Norse in Newfoundland: L'Anse aux Meadows and Vinland," *Newfoundland Studies*, vol. 19, no. 1 (2003): 5–43.

32. Kay, *Norse in Newfoundland*, 66; Holly, *History in the Making*, 113–14.

33. Urve Linnamae, *The Dorset Culture: A Comparative Study in Newfoundland and the Arctic*, Technical Papers of the Newfoundland Museum, no. 1 (St. John's, NL: Newfoundland Museum, 1975); Lisa Mae Fogt, *The Excavation and Analysis of a Dorset Palaeoeskimo Dwelling at Cape Ray, Newfoundland* (master's thesis, Department of Anthropology, Memorial University, St. John's, NL, 1998).

34. James P. Howley, *The Beothucks or Red Indians, The Aboriginal Inhabitants of Newfoundland* (Cambridge: Cambridge University Press, 1915; repr. Toronto: Prospero Books, 2000), 162.

35. Ralph T. Pastore, *Shanawdithit's People: The Archaeology of the Beothuks* (St. John's, NL: Atlantic Archaeology, 1992).

36. M. A. P. Renouf and Trevor Bell, "Maritime Archaic Site Locations on the Island of New-foundland," *The Archaic of the Far Northeast*, ed. David Sanger and M. A. P. Renouf (Orono: University of Maine Press, 2006), 1–46; Trevor Bell and M. A. P. Renouf, "Prehistoric Cultures, Reconstructed Coasts: Maritime Archaic Indian Site Distribution," *World Archaeology*, vol. 35, no. 3 (2004): 350–70, https://doi.org/10.1080/0043824042000185766.

37. K. L. Kvamme, "Magnetometry: Nature's Gift to Archaeology," *Remote Sensing in Archaeology: An Explicitly North American Perspective*, ed. Jay K. Johnson (Tuscaloosa: University of Alabama Press, 2006), 205–33.

38. John J. Mannion, "Settlers and Traders in Western Newfoundland," *The Peopling of Newfoundland: Essays in Historical Geography*, ed. John J. Mannion (St. John's, NL: Institute of Social and Economic Research, Memorial University of Newfoundland, 1977).

39. Peter E. Pope, "Newfoundland and Labrador, 1497–1697," *A Short History of Newfoundland and Labrador*, Newfoundland Historical Society (Portugal Cove–St. Philip's, NL: Boulder Publications, 2008), 23–48.

40. "100 Years of Geodetic Survey in Canada," *Natural Resources Canada*, http://www.nrcan .gc.ca/earth-sciences/geomatics/geodetic-reference-systems/canadian-spatial -reference-system/9110, accessed 7 May 2018.

41. Martin Appelt et al., "Late Dorset," *The Oxford Handbook of the Prehistoric Arctic*, ed. T. Max Friesen and Owen K. Mason (Oxford: Oxford University Press, 2016), 783–805.

42. Edward Chappell, *Voyage of His Majesty's Ship Rosamond to Newfoundland and the Southern Coast of Labrador, of which Countries no account has been published by any British traveler since the Reign of Queen Elizabeth* (London: J. Mawman, 1818).

43. Grant Head, *Eighteenth Century Newfoundland: A Geographer's Perspective*, Carlton Library Series no. 99 (Toronto: McClelland and Stewart, 1976).

44. Birgitta Wallace, "St. Paul's Inlet—the Norse Hóp Site?" (report on file, Historic Resources Division, St. John's, NL, 2003); Donald Wieman, "32 Clues Point to Barachois, Newfoundland as The Vinland Sagas' Settlement of 'Hop,'" *Lavalhallalujah* (blog), 20 October 2015, https://lavalhallalujah.wordpress.com/2015/10/20/32-clues-point-to -barachois-as-hop/, accessed 2 May 2017.

45. Head, *Eighteenth Century Newfoundland*.

46. Scott Brande, personal communication, November 2016.

47. "What Is OSL Dating?" Baylor University, Department of Geosciences, https://www.baylor .edu/geology/index.php?id=868084, accessed 5 May 2018.

Chapter 5

1. Federico Poole, "Tanis (San el Hagar)," *Encyclopedia of the Archaeology of Ancient Egypt*, ed. Kathryn Bard (London: Routledge, 1999), 755–77.

2. Poole, "Tanis (San el Hagar)."

3. John Taylor, "The Third Intermediate Period," *The Oxford History of Ancient Egypt*, ed. Ian Shaw (Oxford: Oxford University Press, 2004), 330–68.

4. For a detailed overview of the Third Intermediate Period, see Kenneth A. Kitchen, *The Third Intermediate Period in Egypt (1100–650 BC)* (Warminster, UK: Aris and Phillips, 1995).

5. Aidan Dodson, *Afterglow of Empire: Egypt from the Fall of the New Kingdom to the Rise of the Saite Renaissance* (Cairo: American University in Cairo Press, 2012), 3–23.

6. Poole, "Tanis (San el Hagar)," 755–77.

7. Poole, "Tanis (San el Hagar)."

8. This would have been quite similar to the palace at Malkata. See Peter Lacovara, *The New Kingdom Royal City* (New York: Kegan Paul International, 1997), 26. Also, a temple wall at Karnak offers evidence for Sheshonq's expedition to Israel in 925 BC, which sought to renew Egypt's imperialism. Sheshonq's troops robbed the main temple and palace in Jerusalem, which implies that the treasures of Tanis may have been forged, in part, from melted-down gold items from Judah, although this has not yet been proven. See Yigal Levin, "Did Pharaoh Sheshonq Attack Jerusalem?" *Biblical Archaeology Review*, vol. 38, no 4 (July/August 2012): 43–52, 66–67.

9. Taylor, "The Third Intermediate Period," 330–68.

10. Pierre Montet, *La nécropole royale de Tanis: Fouilles de Tanis, dirigées par Pierre Montet*, 3 vols. (Paris, 1947–1960).

11. Henri Stierlin and Christiane Ziegler, *Tanis: Trésors des Pharaons* (Paris: Seuil, 1987).

12. Jean Yoyotte, "The Treasure of Tanis," *The Treasures of the Egyptian Museum*, ed. Francesco Tiradritti (Cairo: American University in Cairo Press, 1999), 302–33.

13. Stierlin and Ziegler, *Tanis: Trésors des Pharaons*; Pierre Montet, *Les énigmes de Tanis* (Paris: Payot, 1952).

14. These archaeologists include David O'Connor, Barry Kemp, and Manfred Bietak.

15. "What is Pan-sharpening and how can I create a pan-sharpened image?" US Geological Survey, https://landsat.usgs.gov/what-pan-sharpening-and-how-can-i-create-a-pan-sharpened-image, accessed 2 April 2018.

16. Thomas M. Lillesand et al., *Remote Sensing and Image Interpretation* (Wiley, 2007).

17. Philippe Brissaud, ed., *Cahiers de Tanis I*, Mémoire 75 (Paris: Editions Recherche sur les civilisations, 1987).

18. Just like at Amarna. Barry Kemp, *The City of Akhenaten and Nefertiti: Amarna and Its People* (London: Thames and Hudson, 2012).

19. For overviews of palace waterways and block transportation, see Angus Graham and Kristian Strutt, "Ancient Theban Temple and Palace Landscapes," *Egyptian Archaeology*, vol. 43 (Autumn 2013): 5–7; Angus Graham et al., "Theban Harbours and Waterscapes Survey, 2012," *Journal of Egyptian Archaeology*, vol. 98 (2012): 27–42.

20. Norman de Garis Davies, *Two Ramesside Tombs at Thebes* (New York: Metropolitan Museum of Art, 1927), plate XXX.

21. John H. Taylor, *Unwrapping a Mummy: The Life, Death, and Embalming of Horemkenesi* (London: British Museum Press, 1995), 47.

22. For a detailed overview of ancient Egyptian religious practices, see Donald B. Redford, ed., *The Ancient Gods Speak: A Guide to Ancient Egyptian Religion* (Oxford: Oxford University Press, 2002).

23. For a discussion on a well-excavated New Kingdom house, see Barry J. Kemp and Anna Stevens, *Busy Lives at Amarna: Excavations in the Main City (Grid 12 and the House of Ranefer, N49.18)*, vol. 1, *The Excavations, Architecture and Environmental Remains*, EES Excavation Memoir 90 (London: Egypt Exploration Society and Amarna Trust, 2010).

24. Janine Bourriau and Jacke Phillips, eds., *Invention and Innovation: The Social Context of Technological Change 2, Egypt, the Aegean and the Near East, 1650–1150 B.C.* (Oxford: Oxbow Books, 2016), 85–90.

25. These types of houses are described in detail in Kate Spence, "Ancient Egyptian Houses: Architecture, Conceptualization and Interpretation," *Household Studies in Complex Societies: (Micro) Archaeological and Textual Approaches*, ed. Miriam Müller, Oriental Institute Seminars 10 (Chicago: University of Chicago, 2015), 83–99; Kemp, *The City of Akhenaten and Nefertiti*; Barry J. Kemp and Salvatore Garfi, *A Survey of the Ancient City of El-'Amarna*, Occasional Publications, vol. 9 (London: Egypt Exploration Society, 1993); Leonard Lesko and Barbara Lesko, eds., *Pharaoh's Workers: The Villagers of Deir el Medina* (Ithaca, NY: Cornell University Press, 1994).

26. For plans of a similar palace layout from the New Kingdom site of Malkaka, see Lacovara, *New Kingdom Royal City*.

27. For a discussion of the diverse range of artistic objects made at Amarna, which would have been quite similar to Tanis, see Paul T. Nicholson, *Brilliant Things for Akhenaten: The Production of Glass, Vitreous Materials and Pottery at Amarna Site O45.1*, EES Excavation Memoir 80 (London: Egypt Exploration Society, 2007); Alan J. Shortland, *Vitreous Materials at Amarna. The Production of Glass and Faience in 18th Dynasty Egypt*, British Archaeological Reports International Series 827 (Oxford: Archaeopress, 2000); Kristen Thompson, "Amarna Statuary Project," *Journal of Egyptian Archaeology*, vol. 89 (2003): 17–19.

28. Hilary Wilson, *Egyptian Food and Drink*, Book 9, Shire Egyptology (London: Bloomsbury, 2008).

29. Lacovara, *New Kingdom Royal City*, 26.

30. Kitchen, *Third Intermediate Period in Egypt*.

31. For an overview of what Tanis might look like reconstructed, see Barry Kemp, "A Model of Tell el-Amarna," *Antiquity*, vol. 74, no. 283 (2000): 15–16, https://doi.org/10.1017 /S0003598X00065996.

32. Roger S. Bagnall and Dominic W. Rathbone, eds., *Egypt: From Alexander to the Copts* (London: British Museum Press, 2004), 51.

33. The *Description of Egypt* can be found fully scanned and searchable online. See http:// descegy.bibalex.org/, accessed 2 April 2018.

34. An overview of this new satellite can be found on "WorldView-4," DigitalGlobe, http:// worldview4.digitalglobe.com/#/preload, accessed 2 April 2018.

Chapter 6

1. Like Doggerland, under the North Sea. See Vincent Gaffney et al., *Europe's Lost World: The Rediscovery of Doggerland*, CBA Research Report, no. 160 (York: Council for British Archaeology, 2009).

2. Michael Greshko, "World's Oldest Cave Art Found—And Neanderthals Made It," *National Geographic News*, 22 February 2018, https://news.nationalgeographic.com/2018/02 /neanderthals-cave-art-humans-evolution-science/, accessed 4 April 2018.

3. Lawrence Clayton et al., *The De Soto Chronicles: The Expedition of Hernando de Soto to North America in 1539–1543* (Tuscaloosa: University of Alabama Press, 1993).

4. Fernbank Museum of Natural History, "Archaeologists Track Infamous Conquistador Through Southeast," *ScienceDaily*, 5 November 2009, https://www.sciencedaily.com /releases/2009/11/091105084838.htm, accessed 4 April 2018.

5. Neal Lineback and Mandy L. Gritzner, "Geography in the News: Hernando De Soto's Famous Battle," *National Geographic Blog*, 14 June 2014, https://blog.nationalgeographic .org/2014/06/14/geography-in-the-news-hernando-de-sotos-famous-battle/, accessed 4 April 2018.

6. Nelson J. R. Fagundes et al., "Mitochondrial Population Genomics Supports a Single Pre-Clovis Origin with a Coastal Route for the Peopling of the Americas," *American Journal of Human Genetics*, vol. 82, no. 3 (2008): 583–92, https://doi.org/10.1016/j.ajhg.2007.11 .013.

7. A great deal of controversy surrounds archaeological sites older than 15,000 years. See Brigit Katz, "Found: One of the Oldest North American Settlements," *Smithsonian Smart-News*, 5 April 2017, https://www.smithsonianmag.com/smart-news/one-oldest-north -american-settlements-found-180962750/, accessed 5 April 2017.

8. Hansi Lo Wang, "The Map of Native American Tribes You've Never Seen Before," *NPR Code Switch*, 24 June 2014, https://www.npr.org/sections/codeswitch/2014/06/24 /323665644/the-map-of-native-american-tribes-youve-never-seen-before, accessed 4 April 2018.

9. Kathryn E. Krasinski et al., "Detecting Late Holocene Cultural Landscape Modifications Using LiDAR Imagery in the Boreal Forest, Susitna Valley, Southcentral Alaska," *Journal of Field Archaeology*, vol. 41, no. 3 (2016): 255–70, https://doi.org/10.1080/00934690.2016 .1174764.

10. Brian Daniels, personal communication, 3 March 2018.

11. "Tribal Nations and the United States: An Introduction," National Congress of American Indians, http://www.ncai.org/tribalnations/introduction/Tribal_Nations_and_the _United_States_An_Introduction-web-.pdf, accessed 4 April 2018.

12. René R. Gadacz and Zach Parrott, "First Nations," *The Canadian Encyclopedia*, 2015, http:// www.thecanadianencyclopedia.ca/en/article/first-nations/, accessed 4 April 2018.

13. Arthur Link et al., "United States," *Encyclopædia Britannica*, https://www.britannica.com /place/United-States, accessed 4 April 2018.

14. Sarah E. Baires, "How White Settlers Buried the Truth About the Midwest's Mysterious Mound Cities," Zócalo Public Square, 22 February 2018, http://www.zocalopublicsquare .org/2018/02/22/white-settlers-buried-truth-midwests-mysterious-mounds/ideas /essay/?xid=PS_smithsonian, accessed 5 April 2018.

15. James M. Harmon et al., "LiDAR for Archaeological Landscape Analysis: A Case Study of Two Eighteenth-Century Maryland Plantation Sites," *American Antiquity*, vol. 71, no. 4 (2006): 649–70, https://doi.org/10.2307/40035883.
16. Mark J. Rochelo et al., "Revealing Pre-Historic Native American Belle Glade Earthworks in the Northern Everglades Utilizing Airborne LiDAR," *Journal of Archaeological Science: Reports*, vol. 2 (2015): 624–43, https://doi.org/10.1016/j.jasrep.2014.11.009.
17. Katharine M. Johnson and William B. Ouimet, "Rediscovering the Lost Archaeological Landscape of Southern New England Using Airborne Light Detection and Ranging (LiDAR)," *Journal of Archaeological Science*, vol. 43 (2014): 9–20, https://doi.org/10.1016/j.jas.2013.12.004.
18. Harmon et al., "LiDAR for Archaeological Landscape Analysis."
19. Calculated based on the known area for Maya remains, with an average of the total forested area in that region.
20. Adrian S. Z. Chase et al., "LiDAR for Archaeological Research and the Study of Historical Landscapes," *Sensing the Past: From Artifact to Historical Site*, ed. Nicola Masini and Francesco Soldovieri (Cham: Switzerland: Springer International Publishing, 2017), 89–100, https://doi.org/10.1007/978-3-319-50518-3_4; Arlen Chase et al., "Geospatial Revolution and Remote Sensing LiDAR in Mesoamerican Archaeology," *Proceedings of the National Academy of Sciences*, vol. 109, no. 32 (2012): 12916–21, https://doi.org/10.1073/pnas.1205198109.
21. Tom Clynes, "Exclusive: Laser Scans Reveal Maya 'Megalopolis' Below Guatemalan Jungle," *National Geographic News*, 1 February 2018, https://news.nationalgeographic.com/2018/02/maya-laser-lidar-guatemala-pacunam/, accessed 5 April 2018.
22. Francisco Estrada-Belli, personal communication, 7 November 2018.
23. "Amazon Rainforest," *Encyclopedia Britannica*, 2018, https://www.britannica.com/place/Amazon-Rainforest, accessed 5 April 2018.
24. Evan Andrews, "The Enduring Mystery Behind Percy Fawcett's Disappearance," *History*, 29 May 2015, https://www.history.com/news/explorer-percy-fawcett-disappears-in-the-amazon, accessed 5 April 2018.
25. Michael J. Heckenberger et al., "Amazonia 1492: Pristine Forest or Cultural Parkland?" *Science*, vol. 301, no. 5640 (2003): 1710–14, https://doi.org/10.1126/science.1086112.
26. Michael J. Heckenberger et al., "Pre-Columbian Urbanism, Anthropogenic Landscapes, and the Future of the Amazon," *Science*, vol. 321, no. 5893 (2008): 1214–17, https://doi.org/10.1126/science.1159769.
27. Martti Pärssinen et al., "Pre-Columbian Geometric Earthworks in the Upper Purús: A Complex Society in Western Amazonia," *Antiquity*, vol. 83, no. 322 (2009): 1084–95, https://doi.org/10.1017/S0003598X00099373.
28. Hiram Bingham, "In the Wonderland of Peru—Rediscovering Machu Picchu," *National Geographic Magazine*, April 1913, https://www.nationalgeographic.com/magazine/1913/04/machu-picchu-peru-inca-hiram-bingham-discovery/, accessed 3 April 2018.
29. Rosa Lasaponara and Nicola Masini, "Facing the Archaeological Looting in Peru by Using Very High-Resolution Satellite Imagery and Local Spatial Autocorrelation Statistics," *Computational Science and Its Applications—ICCSA 2010*, ed. David Taniar et al. (Berlin and Heidelberg: Springer, 2010), 254–61, https://doi.org/10.1007/978-3-642-12156-2_19.
30. Rosa Lasaponara et al., "New Discoveries in the Piramide Naranjada in Cahuachi (Peru) Using Satellite, Ground Probing Radar and Magnetic Investigations," *Journal of Archaeological Science*, vol. 38, no. 9 (2011): 2031–39, https://doi.org/10.1016/j.jas.2010.12.010.
31. William Neuman and Ralph Blumenthal, "New to the Archaeologist's Toolkit: The Drone," *New York Times*, 13 August 2014, https://www.nytimes.com/2014/08/14/arts/design/drones-are-used-to-patrol-endangered-archaeological-sites.html, accessed 6 April 2018.
32. Terry L. Hunt and Carl P. Lipo, "Late Colonization of Easter Island," *Science*, vol. 311, no. 5767 (2006): 1603–6, https://doi.org/10.1126/science.1121879.

33. Carl P. Lipo and Terry L. Hunt, "Mapping Prehistoric Statue Roads on Easter Island," *Antiquity*, vol. 79, no. 303 (2005): 158–68, https://doi.org/10.1017/S0003598X00113778.

34. Carl P. Lipo et al., "The 'Walking' Megalithic Statues (Moai) of Easter Island," *Journal of Archaeological Science*, vol. 40, no. 6 (2013): 2859–66, https://doi.org/10.1016/j.jas.2012.09.029.

35. Terry Hunt and Carl Lipo, *The Statues That Walked: Unraveling the Mystery of Easter Island* (New York: Simon and Schuster, 2011).

36. Robert DiNapoli et al., "Rapa Nui (Easter Island) monument (*ahu*) locations explained by freshwater sources," *PLOS ONE* (10 January 2019): e0210409, https://doi.org/10.1371/journal.pone.0210409.

37. Terry L. Hunt and Carl Lipo, "The Archaeology of Rapa Nui (Easter Island)," *The Oxford Handbook of Prehistoric Oceania*, ed. Ethan E. Cochrane and Terry L. Hunt (New York: Oxford University Press, 2017), https://doi.org/10.1093/oxfordhb/9780199925070.013.026.

38. Dominic Hosner et al, "Archaeological Sites in China During the Neolithic and Bronze Age," *PANGAEA*, 2016, https://doi.org/10.1594/PANGAEA.860072, supplement to Hosner et al., "Spatiotemporal and Distribution Patterns of Archaeological Sites in China During the Neolithic and Bronze Age: An Overview," *The Holocene*, https://doi.org/10.1177/0959683616641743.

39. N. K. Hu and X. Li, "Historical Ruins of Remote Sensing Archaeology in Arid Desertified Environment, Northwestern China," *IOP Conference Series: Earth and Environmental Science*, vol. 57, no. 1 (2017), https://doi.org/10.1088/1755-1315/57/1/012028.

40. V. Pawar et al., "Satellite Remote Sensing on the Plains of NW India—The Approaches Used by the Land, Water and Settlement Project," *Proceedings of National Workshop on Space Technology and Archaeology, 29–30 April 2015* (Haryana Space Applications Centre, Hisar, Haryana, India, 2016), 22–26.

41. Hector A. Orengo and Cameron A. Petrie, "Multi-Scale Relief Model (MSRM): A New Algorithm for the Visualization of Subtle Topographic Change of Variable Size in Digital Elevation Models," *Earth Surface Processes and Landforms*, vol. 43, no. 6 (2018): 1361–69, https://doi.org/10.1002/esp.4317.

42. Ajit Singh et al., "Counter-Intuitive Influence of Himalayan River Morphodynamics on Indus Civilisation Urban Settlements," *Nature Communications*, vol. 1617, no. 8 (2017), https://doi.org/10.1038/s41467-017-01643-9.

43. Paige Williams, "Digging for Glory," *New Yorker*, 27 June 2016, https://www.newyorker.com/magazine/2016/06/27/lee-berger-digs-for-bones-and-glory, accessed 7 April 2018.

44. Shadreck Chirikure et al., "Seen but Not Told: Re-mapping Great Zimbabwe Using Archival Data, Satellite Imagery and Geographical Information Systems," *Journal of Archaeological Method and Theory*, vol. 24, no. 2 (2017): 489–513, https://doi.org/10.1007/s10816-016-9275-1.

45. Shadreck Chirikure et al., "Zimbabwe Culture Before Mapungubwe: New Evidence from Mapela Hill, South-Western Zimbabwe," *PLOS ONE* (31 October 2014), https://doi.org/10.1371/journal.pone.0111224.

46. M. G. Meredith-Williams et al., "Mapping, Modelling and Predicting Prehistoric Coastal Archaeology in the Southern Red Sea Using New Applications of Digital-Imaging Techniques," *World Archaeology*, vol. 46, no. 1 (2014): 10–24, https://doi.org/10.1080/00438243.2014.890913; M. G. Meredith-Williams et al., "4200 New Shell Mound Sites in the Southern Red Sea," *Human Exploitation of Aquatic Landscapes*, ed. Ricardo Fernandes and John Meadows, special issue of *Internet Archaeology*, no. 37 (2014), https://doi.org/10.11141/ia.37.2.

47. Enrico Borgogno Mondino et al., "High Resolution Satellite Images for Archeological Applications: The Karima Case Study (Nubia Region, Sudan)," *European Journal of Remote Sensing*, vol. 45, no. 1 (2012): 243–59, https://doi.org/10.5721/EuJRS20124522.

48. Amy Maxmen, "A Race Against Time to Excavate an Ancient African Civilization: Archaeologists in Nubia Are Struggling Against Erosion, Desertification, and Government Plans to Develop the Land," *Atlantic*, 23 February 2018, https://www.theatlantic.com/science/archive/2018/02/erosion-and-development-threaten-ancient-nubian-sites/554003/, accessed 6 April 2018.

49. David J. Mattingly and Martin Sterry, "The First Towns in the Central Sahara," *Antiquity*, vol. 87, no. 336 (2013): 503–18, https://doi.org/10.1017/S0003598X00049097.

50. Carrie Hirtz, "Contributions of GIS and Satellite-Based Remote Sensing to Landscape Archaeology in the Middle East," *Journal of Archaeological Research*, vol. 22, no. 3 (2014): 229–76, https://doi.org/10.1007/s10814-013-9072-2.

51. Bjoern H. Menze and Jason A. Ur, "Mapping Patterns of Long-Term Settlement in Northern Mesopotamia at a Large Scale," *Proceedings of the National Academy of Sciences*, vol. 109, no. 14 (2012): E778–87, https://doi.org/10.1073/pnas.1115472109.

52. Warwick Ball and Jean-Claude Gardin, *Archaeological Gazetteer of Afghanistan*, Synthèse, no. 8 (Paris: Éditions Recherche sur les civilisations, 1982).

53. David Thomas, personal communication, 8 November 2018.

54. David C. Thomas et al., "The Archaeological Sites of Afghanistan in Google Earth," *AARGnews*, no. 37 (September 2008): 22–30.

55. Andrew Lawler, "Spy Satellites Are Revealing Afghanistan's Lost Empires," *Science*, 13 December 2017, http://www.sciencemag.org/news/2017/12/spy-satellites-are-revealing -afghanistan-s-lost-empires, accessed 2 April 2017.

56. David Kennedy and Robert Bewley, "APAAME: Aerial Photographic Archive for Archaeology in the Middle East," APAAME, http://www.apaame.org/, accessed 4 April 2018.

57. David Kennedy and Robert Bewley, "Aerial Archaeology in Jordan," *Antiquity*, vol. 83, no. 319 (2009): 69–81, https://doi.org/10.1017/S0003598X00098094.

58. "EAMENA: Endangered Archaeology in the Middle East and North Africa," University of Oxford, 2015, www.eamena.org, accessed 31 March 2018.

59. "Mega-Jordan: The National Heritage Documentation and Management System," MEGA-Jordan, Getty Conservation Institute and World Monuments Fund, 2010, http://www .megajordan.org, accessed 31 March 2018.

60. I went to the website and selected all site types, finding more than 68,000 sites listed, but sites are listed multiple times across categories and time periods. It is likely that there are ca. 27,000 sites, according to direct information from the Department of Antiquities. Stephen Savage, personal communication, 8 April 2018.

61. Rosa Lasaponara et al., "On the LiDAR Contribution for the Archaeological and Geomorphological Study of a Deserted Medieval Village in Southern Italy," *Journal of Geophyics and Engineering*, vol. 7, no. 2 (2010): 155, https://doi.org/10.1088/1742 -2132/7/2/S01.

62. R. Coluzzi et al., "On the LiDAR Contribution for Landscape Archaeology and Palaeoenvironmental Studies: The Case Study of Bosco dell'Incoronata (Southern Italy)," *Advances in Geosciences*, vol. 24 (2010): 125–32, https://doi.org/doi:10.5194/adgeo-24-125 -2010.

63. Paolo Mozzi et al., "The Roman City of Altinum, Venice Lagoon, from Remote Sensing and Geophysical Prospection," *Archaeological Prospection*, vol. 23, no. 1 (2016): 27–44, https://doi.org/10.1002/arp.1520.

64. "Learn the Knowledge of London," Transport for London, https://tfl.gov.uk/info-for /taxis-and-private-hire/licensing/learn-the-knowledge-of-london, accessed 3 April 2018.

65. "ARCHI UK," Archaeological Data Service, ARCHI UK, http://www.archiuk.com/, accessed 1 April 2018.

66. "Lasers Reveal 'Lost' Roman Roads," GOV.UK, 3 February 2016, https://www.gov.uk /government/news/lasers-reveal-lost-roman-roads, accessed 2 April 2018.

67. Maev Kennedy, "'Millennia of Human Activity': Heatwave Reveals Lost UK Archaeological Sites," *Guardian*, 14 August 2018, https://www.theguardian.com/science/2018/aug /15/millennia-of-human-activity-heatwave-reveals-lost-uk-archaeological-sites, accessed 8 November 2018.

68. Erwin Meylemans et al., "It's All in the Pixels: High-Resolution Remote-Sensing Data and the Mapping and Analysis of the Archaeological and Historical Landscape," *Internet Archaeology*, vol. 43 (2017), https://doi.org/10.11141/ia.43.2.

69. Nick Allen, "1,000-Year-Old Fishing Trap Found on Google Earth," *Telegraph*, 16 March 2009, https://www.telegraph.co.uk/news/newstopics/howaboutthat/5000835 /1000-year-old-fishing-trap-found-on-Google-Earth.html, accessed 7 April 2018.

70. Laura Rocchio, "Satellites and Shipwrecks: Landsat Satellite Spots Foundered Ships in Coastal Waters," NASA, 11 March 2016, https://www.nasa.gov/feature/goddard/2016/landsat-spots-shipwrecks-in-coastal-waters, accessed 5 April 2018.

71. "Drones Seek Out Lost Shipwrecks Below Lake Huron." *DroneDeploy* (blog), 20 September 2017, https://blog.dronedeploy.com/drones-seek-out-lost-shipwrecks-below-lake-huron-1420f8b407b4, accessed 5 April 2018.

72. "Trident Underwater Drone," OpenROV, https://www.openrov.com/, accessed 4 April 2018.

73. Toshiko Kaneda and Carl Haub, "How Many People Have Ever Lived on Earth?" Population Reference Bureau, https://www.prb.org/howmanypeoplehaveeverlivedonearth/, accessed 7 April 2018.

74. Richard Gray, "How Can We Manage Earth's Land?" BBC Futurenow, 29 June 2017, http://www.bbc.com/future/story/20170628-how-to-best-manage-earths-land, accessed 7 April 2018.

Chapter 7

1. David Jeffreys and Ana Tavares, "The Historic Landscape of Early Dynastic Memphis," *Mitteilungen des Deutschen Archäologischen Instituts Abteilung Kairo*, vol. 50 (1994): 143–73.

2. I. E. S. Edwards, *The Pyramids of Egypt*, 5th ed. (New York: Harmondsworth, 1993).

3. Mark Lehner, *The Complete Pyramids* (London: Thames and Hudson, 1997), 115.

4. For a comprehensive overview of administration in the Old Kingdom, see Klaus Baer, *Rank and Title in the Old Kingdom: The Structure of the Egyptian Administration in the Fifth and Sixth Dynasties* (Chicago: University of Chicago Press, 1960).

5. James P. Allen, *The Ancient Egyptian Pyramid Texts* (Atlanta: Society of Biblical Literature Press, 2015).

6. Gregory Mumford, "Tell Ras Budran (Site 345): Defining Egypt's Eastern Frontier and Mining Operations in South Sinai During the Late Old Kingdom (Early EB IV/MB I)," *Bulletin of the American Schools of Oriental Research*, no. 342 (May 2006): 13–67; Gregory Mumford, "Ongoing Investigations at a Late Old Kingdom Coastal Fort at Ras Budran in South Sinai," *Journal of Ancient Egyptian Interconnections*, vol. 4, no. 4 (2012): 20–28, https://doi.org/10.2458/azu_jaei_v04i4_mumford.

7. Archaeologists have noted Old Kingdom sherds at Tell Abassiya, Tell Haddidin, Tell Iswid North, Tell Iswid South, Tell Hasanin, Tell Umm el Zayat, Tell Mashala, Tell el-Akhdar, Tell Dirdir, and Tell Gherir (Edwin C. M. van den Brink et al., "A Geo-Archaeological Survey in the East Delta, Egypt: The First Two Seasons, a Preliminary Report," *Mitteilungen des Deutschen Archäologischen Instituts Abteilung Kairo*, vol. 43 [1987]: 4–31; Edwin C. M. van den Brink et al., "The Amsterdam University Survey Expedition to the East Nile Delta [1984–1986]," *The Archaeology of the Nile Delta: Problems and Priorities*, ed. Edwin van den Brink [Amsterdam: Netherlands Foundation for Archaeological Research in Egypt, 1988], 65–114); Tell Diba, Tell Farkha (Jean Leclant and Anne Minault-Gout, "Fouilles et travaux en Égypte et au Soudan, 1997–1998. Seconde partie," *Orientalia*, vol. 69 [2000]: 141–70); Abu Daoud (Marek Chlodnicki et al., "The Nile Delta in Transition: A View from Tell el-Farkha," *The Nile Delta in Transition, 4th–3rd Millennium B.C. Proceedings of the Seminar Held in Cairo, 21–24 October 1990, at the Netherlands Institute of Archaeology and Arabic Studies*, ed. Edwin C. M. van den Brink [Tel Aviv: Edwin C. M. van den Brink, 1992], 171–90); and Geziret el-Faras (Van den Brink et al., "A Geo-Archaeological Survey in the East Delta, Egypt," 20; Van den Brink et al., "The Amsterdam University Survey Expedition to the East Nile Delta [1984–1986]"). Tell Ibrahim Awad has an Old Kingdom settlement, cemetery, and evidence for a temple deposit (Willem M. van Haarlem, "Temple Deposits at Tell Ibrahim Awad II—An Update," *Göttinger Miszellen*, vol. 154 [1996]: 31–34). Mendes contains a necropolis measuring 150,000 square miles, with a settlement and a large temple complex (Donald B. Redford, *Excavations at Mendes: Volume I. The Royal Necropolis* [Leiden: Brill, 2004]; Donald B. Redford, *City of the Ram-Man: The Story of Ancient Mendes* [Princeton, NJ: Princeton University Press, 2010]). The survey discovered several previously unrecorded sites with Old Kingdom pottery at the sites of Tell Tarha, Tell Museya, Tell Gabar, and Tell

Sharufa. The construction of a water filtration plant has obscured Tell Tebilla's Old Kingdom strata but yielded ex-situ potsherds (Gregory Mumford, "The First Intermediate Period: Unravelling a 'Dark Age' at Mendes and Tell Tebilla," *Akhenaten Temple Project Newsletter*, no. 1 [2000]: 3–4). Old Kingdom sherds appeared at Tell Fagi, Tell el-Ein (Van den Brink et al., "A Geo-Archaeological Survey in the East Delta, Egypt," 23); and Tell Mara (Van den Brink et al., "The Amsterdam University Survey Expedition to the East Nile Delta [1984–1986]"). Kufr Nigm has extensive structures visible within the excavation units (Mohammed I. Bakr, "The New Excavations at Ezbet et-Tell, Kufr Nigm: The First Season [1984]," in Van den Brink, *The Archaeology of the Nile Delta: Problems and Priorities*, 49–62).

8. Gregory Mumford, *The Late Old Kingdom to First Intermediate Period Settlement at Tell er-Ru'ba (Mendes)* (forthcoming).

9. Seen in the 2003 surface survey.

10. Van den Brink et al., "A Geo-Archaeological Survey in the East Delta, Egypt," 20.

11. Willem van Haarlem, "Tell Ibrahim Awad," *Egyptian Archaeology*, vol. 18 (2001): 33–35.

12. For a comprehensive study on ancient Egyptian materials, see Paul T. Nicholson and Ian Shaw, eds., *Ancient Egyptian Materials and Technologies* (Cambridge: Cambridge University Press, 2009).

13. Rushdi Said, *Geological Evolution of the Nile Valley* (New York: Springer, 1988), 1–7.

14. Rushdi Said, *The River Nile: Geology, Hydrology and Utilization* (Oxford and New York: Pergamon Press, 1993), 1–7.

15. Gregory Mumford, "New Investigations at Tell Tebilla in the Mendesian Nome," *Akhenaten Temple Project Newsletter*, vol. 2 (2000): 1–3.

16. If you take a core sample on any settlement site in the Delta or Nile Valley, and you go deep enough, you'll hit sand. That's because Egypt's original population settled on sandy mounds called *gezirahs*, or "turtlebacks." The formation of *gezirahs* is connected to Late Pleistocene glaciation. The exact date of *gezirah* formation is not known. When the subpolar glaciers melted during the Late Pleistocene (38,000–12,000 BC), the height of the Mediterranean increased more than 100 meters. That put the coastline 50 kilometers inland from where it is today. The above-sea-level height of the land increased more than 25 meters from the coastline to present-day Mit Rahina (Memphis), and the increase in water caused this sloping surface to erode away. Eventually, the alluvium carried down the Nile created lagoons due to its volume. The *gezirahs* on which so many Deltaic settlements were formed began to emerge in this Late Pleistocene Period as parts of the Delta eroded away, caused by the gradual dropping of the sea level following the previous increase. Karl Butzer took a number of deep cores in the Delta, from Alexandria to Port Said. The later Paleolithic record can be found 10 meters below the present surface. Karl W. Butzer, "Geoarchaeological Implications of Recent Research in the Nile Delta," *Egypt and the Levant: Interrelations from the 4th Through Early 3rd Millennium BCE*, ed. Edwin C. M. van den Brink and Thomas Evan Levy (London: Leicester University Press, 2002), 83–97.

17. Lehner, *Complete Pyramids*, 115.

18. John Coleman Darnell, "The Message of King Wahankh Antef II to Khety, Ruler of Heracleopolis," *Zeitschrift für ägyptische Sprache und Altertumskunde*, vol. 124, no. 2 (1997): 101–8.

19. Detlef Franke, "The Career of Khnumhotep III of Beni Hasan and the So-called 'Decline of the Nomarchs,'" *Middle Kingdom Studies*, ed. Stephen Quirke (New Malden, Δ255Surrey: SIA Publishing, 1991), 51–67; Labib Habachi, *Elephantine IV. The Sanctuary of Heqaib*, Deutsches Archäeologisches Institut, Abteilung Cairo, Archäeologische Veröffentlichungen, 33 (Mainz: Phillip von Zabern, 1985); Percy Newberry, *El Bersheh, Part I (The Tomb of Tehuti-hetep)* (London: The Egypt Exploration Fund, 1895, 33; repr. Phillip von Zabern: Mainz, 1985); P. Newberry, *El-Berhseh I The Tomb of Djeutyhetep* (London, 1895).

20. Jaromir Malek, "The Old Kingdom (ca. 2686–2160 BC)," *The Oxford History of Ancient Egypt*, ed. Ian Shaw (Oxford: Oxford University Press, 2000), 89–117; Stephan Seidlmayer,

"First Intermediate Period (ca. 2160–2055 BC)," in Shaw, *Oxford History of Ancient Egypt*, 118–47.

21. Malek, "The Old Kingdom (ca. 2686–2160 BC)."

22. Barbara Bell, "Climate and the History of Egypt: The Middle Kingdom," *American Journal of Archaeology*, vol. 79, no. 3 (1975): 223–69, https://doi.org/10.2307/503481; Barbara Bell, "The Dark Ages in Ancient History. I. The First Dark Age in Egypt," *American Journal of Archaeology*, vol. 75, no. 1 (1971): 1–26, https://doi.org/10.2307/503678; Barbara Bell, "The Oldest Record of the Nile Floods," *Geographical Journal*, vol. 136, no. 4 (1970): 569–73; Harvey Weiss and Raymond S. Bradley, "What Drives Societal Collapse?" *Science*, vol. 291, no. 5504 (2001): 609–10, https://doi.org/10.1126/science.1058775; Fekri Hassan, "The Fall of the Egyptian Old Kingdom," BBC, 2011, http://www.bbc.co.uk/history/ancient/egyptians/apocalypse_egypt_01.shtml, accessed 5 May 2018; Kent R. Weeks, *The Illustrated Guide to Luxor* (Cairo: American University in Cairo Press, 2005), 35.

23. Said, *River Nile: Geology, Hydrology and Utilization*, 165.

24. Weiss and Bradley, "What Drives Societal Collapse?" 609–10.

25. Françoise Gasse, "Hydrological Changes in the African Tropics Since the Last Glacial Maximum," *Quaternary Science Reviews*, vol. 19, nos. 1–5 (2000): 189–212, https://doi.org/10.1016/S0277-3791(99)00061-X.

26. Michael D. Krom et al., "Nile River Sediment Fluctuations over the Past 7000 Yrs and Their Key Role in Sapropel Development," *Geology*, vol. 30, no. 1 (2002): 71–74, https://doi.org/10.1130/0091-7613(2002)030<0071:NRSFOT>2.0.CO;2.

27. Said, *River Nile: Geology, Hydrology and Utilization*, chapter 5.

28. Joe Morrissey and Mary Lou Guerinot, "Iron Uptake and Transport in Plants: The Good, the Bad, and the Ionome," *Chemical Reviews*, vol. 109, no. 10 (2009): 4553–67, https://doi.org/10.1021/cr900112r.

29. Jean-Daniel Stanley et al., "Short Contribution: Nile Flow Failure at the End of the Old Kingdom, Egypt: Strontium Isotopic and Petrologic Evidence," *Geoarchaeology*, vol. 18, no. 3, (2003): 395–402, https://doi.org/10.1002/gea.10065.

30. Thomas von der Way, *Tell el-Fara'in/Buto I*, Archäologische Veröffentlichungen (Deutsches Archäologisches Institut. Abteilung Kairo), 83 (Mainz: Philip Von Zabern, 1997); Thomas von der Way, "Excavations at Tell el-Fara'in/Buto in 1987–1989," in Van den Brink, *Nile Delta in Transition*, 1–10.

31. For a detailed overview of the Buto chronology, see von der Way, *Tell el-Fara'in/Buto I*.

32. Lisa Giddy and David Jeffreys, "Memphis 1991," *Journal of Egyptian Archaeology*, vol. 78 (1992): 1–11, https://doi.org/10.2307/3822063.

33. Nicole Alexanian and Stephan Johannes Seidelmeyer, "Die Residenznekropole von Daschur Erster Grabungsbericht," *Mitteilungen des Deutschen Archäologischen Instituts, Abteilung Kairo*, vol. 58 (2002): 1–29.

34. William Ellis, "Africa's Sahel: The Stricken Land," *National Geographic Magazine*, August 1987, 140–79.

35. Harvey Weiss, "Beyond the Younger Dryas," *Environmental Disaster and the Archaeology of Human Response*, ed. Garth Bawden and Richard Martin Reycraft, Maxwell Museum of Anthropology, Anthropological Papers no. 7 (Albuquerque: University of New Mexico, 2000), 75–98. At the Soreq Cave in the Judean hills of Israel, deposits reveal a 20 to 30 percent precipitation decrease between 4,200 and 4,000 years ago. (See Miryam Bar-Matthews et al., "Late Quaternary Paleoclimate in the Eastern Mediterranean Region from Stable Isotope Analysis of Speleothems at Soreq Cave, Israel," *Quaternary Research*, vol. 47, no. 2 [1997]: 155–68, https://doi.org/10.1006/qres.1997.1883.) In Palestine, we see Early Bronze IV (2250–2000 BC) sites abandoned. At Tell Leilan in Syria, archaeologists found a 1-meter-thick sterile layer of silts corresponding to post–Old Kingdom times, much like what seems to appear in a core sample from Tell Tebilla. (See H. Weiss et al., "The Genesis and Collapse of Third Millennium North Mesopotamian Civilization," *Science*, vol. 261, no. 5124 [1993]: 995–1004, https://doi.org/10.1126/science.261.5124.995; Larry A. Pavlish, "Archaeometry at Mendes: 1990–2002," *Egypt, Israel and the Ancient Mediterranean World: Studies in Honor of Donald B. Redford*, ed. Gary N. Knoppers

and Antoine Hirsch, Problem der Ägyptologie series, vol. 20 [Leiden: Brill, 2004], 61–112.) In Syria and Iraq, there is evidence for the disappearance of the Akkadian Empire around 2170 BC, or 4,170 +/-150 years before present. At Lake Van, located between the Caspian Sea and the Black Sea in Turkey, archaeologists have collected an annual record of silt and clay deposits covering the past 20,000 years. Such layers, called varves, typically reveal the deposition cycles associated with all bodies of water. Here they show that the airborne dust rose five times between 2290 and 2000 BC. Also, lake levels and oak pollens decreased, while wind-borne quartz deposition increased—something that occurs during times of aridity. (See Gerry Lemcke and Michael Sturm, "δ^{18}o and Trace Element Measurements as Proxy for the Reconstruction of Climate Changes at Lake Van [Turkey]: Preliminary Results," *Third Millennium B.C. Climate Change and Old World Collapse*, NATO ASI Series I, Global Environmental Change, vol. 49, ed. H. Nüzhet Dalfes et al. [Berlin: Springer, 1997], 653–78.) Looking eastward, a study from India that analyzed core samples of sediments from the Indus River delta found major changes in the oxygen isotope ratios of plankton around 4,200 years ago, suggesting decreased monsoon rainfalls. (See M. Staubwasser et al., "Climate Change at the 4.2 ka BP Termination of the Indus Valley Civilization and Holocene South Asian Monsoon Variability," *Geophysical Research Letters*, vol. 30, no. 8 [2003]: 1425, https://doi.org/10.1029/2002GL016822.)

36. Staubwasser et al., "Climate Change at the 4.2 ka BP Termination of the Indus Valley," 1425.

37. Donald B. Redford, "Mendes & Environs in the Middle Kingdom," *Studies in Honor of William Kelly Simpson*, vol. 2, ed. Peter Der Manuelian (Boston: Museum of Fine Arts, 1996), 679–82.

38. Peter deMenocal, "Cultural Responses to Climate Change During the Late Holocene," *Science*, vol. 292, no. 5517 (2001): 667–73, https://doi.org/10.1126/science.1059287; H. M. Cullen et al., "Climate Change and the Collapse of the Akkadian Empire: Evidence from the Deep Sea," *Geology*, vol. 28, no. 4 (2000): 379–82, https://doi.org/10.1130/0091-7613(2000)28<379:CCATCO>2.0.CO;2.

39. John Baines and Jaromir Malek, *Atlas of Ancient Egypt* (New York: Facts on File, 1984).

40. Van Haarlem, "Tell Ibrahim Awad," 33–35. The cemetery of this site contained the remains of people who lived between the end of the Old Kingdom and the beginning of the First Intermediate Period. Delia L. Phillips et al., "Bioarchaeology of Tell Ibrahim Awad," *Ägypten und Levante / Egypt and the Levant*, vol. 19 (2009): 157–210.

41. Jacques Vandier, *Mo'alla: La tombe d'Ankhtifi et la tombe de Sébekhotep* (Cairo: l'Institut français d'archéologie orientale, 1950); Miriam Lichtheim, *Ancient Egyptian Autobiographies Chiefly of the Middle Kingdom* (Göttingen: Vandenhoek and Ruprecht, 1988), 23–26; Miriam Lichtheim, *Ancient Egyptian Literature. Volume I: The Old and Middle Kingdoms* (Berkeley: University of California Press, 2006).

Inscription #1: The Butler Merer of Edfu said: *"I buried the dead and I nourished the living, wherever I went in the drought that occurred. I closed off all their fields and mounds in town and countryside, not letting their water inundate for someone else, as does a worthy citizen so that his family may swim."* (See Lichtheim, *Ancient Egyptian Literature. Volume I: The Old and Middle Kingdoms*, 87.) This man refers directly to a drought. When he talks about "closing off fields," he means that he prevented the vital floodwaters from escaping from the fields of those who lived in his province. If he had not done so, the waters would have flowed away to irrigate another province's crops.

Inscription #2: The Treasurer Iti of Imyotru (near modern Gebelein, 30 kilometers south of Luxor) explained: *"I nourished Imyotru in years of misery. Though four hundred men were in straits through it, I did not seize a man's daughter, nor did I seize his field."* (See Lichtheim, *Ancient Egyptian Literature. Volume I: The Old and Middle Kingdoms*, 88.) In this case, Iti makes reference to not just one instance, but multiple years of "misery." We do not know precisely what that means, but clearly people were suffering.

Inscription #3: In the stele of the Steward Senisi of Coptus (modern Quft, 30 kilometers north of Luxor), we can read: *"I measured out Upper Egyptian barley as sustenance for this whole town in the gateway of the Count and Chief Priest Djefi, in the painful years of distress."*

(See Lichtheim, *Ancient Egyptian Literature. Volume I: The Old and Middle Kingdoms*, 89.) Again, we see a reference to extended suffering. In this case, people needed measures of barley to survive, which suggests a period of starvation.

Inscription #4: In the autobiography of the Nomarch Henqu, the inscription states: *"I also resettled the towns that were enfeebled in this nome with persons of other nomes."* (See Lichtheim, *Ancient Egyptian Literature. Volume I: The Old and Middle Kingdoms*, 89.) These towns might have been enfeebled due to disease, starvation, or war, hence an influx of people from other nomes. These things suggest a period of instability.

Inscription #5: From the autobiography of a nomarch named Khety: *"I made a sluice-way for this town, while Upper Egypt was in a bad way, no water to be seen. I sealed the borders . . . I made the high ground into marshland. I made the inundation flood the old mounds. I let the plowlands be (inundated) while every neighborhood thirsted."* (See Lichtheim, *Ancient Egyptian Autobiographies*, 23–24.) This is clear evidence of a drought, with the nomarch using innovative water retention techniques by digging a series of canals and levees. Basically, he hacked the floodplain.

Inscription #6: From the door stele of the Treasurer Neferyu, *"I nourished the great in the year of 'belt tightening.'"* (See Lichtheim, *Ancient Egyptian Autobiographies*, 26–27.) A drought would be accompanied by a year of poor harvests. This is another piece of evidence for at least one arid year in the First Intermediate Period.

Inscription #7: From the tomb of Ankhtifi of Mo'alla (just outside Luxor): *"All of Upper Egypt was dying of hunger but I did not allow anyone to die of hunger in this nome . . . the whole country has become like locusts going up and down stream (in search of food)."* Egyptologists have downplayed the significance of texts such as this (see Stephan Seidlmayer, "First Intermediate Period [ca. 2160–2055 BC]"), saying Ankhtifi is repeating what numerous other tomb owners have stated while also greatly exaggerating (see D. B. Spaniel, "The Date of Ankhtifi of Mo'alla," *Göttinger Miszellen*, vol. 78 [1984]: 87–94). Ankhtifi also makes reference to the ancient Egyptians eating their children, which most modern Egyptologists discredit. While Ankhtifi's tomb inscription follows formulae that are similar to those appearing in other tombs, he goes a step further. Because of the drought, Ankhtifi takes pride in telling posterity that he did not allow anyone in his nome to go hungry. The normal descriptive formula takes an entirely different meaning: Ankhtifi performed the custodial duties of a nomarch in a time of great need, thus showing his leadership abilities.

42. Edward Brovarski, "Ahanakht of Bersheh and the Hare Nome in the First Intermediate Period and Middle Kingdom," *Studies in Ancient Egypt, the Aegean, and the Sudan: Essays in Honor of Dows Dunham on the Occasion of his 90th birthday, June 1, 1980*, ed. William Kelly Simpson and Whitney M. Davis (Boston: Museum of Fine Arts, 1981), 14–30.

43. Brovarski, "Ahanakht of Bersheh and the Hare Nome in the First Intermediate Period and Middle Kingdom."

Chapter 8

1. My favorite history of the Middle Kingdom is Wolfram Grajetzki, *The Middle Kingdom of Ancient Egypt* (London: Gerald Duckworth, 2006).

2. Grajetzki, *Middle Kingdom of Ancient Egypt*, 19.

3. Grajetzki, *Middle Kingdom of Ancient Egypt*, 19–23.

4. Grajetzki, *Middle Kingdom of Ancient Egypt*, 28.

5. For overviews of the site, see William Kelly Simpson, "Lischt," *Lexikon der Ägyptologie*, vol. 3, ed. Wolfgang Helck and Wolfhart Westendorf (Wiesbaden: Otto Harrassowitz, 1979), 1058–61.

6. Dieter Arnold, *The Pyramid Complex of Amenemhat I at Lisht: The Architecture*, Egyptian Expedition Publications of the Metropolitan Museum of Art, vol. 29 (New York: Metropolitan Museum of Art, 2015).

7. Grajetzki, *Middle Kingdom of Ancient Egypt*, 29–32.

8. Dieter Arnold and Peter Jánosi, "The Move to the North: Establishing a New Capital," *Ancient Egypt Transformed: The Middle Kingdom*, ed. Adela Oppenheim et al. (New York: Metropolitan Museum of Art, 2015), 54–67. This co-regency is debated, though. See Grajetzki, *Middle Kingdom of Ancient Egypt*, 33.

9. Arnold and Jánosi, "The Move to the North," 54–67; Grajetzki, *Middle Kingdom of Ancient Egypt*, 55.

10. William Kelly Simpson, *The Literature of Ancient Egypt: An Anthology of Stories, Instructions, Stelae, Autobiographies, and Poetry*, 3rd ed. (New Haven, CT: Yale University Press, 2003), 54–66.

11. See Dieter Arnold, *The South Cemeteries of Lisht, Volume III: The Pyramid Complex of Senwosret I*, Egyptian Expedition Publications of the Metropolitan Museum of Art, vol. 25 (New York: Metropolitan Museum of Art, 1992); Dieter Arnold, *The South Cemeteries of Lisht, Volume I: The Pyramid of Senwosret I*, Egyptian Expedition Publications of the Metropolitan Museum of Art, vol. 22 (New York: Metropolitan Museum of Art, 1988).

12. Wolfram Grajetzki, *Court Officials of the Egyptian Middle Kingdom* (London: Gerald Duckworth, 2009), 132–33.

13. Seen in the tomb of Khnumhotep II: Naguib Kanawati and Linda Evans, *Beni Hasan, Volume 1: The Tomb of Khnumhotep II*, The Australian Centre for Egyptology, Report 36 (Oxford: Aris and Phillips, 2014).

14. For overviews of Middle Egyptian, see James P. Allen, *Middle Egyptian: An Introduction to the Language and Culture of Hieroglyphs* (Cambridge: Cambridge University Press, 2000); Mark Collier and Bill Manley, *How to Read Egyptian Hieroglyphs: A Step-by-Step Guide to Teach Yourself*, rev. ed. (Berkeley: University of California Press, 2003); Richard B. Parkinson, "The Impact of Middle Kingdom Literature: Ancient and Modern," in Oppenheim et al., *Ancient Egypt Transformed*, 180–87.

15. R. B. Parkinson, *Voices from Ancient Egypt: An Anthology of Middle Kingdom Writings*, Oklahoma Series in Classical Culture, vol. 9 (Norman: University of Oklahoma Press, 1991), 5–6.

16. For an overview of Itj-Tawy, see Grajetzki, *Middle Kingdom of Ancient Egypt*, 29–31.

17. Although not necessarily for everyone. See Wolfram Grajetzki, *Burial Customs in Ancient Egypt: Life in Death for Rich and Poor* (London: Gerald Duckworth, 2003).

18. Dieter Arnold, *Middle Kingdom Tomb Architecture at Lisht*, Egyptian Expedition Publications of the Metropolitan Museum of Art, vol. 28 (New York: Metropolitan Museum of Art, 2008).

19. Mud-brick construction ramps survive in varying types and quantities at and near Old through Middle Kingdom pyramids. See Dieter Arnold, *Building in Egypt: Pharaonic Stone Masonry* (Oxford: Oxford University Press, 1991), 81–90.

20. Middle Kingdom quarries for hard and soft stones occur mainly in the Eastern Desert, but there are also some in the Western Desert. See Barbara G. Aston et al., "Stone," *Ancient Egyptian Materials and Technology*, ed. Paul T. Nicholson and Ian Shaw (Cambridge: Cambridge University Press, 2000), 5–77, esp. 8–15, figs. 2.1–2 maps, table 2.1; for quarries, see Rosemarie Klemm and Dietrich D. Klemm, *Stones and Quarries in Ancient Egypt*, trans. and ed. Nigel Strudwick (London: British Museum Press, 2008).

21. See Arnold, *South Cemeteries of Lisht, Volume I: The Pyramid of Senwosret I*, 14.

22. Felix Arnold, "Settlement Remains at Lisht-North," *House and Palace in Ancient Egypt: International Symposium in Cairo, April 8 to 11, 1992*, vols. 1 and 2, ed. Manfred Bietak, Österreichische Akademie der Wissenschaften, Denkschriften der Gesamtakademie, vol. 14 (Vienna: Österreichische Akademie der Wissenschaften, 1996), 13–21.

23. "Necklace of Sithathoryunet," Metropolitan Museum of Art, https://www.metmuseum.org/art/collection/search/545532, accessed 5 May 2018; Wolfram Grajetzki, *Tomb Treasures of the Late Middle Kingdom: The Archaeology of Female Burials* (Philadelphia: University of Pennsylvania Press, 2014), 36–45.

24. "Amenemhet and Khnumhotep II at Beni Hasan," in Simpson, *Literature of Ancient Egypt*, 418–24.

25. As the power center shifted from Itj-Tawy to the northeast Delta during what's known as the Second Intermediate Period (ca. 1648–1540 BC), the city must still have had occupants. We believe this because the Victory Stele of Piye—an inscribed stone slab from the Twenty-fifth Dynasty, now in the Egyptian Museum in Cairo—mentions Itj-Tawy. That was some 1,100 years after the city served as Egypt's capital. This identification is not certain, though. The stele may have referred not to the old capital, but to another city, or to the general region.

26. The phrase "White Walls" (*Inbu-Hedj*) refers to pharaonic Memphis. Steven Snape, *The Complete Cities of Ancient Egypt* (London: Thames and Hudson, 2014), 170; see also Nadine Moeller, *The Archaeology of Urbanism in Ancient Egypt, From the Predynastic Period to the End of the Middle Kingdom* (Cambridge: Cambridge University Press, 2016), 158–60.

27. Unlike some early Middle Kingdom "soul house" models (Aikaterini Koltsida, *Social Aspects of Ancient Egyptian Domestic Architecture*, British Archaeological Reports International Series, book 1608 [Oxford: Archaeopress, 2007], pls. 11–15) and New Kingdom and later housing (Dieter Arnold, *The Encyclopedia of Ancient Egyptian Architecture* [Princeton, NJ: Princeton University Press, 2003], 112), including Late Period multistory house models, the archaeology of the Middle Kingdom features less evidence for multiple floors (versus rooftop access) from the many state-founded communities and portions of a few organic settlements. Many dwellings might have an upper floor implied, but not necessarily confirmed, by the presence of stairways and other features found in housing at Lahun (where staircases are often affiliated with granaries), Elephantine (a potential multistory building H84; houses H70 and H93), Tell el-Dab'a (a palatial complex), North Lisht (Houses A 1.3 and A 3.3), and elsewhere (Moeller, *Archaeology of Urbanism in Ancient Egypt*, 285, 311, 314, fig. 8.44, 336–37, 341, 352–55, fig. 9.10, 361–64, figs. 9.18–19, 370; see also Stephen Quirke, *Egyptian Sites: Lahun. A Town in Egypt 1800 B.C., and the History of Its Landscape* [London: Golden House Publications, 2005], 49).

28. Percy Newberry, *El Bersheh, Part I: The Tomb of Tehuti-hetep* (London: Egypt Exploration Fund, 1895).

29. Sarah Parcak et al., "Satellite Evidence of Archaeological Site Looting in Egypt: 2002–2013," *Antiquity*, vol. 90, no. 349 (2016): 185–205, https://doi.org/10.15184/aqy.2016.1.

30. Seen in the rock-cut tombs of Tell el Amarna. See Norman de Garis Davies, *The Rock Tombs of el Amarna* (London: Egypt Exploration Fund, 1903).

31. But this cemetery has had few tombs excavated. See Wolfram Grajetzki, "Multiple Burials in Ancient Egypt to the End of the Middle Kingdom," *Life and Afterlife in Ancient Egypt During the Middle Kingdom and Second Intermediate Period*, ed. Silke Grallert and Wolfram Grajetzki, GHP Egyptology 7 (London: Golden House Publications, 2007), 16–34.

32. For another example of a tomb with a mud-brick causeway, see Alexander Badawy, *A History of Egyptian Architecture, Volume 2: The First Intermediate Period, the Middle Kingdom, and the Second Intermediate Period* (Berkeley: University of California Press, 1966), 152, fig. 59; and at Lisht, Grajetzki, *Tomb Treasures of the Late Middle Kingdom*, 18, fig. 2.

33. For an overview of painting and artistic styles in ancient Egypt, see W. Stevenson Smith, *The Art and Architecture of Ancient Egypt*, rev. with additions by William Kelly Simpson (New Haven, CT: Yale University Press, 1998).

34. Numerous examples of Middle Kingdom painting can be found in Oppenheim et al., *Ancient Egypt Transformed*.

35. Discussions of these and other Middle Kingdom titles can be seen in Henry George Fischer, *Egyptian Titles of the Middle Kingdom: A Supplement to Wm. Ward's Index*, 2nd ed., rev. and augmented (New York: Metropolitan Museum of Art, 1997).

36. See Collier and Manley, *How to Read Egyptian Hieroglyphs*, 41; and Grajetzki, *Court Officials of the Egyptian Middle Kingdom*, 101.

37. See Ingrid Melandri, "Female Burials in the Funerary Complexes of the Twelfth Dynasty: An Architectonic Approach," *The World of Middle Kingdom Egypt (2000–1550 BC), Volume II: Contributions on Archaeology, Art, Religion, and Written Records*, ed. Gianluca Miniaci and Wolfram Grajetzki, Middle Kingdom Studies, book 2 (London: Golden House Publications, 2016), 161–79.

38. For a discussion on the types of Middle Kingdom kilts and garments in general for commoners, the military, priests, the elite, royalty, and foreigners in Egypt, see Philip J. Watson, *Costume of Ancient Egypt*, Costume Reference (London: B. T. Batsford, 1987), 12–17, 30, 39–40, 47–48, 51, 55.

39. Although women rarely received their own tomb chapels in ancient Egypt, a few examples exist, such as a Middle Kingdom vizier, Intefiqer, building his mother, Senet, a tomb in Thebes (Gay Robins, *Women in Ancient Egypt* [Cambridge, MA: Harvard University Press, 1993], 100, 165), whereas mothers were honored widely in ancient Egyptian

society, inscriptions (e.g., the Middle Kingdom text known as *Teaching of Duaf's son Khety*), and male-dominated mortuary settings (Robins, *Women in Ancient Egypt*, 106–7).

40. See Janine Bourriau, *Pharaohs and Mortals: Egyptian Art in the Middle Kingdom*, Fitzwilliam Museum Publications (Cambridge and New York: Cambridge University Press, 1998), 144, pl. 149.

41. Carol Andrews, *Amulets of Ancient Egypt* (London: British Museum Press, 1994).

42. Janet Richards, *Society and Death in Ancient Egypt: Mortuary Landscapes of the Middle Kingdom* (Cambridge: Cambridge University Press, 2005), 196–97, E830 N 780 Burial 9, fig. 97.

43. Aidan Dodson and Salima Ikram, *The Tomb in Ancient Egypt: Royal and Private Sepulchres from the Early Dynastic Period to the Romans* (Cairo: American University in Cairo Press, 2008), 36–38.

Chapter 9

1. Christine Finn, "Recreating the Sounds of Tutankhamun's Trumpets," BBC News, 18 April 2011, http://www.bbc.com/news/world-middle-east-13092827, accessed 9 March 2018.

2. Brad Jones, "We Just Discovered One of Our Closest Earth-Like Planets Ever," *Futurism*, 15 November 2017, https://futurism.com/discovered-closest-earth-like-planets/, accessed 10 March 2018.

3. "Number of Smartphone Users Worldwide from 2014 to 2020 (in Billions)," Statista, the Statistics Portal, 2016, https://www.statista.com/statistics/330695/number-of-smartphone-users-worldwide/, accessed 10 March 2018.

4. Rebecca J. Rosen, "Why Today's Inventors Need to Read More Science Fiction," *Atlantic*, 20 September 2013, https://www.theatlantic.com/technology/archive/2013/09/why-todays-inventors-need-to-read-more-science-fiction/279793/, accessed 10 March 2018.

5. "Sub-$50 Small Multirotor Drone Mini Reviews," RotorCopters, http://www.rotorcopters.com/sub-50-multirotor-drone-mini-reviews/, accessed 30 March 2018.

6. "Micro and Nano Drones—the Smaller the Better," Dronethusiast, https://www.dronethusiast.com/best-micro-mini-nano-drones/, accessed 30 March 2018.

7. Telmo Adão et al., "Hyperspectral Imaging: A Review on UAV-Based Sensors, Data Processing and Applications for Agriculture and Forestry," *Remote Sensing*, vol. 9, no. 11 (2017): 1110, https://doi.org/10.3390/rs9111110.

8. Eyal Ben-Dor, ed., "Hyperspectral Remote Sensing," *Remote Sensing*, special issue, vol. 12, no. 2 (2012), http://www.mdpi.com/journal/remotesensing/special_issues/hyperspectral-remote-sens, accessed 8 March 2018.

9. Andy Extance, "Spectroscopy in Your Hands," *Chemistry World*, 2 February 2018, https://www.chemistryworld.com/feature/handheld-spectrometers/3008475.article, accessed 9 March 2018.

10. "ASD Terraspec 4 Hi-Res Mineral Spectrometer," Malvern Panalytical, https://www.asd.com/products-and-services/terraspec/terraspec-4-hi-res-mineral-spectrometer, accessed 31 March 2018.

11. Sarah Parcak and Gregory Mumford, "Satellite Imagery Detection of a Possible Hippodrome and Other Features at the Ptolemaic-Roman Port Town of Taposiris Magna," *Journal of Ancient Egyptian Interconnections*, vol. 4, no. 4 (2012): 30–34, https://doi.org/10.2458/azu_jaei_v04i4_gregory_mumford.

12. Janet Nichol and Pui Hang To, "Temporal Characteristics of Thermal Satellite Sensors for Urban Heat Island Analysis," *Earthzine*, 8 July 2011, https://earthzine.org/2011/07/08/temporal-characteristics-of-thermal-satellite-sensors-for-urban-heat-island-analysis/, accessed 31 March 2018.

13. Jesse Casana et al., "Archaeological Aerial Thermography: A Case Study at the Chaco-Era Blue J Community, New Mexico," *Journal of Archaeological Science*, vol. 45 (2014): 207–19, https://doi.org/10.1016/j.jas.2014.02.015.

14. See "Remote Sensing," Harris Aerial, https://www.harrisaerial.com/remote-sensing/, accessed 12 March 2018.

15. Sarah Parcak et al., "Satellite Evidence of Archaeological Site Looting in Egypt: 2002–2013," *Antiquity*, vol. 90, no. 349 (2016): 188–205, https://doi.org/10.15184/aqy.2016.1.

16. See "Magnitude Surveys Ltd," http://www.magnitudesurveys.co.uk/, accessed 31 March 2018.

17. Alex Davies, "What Is LiDAR, Why Do Self-Driving Cars Need It, and Can It See Nerf Bullets?" *Wired*, 6 February 2018, https://www.wired.com/story/lidar-self-driving-cars-luminar-video/, accessed 31 March 2018.

18. Kazuya Nakajima et al., "3D Environment Mapping and Self-Position Estimation by a Small Flying Robot Mounted with a Movable Ultrasonic Range Sensor," *Journal of Electrical Systems and Information Technology*, vol. 4, no. 2 (2017): 289–98, https://doi.org/10.1016/j.jesit.2017.01.007.

19. Susanne Brinkmann et al., "Laser Cleaning Tomb Paintings at Luxor (TT49)," *Kmt: A Modern Journal of Ancient Egypt*, vol. 21, no. 3 (2010): 18–34.

20. I. Bukreeva et al., "Virtual Unrolling and Deciphering of Herculaneum Papyri by X-Ray Phase-Contrast Tomography," *Nature: Scientific Reports*, vol. 6, no. 27227 (2016): https://doi.org/10.1038/srep27227.

21. Vito Mocella et al., "Revealing Letters in Rolled Herculaneum Papyri by X-Ray Phase-Contrast Imaging," *Nature Communications*, vol. 6, no. 5895 (2015): https://doi.org/10.1038/ncomms6895.

22. Robert Perkins, "A Birder in the Hand: Mobile Phone App Can Recognize Birds from Photos," *Caltech News*, 14 December 2016, http://www.caltech.edu/news/birder-hand-mobile-phone-app-can-recognize-birds-photos-53288, accessed 14 December 2016.

23. Nikki Aldeborgh, "GBDX + PoolNet: Identifying Pools on Satellite Imagery," DigitalGlobe, 13 July 2016, https://platform.digitalglobe.com/gbdx-poolnet-identifying-pools-satellite-imagery/, accessed 31 March 2018.

24. See "Google Books Ngram Viewer," Google, https://books.google.com/ngrams, accessed 31 March 2018.

25. Michael Blanding, "Plagiarism Software Reveals a New Source for 11 of Shakespeare's Plays," *New York Times*, 7 February 2018, https://www.nytimes.com/2018/02/07/books/plagiarism-software-unveils-a-new-source-for-11-of-shakespeares-plays.html, accessed 31 March 2018.

26. Marc Raibert, "Meet Spot, the Robot Dog That Can Run, Hop, and Open Doors," TED2017, https://www.ted.com/talks/marc_raibert_meet_spot_the_robot_dog_that_can_run_hop_and_open_doors, accessed 24 March 2018.

27. Christina Poletto, "When Roomba Met Dog Poop: Man's 'Poopocalypse' Goes Viral," *Today*, 16 August 2016, https://www.today.com/home/when-roomba-met-dog-poop-man-s-poopocalypse-goes-viral-t101883, accessed 24 March 2018.

28. Anthony Cuthbertson, "DARPA Plans Autonomous 'Flying Insect' Drones with Skills to Match Birds of Prey," *International Business Times*, 2 January 2015, http://www.ibtimes.co.uk/darpa-plans-autonomous-flying-insect-drones-skills-match-birds-prey-1481554, accessed 15 February 2018.

29. Antoinette Mercurio, "The Little Robot That Could: Professors of History and Computer Science Collaborate on Robot Archaeology Project," Ryerson University, 13 October 2017, https://www.ryerson.ca/news-events/news/2017/10/the-little-robot-that-could/, accessed 14 February 2018.

30. "Geno DNA Ancestry Kit," *National Geographic*, https://genographic.nationalgeographic.com/, accessed 14 February 2018.

31. Zahi Hawass et al., "Ancestry and Pathology in King Tutankhamun's Family," *Journal of the American Medical Association*, vol. 303, no. 7 (2010): 638–47, https://doi.org/10.1001/jama.2010.121.

32. Christina Warinner et al., "A New Era in Palaeomicrobiology: Prospects for Ancient Dental Calculus as a Long-Term Record of the Human Oral Microbiome," *Philosophical Transactions of the Royal Society B: Biological Sciences*, vol. 370, no. 1660 (2015), https://doi.org/10.1098/rstb.2013.0376.

33. "Face of First Brit Revealed," UCL News, University College London, 7 February 2018, https://www.ucl.ac.uk/news/news-articles/0218/070218-Face-of-cheddar-man -revealed, accessed 6 February 2018.

34. Jane Wakefield, "TED2017: Scary Robots That Want to Be Useful," BBC News, 17 April 2017, http://www.bbc.com/news/technology-39656040, accessed 31 March 2018.

35. Douglas Gantenbein, "Kinect Launches a Surgical Revolution," Microsoft Research Blog, 7 June 2012, https://www.microsoft.com/en-us/research/blog/kinect-launches-surgical -revolution/, accessed 31 March 2018.

36. "Surgical Simulation Training," CAE Healthcare, https://caehealthcare.com/surgical -simulation, accessed 30 March 2018.

37. "MorphoSource," MorphoSource by Duke University, https://www.morphosource.org/, accessed 8 February 2018.

38. Kristina Killgrove, "How to Print Your Own 3D Replicas of Homo Naledi and Other Hominin Fossils," Forbes, 19 September 2015, https://www.forbes.com/sites /kristinakillgrove/2015/09/19/how-to-print-your-own-3d-replicas-of-homo-naledi-and -other-hominin-fossils/#657a831112c0, accessed 4 February 2018.

39. David L. Chandler, "Surfaces Get Smooth or Bumpy on Command," MIT News, 11 June 2015, http://news.mit.edu/2015/controllable-surface-textures-0611, accessed 7 February 2018.

40. Jennifer Chu, "New 3D Printer Is 10 Times Faster Than Commercial Counterparts," MIT News, 29 November 2017, http://news.mit.edu/2017/new-3-d-printer-10-times-faster -commercial-counterparts-1129, accessed 6 February 2018.

41. "Sir Arthur's Quotations," The Arthur C. Clarke Foundation, https://www.clarkefoundation .org/about-sir-arthur/sir-arthurs-quotations/, accessed 19 February 2018.

42. Brad Jones, "Planet Hunter," Futurism, 15 November 2017, https://futurism.com /discovered-closest-earth-like-planets/, accessed 19 February 2018.

43. "The Drake Equation," SETI Institute, https://www.seti.org/drakeequation, accessed 15 February 2018.

44. "The Drake Equation."

45. As presented in Erich von Däniken, Chariots of the Gods? Unsolved Mysteries of the Past (New York: G. P. Putnam's Sons, 1968).

46. "How the World Reacted to Elon Musk's Falcon Heavy Launch," BBC News, 7 February 2018, http://www.bbc.com/news/world-us-canada-42973449, accessed 31 March 2018.

47. Viviane Slon et al., "Neandertal and Denisovan DNA from Pleistocene Sediments," Science, vol. 356, no. 6338 (2017): 605–8, http://doi.org/10.1126/science.aam9695.

Chapter 10

1. Jean-François Champollion, Lettre à M. Dacier relative à l'alphabet des hiéroglyphes phonétiques (Paris: Firmin Didot Père et Fils, 1822).

2. Stephens & Catherwood Revisited: Maya Ruins and the Passage of Time (Washington, DC: Dumbarton Oaks Research Library and Collection, Trustees for Harvard University, 2015).

3. Hiram Bingham, "In the Wonderland of Peru—Rediscovering Machu Picchu," National Geographic Magazine, April 1913, https://www.nationalgeographic.com/magazine/1913 /04/machu-picchu-peru-inca-hiram-bingham-discovery/, accessed 20 February 2018.

4. "Helena, St. (c. 255–c. 230)," The Oxford Dictionary of the Christian Church, ed. F. L. Cross and E. A. Livingstone (Oxford: Oxford University Press, published online 2009), https:// doi.org/10.1093/acref/9780192802903.001.0001.

5. Georgina Howell, Gertrude Bell: Queen of the Desert, Shaper of Nations (New York: Sarah Crichton Books, Farrar, Straus and Giroux, 2008).

6. Kathleen Kenyon, Digging Up Jericho (London: Ernest Benn, 1957).

7. Agatha Christie, Agatha Christie: An Autobiography (New York: Berkley Books, 1991).

8. Agatha Christie Mallowan, "A-sitting on a Tell," Come, Tell Me How You Live (London: Agatha Christie Limited, A Chorian Company, 1946). Reprinted by permission of Harper Collins Publishers.

9. Daniel E. Slotnik, "Barbara Mertz, Egyptologist and Mystery Writer, Dies at 85," *New York Times*, 13 August 2013, http://www.nytimes.com/2013/08/14/arts/barbara-mertz-egyptologist-and-mystery-writer-dies-at-85.html, accessed 18 February 2018.

10. "Meet the Egyptian Female Archaeologist Leading Her Own Excavation at Just 27 Years Old," *Cairoscene*, 19 May 2017, http://www.cairoscene.com/ArtsAndCulture/Meet-the-Egyptian-Female-Archaeologist-Leading-Her-Own-Excavation-at-Just-27-Years-Old, accessed 17 February 2018.

11. See "Archaeology/In Your Hands," https://digventures.com/, accessed 17 February 2018.

12. "Chocolate Artefact," *DigVentures*, https://digventures.com/shop/chocolate-artefact/, accessed 19 May 2018.

13. See Lyminge Archaeological Project, http://www.lymingearchaeology.org/, accessed 19 February 2018.

14. François Dubé, "Breaking New Ground," *ChinAfrica*, 8 September 2017, http://www.chinafrica.cn/Africa/201709/t20170908_800104306.html, accessed 19 February 2018.

15. Natan Kellermann, "Epigenetic Transmission of Holocaust Trauma: Can Nightmares Be Inherited?" *Israeli Journal of Psychiatry and Related Sciences*, vol. 50, no. 1 (2013): 33–39.

16. Amy Boddy et al., "Fetal Microchimerism and Maternal Health: A Review and Evolutionary Analysis of Cooperation and Conflict Beyond the Womb," *BioEssays*, vol. 37, no. 10 (2015): 1106–18, https://doi.org/10.1002/bies.201500059.

17. Alan Rogers et al., "Early History of Neanderthals and Denisovans," *Proceedings of the National Academy of Sciences*, vol. 114, no. 37 (2017): 9859–63, https://doi.org/10.1073/pnas.1706426114.

18. Ann Gibbons, "Signs of Symbolic Behavior Emerged at the Dawn of Our Species in Africa," *Science News*, 15 March 2018, http://www.sciencemag.org/news/2018/03/signs-symbolic-behavior-emerged-dawn-our-species-africa, accessed 26 April 2018.

19. Richard Potts et al., "Environmental Dynamics During the Onset of the Middle Stone Age in Eastern Africa," *Science*, vol. 360, no. 6384 (2018), https://doi.org/10.1126/science.aao2200.

20. Douglas Fry and Patrik Söderberg, "Lethal Aggression in Mobile Forager Bands and Implications for the Origins of War," *Science*, vol. 341, no. 6143 (2013): 270–73, https://doi.org/10.1126/science.1235675.

21. Colin K. Khoury et al., "Origins of Food Crops Connect Countries Worldwide," *Proceedings of the Royal Society B: Biological Sciences*, vol. 283, no. 1832 (2016), https://doi.org/10.1098/rspb.2016.0792.

22. Jeremy Cherfas, "A Map of Where Your Food Originated May Surprise You," *The Salt*, National Public Radio, 13 June 2016, www.npr.org/sections/thesalt/2016/06/13/481586649/a-map-of-where-your-food-originated-may-surprise-you, accessed 20 March 2018.

23. Luke Fleming, "Linguistic Exogamy and Language Shift in the Northwest Amazon," *International Journal of the Sociology of Language*, vol. 2016, no. 240 (2016): 9–27, https://doi.org/10.1515/ijsl-2016-0013; Jean E. Jackson, *The Fish People: Linguistic Exogamy and Tukanoan Identity in Northwest Amazonia*, Cambridge Studies in Social Anthropology, (Cambridge: Cambridge University Press, 1983), xix, 287.

24. Peter Ralph and Graham Coop, "The Geography of Recent Genetic Ancestry Across Europe," *PLOS Biology*, vol. 11, no. 5 (2013): e1001555, https://doi.org/10.1371/journal.pbio.1001555; Susan Bell, "Researcher Uses DNA to Demonstrate Just How Closely Everyone on Earth Is Related to Everyone Else," *PHYSORG*, 8 August 2013, https://phys.org/news/2013-08-dna-earth.html, accessed 21 March 2018.

25. Colin McEvedy and Richard M. Jones, *Atlas of World Population History* (Middlesex, UK: Penguin Books, 1978); John Carl Nelson, *Historical Atlas of the Eight Billion: World Population History 3000 BCE to 2020* (CreateSpace Independent Publishing Platform, 2014).

26. Peter Brand, "Reuse and Restoration," *UCLA Encyclopedia of Egyptology*, ed. Willeke Wendrich, 2010, https://escholarship.org/uc/item/2vp6065d, accessed 19 March 2018.

27. Thomas Asbridge, *The Crusades: The War for the Holy Land* (London: Simon and Schuster, 2010).

28. Olivia Solon, "Elon Musk: We Must Colonise Mars to Preserve Our Species in a Third World War," *Guardian*, 11 March 2018, www.theguardian.com/technology/2018/mar/11/elon-musk-colonise-mars-third-world-war, accessed 21 March 2018.

29. Stephen Petranek, *How We'll Live on Mars*, TED Books (New York: Simon and Schuster, 2015).

30. Michael Emslie et al., "Expectations and Outcomes of Reserve Network Performance Following Re-zoning of the Great Barrier Reef Marine Park," *Current Biology*, vol. 25, no. 8 (2015): 983–92, https://doi.org/10.1016/j.cub.2015.01.073.

31. Karen Frances Eng, "The Man Who Plants Trees: Shubhendu Sharma Is Reforesting the World, One Patch at a Time," *TEDBlog*, 9 May 2014, https://blog.ted.com/shubhendu sharma/, accessed 21 March 2018.

Chapter 11

1. Jaromir Malek et al., "Howard Carter's Notes on Various Objects Found in the Tomb of Tutankhamun (TAA i.2.10)," Griffith Institute, University of Oxford, http://www.griffith.ox.ac.uk/gri/taa_i_2_10.html, accessed 31 March 2018. On object # 435: "(H. 47.6). Crater with flanking ornament Finger marks of thieves on interior walls."

2. "The Antiquities Coalition Warns American Heritage Is a Casualty of Government Shutdown," *Antiquities Coalition* (blog), 22 January 2018, https://theantiquitiescoalition.org/blog-posts/american-heritage-casualty-of-shutdown/, accessed 22 January 2018.

3. Brian Vastag, "Amid Protests and Looting, Officials Work to Preserve Egypt's Treasures," *Washington Post*, 30 January 2011, http://www.washingtonpost.com/wp-dyn/content/article/2011/01/30/AR2011013003244.html, accessed 11 March 2018.

4. Elizabeth C. Stone, "Patterns of Looting in Southern Iraq," *Antiquity*, vol. 82, no. 315 (2008): 125–38, https://doi.org/10.1017/S0003598X00096496.

5. Sarah Parcak et al., "Satellite Evidence of Archaeological Site Looting in Egypt: 2002–2013," *Antiquity*, vol. 90, no. 349 (2016): 188–205, https://doi.org/10.15184/aqy.2016.1.

6. Sarah Parcak et al., "Using Open Access Satellite Data Alongside Ground Based Remote Sensing: An Assessment, with Case Studies from Egypt's Delta," *Geosciences*, vol. 7, no. 4 (2017): 94, https://doi.org/10.3390/geosciences7040094.

7. Across the world, colleagues are asking the same questions in their areas. Following on Elizabeth Stone's work, many projects are now monitoring Iraq and Syria, where the level of intentional site destruction and looting has become mind-boggling. (See Michael Danti et al., "The American Schools of Oriental Research Cultural Heritage Initiatives: Monitoring Cultural Heritage in Syria and Northern Iraq by Geospatial Imagery," *Geosciences*, vol. 7, no. 4 [2017]: 95, https://doi.org/10.3390/geosciences7040095; and Jesse Casana and Mitra Panahipour, "Notes on a Disappearing Past: Satellite-Based Monitoring of Looting and Damage to Archaeological Sites in Syria," *Journal of Eastern Mediterranean Archaeology and Heritage Studies*, vol. 2, no. 2 [2014]: 128–51, https://doi.org/10.5325/jeasmedarcherstu.2.2.0128.) There are multiple videos of mindless brutes smashing 4,000-year-old stone monuments with hammers ("Casualties of War," *PBS NewsHour*, 27 February 2015, https://www.youtube.com/watch?v=DBrHUrUMifk, accessed 11 March 2018). But here's a bit of perspective: the looting got bad following ISIL's takeover—bad guys who hate culture destroy culture—but similar to what we saw in Egypt, I would guess that looting in Syria started to worsen in 2010 following the 2006–9 drought, alongside the global recession. The looting since the civil war began likely exacerbated an already bad situation and may represent ISIL cashing in on an already established market.

8. Protect and Preserve International Cultural Property Act, H.R. 1493, United States House of Representatives, https://www.congress.gov/bill/114th-congress/house-bill/1493 (19 March 2015), accessed 28 October 2017.

9. "Secretary Kerry Signs Cultural Property Protection Agreement with Egypt," US Department of State, https://2009-2017.state.gov/r/pa/prs/ps/2016/11/264632.htm, accessed 26 October 2017.

10. Julie Zauzmer and Sarah Pulliam Bailey, "Hobby Lobby's $3 Million Smuggling Case Casts a Cloud over the Museum of the Bible," *Washington Post*, 6 July 2017, https://www.washingtonpost.com/news/acts-of-faith/wp/2017/07/06/hobby-lobbys-3-million

-smuggling-case-casts-a-cloud-over-the-museum-of-the-bible/?utm_term=
.e8d7123583da, accessed 7 March 2018.

11. Patty Gerstenblith, "Controlling the International Market in Antiquities: Reducing the Harm, Preserving the Past," *Chicago Journal of International Law*, vol. 8, no. 1 (2007): 169–95.

12. Zauzmer and Bailey, "Hobby Lobby's $3 Million Smuggling Case."

13. Sarah Parcak, "Moving from Space-Based to Ground-Based Solutions in Remote Sensing for Archaeological Heritage: A Case Study from Egypt," *Remote Sensing*, vol. 9, no. 12 (2017): 1297, https://doi.org/10.3390/rs9121297.

14. Tom Mueller, "How Tomb Raiders Are Stealing Our History," *National Geographic Magazine*, June 2016, https://www.nationalgeographic.com/magazine/2016/06/looting-ancient-blood-antiquities/, accessed 28 October 2017.

15. Danny Lewis, "How 'Operation Mummy's Curse' Is Helping Fight Terrorism," *Smithsonian SmartNews*, 28 April 2015, https://www.smithsonianmag.com/smart-news/federal-agents-are-fighting-terrorism-tracking-down-missing-mummies-180955113/, accessed 28 October 2017; "ICE Returns Ancient Artifacts to Egypt," US Immigration and Customs Enforcement, 1 December 2016, https://www.ice.gov/news/releases/ice-returns-ancient-artifacts-egypt#wcm-survey-target-id, accessed 6 March 2018.

16. Kathleen Caulderwood, "US Returns $2.5M In Egyptian Antiquities as Experts Call for Tougher Punishment on Smugglers," *International Business Times*, 22 April 2015, http://www.ibtimes.com/us-returns-25m-egyptian-antiquities-experts-call-tougher-punishment-smugglers-1892622, accessed 28 October 2017.

17. Caulderwood, "US Returns $2.5M In Egyptian Antiquities."

18. "18 U.S. Code § 2315-Sale or Receipt of Stolen Goods, Securities, Moneys, or Fraudulent State Tax Stamps," *Legal Information Institute*, https://www.law.cornell.edu/uscode/text/18/2315, accessed 28 October 2017.

19. David Silverman and Jennifer Houser Wegner, "Unpublished Report on the Tripartite Coffin Set, Penn Museum, University of Pennsylvania Museum," provided by a confidential source at US Homeland Security in January 2015.

20. "Ancient Art," https://caryatidconservation.sharepoint.com/Pages/ancient.aspx, accessed 28 October 2017, link no longer working.

21. Jaromir Malek, *Topographical Bibliography of Ancient Egyptian Hieroglyphic Texts, Statues, Reliefs and Paintings. Volume VIII: Objects of Provenance Not Known: Statues* (Leuven: Peeters, 1999), 846–47.

22. Blythe Bowman Proulx, "Archaeological Site Looting in 'Glocal' Perspective: Nature, Scope, and Frequency," *American Journal of Archaeology*, vol. 117, no. 1 (2013): 111–25, https://doi.org/10.3764/aja.117.1.0111.

23. Louisa Loveluck, "Islamic State Sets Up 'Ministry of Antiquities' to Reap the Profits of Pillaging," *Telegraph*, 30 May 2015, http://www.telegraph.co.uk/news/worldnews/islamic-state/11640670/Islamic-State-sets-up-ministry-of-antiquities-to-reap-the-profits-of-pillaging.html, accessed 3 February 2018.

24. "Notice: Two Sentry Guards Killed at the Archaeological Site at Deir el-Bersha in Egypt," *Association for Research into Crimes Against Art*, 22 February 2016, http://art-crime.blogspot.com/2016/02/one-killed-one-injured-at.html, accessed 8 March 2018.

25. Morag M. Kersel, "Go, Do Good! Responsibility and the Future of Cultural Heritage in the Eastern Mediterranean in the 21st Century," *The Future of the Past: From Amphipolis to Mosul, New Approaches to Cultural Heritage Preservation in the Eastern Mediterranean*, ed. Konstantinos Chalikias et al. (Boston: Archaeological Institute of America, 2016), 5–10.

26. Morag Kersel and Andrew C. Hill, "Aerial Innovations: Using Drones to Document Looting," *Oriental Institute News and Notes*, no. 224 (2015): 8–9.

Chapter 12

1. See "Galaxy Zoo," https://www.zooniverse.org/projects/zookeeper/galaxy-zoo/, accessed 19 February 2018.

2. See "Eyewire," https://eyewire.org/explore, accessed 19 February 2018.

3. See "Levantine Ceramics Project," https://www.levantineceramics.org/, accessed 17 February 2018.

4. Karen Eng, "GlobalXplorer° Completes Its First Expedition: What the Crowd Found in Peru," Medium, 10 April 2018, https://medium.com/@globalxplorer/globalxplorer-completes-its-first-expedition-what-the-crowd-found-in-peru-7897ed78ce05, accessed 10 April 2018.

5. Eli Rosenberg, "A Protest Damaged Ancient Monuments in Peru. The Repair Effort Led to the Discovery of Even More," Washington Post, 5 April 2018, https://www.washingtonpost.com/news/speaking-of-science/wp/2018/04/05/a-protest-damaged-ancient-monuments-in-peru-the-repair-effort-led-to-the-discovery-of-even-more/?noredirect=on&utm_term=.ec70c0b29980, accessed 5 April 2018.

6. Chris Hadfield, An Astronaut's Guide to Life on Earth: What Going to Space Taught Me About Ingenuity, Determination, and Being Prepared for Anything (New York: Back Bay Books, Little, Brown, 2015).

7. Chris Hadfield, "We Should Treat Earth as Kindly as We Treat Spacecraft," Wired, 25 November 2013, https://www.wired.com/2013/11/chris-hadfield-wired/, accessed 29 April 2018.

Index

Page numbers in *italics* refer to maps.

Abira (Egyptology student), 215
Abusir el-Malik, 210–12, *211*
Abusir pyramids, 153
Abydos, 127
academic journals, 188–89
Acheulean era, 14
Acre geoglyphs, 110–11
Adams, R. E., 38
aerial laser mapping. *See* LIDAR
aerial photos, 15, 29, 32–36, 63, 75, 110,
    119. *See also* drones
    forestry and, 3–4, 230
    georeferencing and, 21
Afghanistan, 16, 19, 118–19
Africa, 115–18
agate, 151, 161
Ahmed, Ahmed Ibrahim, 162
ahu (megalithic platforms), 113
Akhilesh, Kumar, 14
Akkadian Empire, 137
alabaster vessels, 161
Alaska, 106
Alexander the Great, 42
Alexandria, 28, 62, 100
algorithms, 31
Ali, Mohammed Youssef, 153–54
Al Jazeera English, 202
Allam, Mahmoud, 162
Altinum, 120
Amarna, 91, 99, 154
Amazon, 6, 110–11, 194
Amenemhet I, 146–48, 161, 196
    pyramid of, 148, 153
American Research Center (Egypt), 202
American Schools of Oriental Research,
    187
Amerindians, 85
amethyst, 151, 161
amulets, 143, 161

Amun-Re (Egyptian god), 23, 89, 92
    temple of (Tanis), 90
Ancestry.com, 178
ancient art, 147, 175–76
ancient lives and cultures
    assessing value of objects and, 199–200
    cemeteries and, 11–13
    context and, 45, 47–50
    ever presence of, 196–97
    human signs in objects, 11
    learning from, 7, 195–96
    reconstructing life spans of, 15–16
    reconstructing technologies of, 13–14
Anderson, Chris, 219–20
Angamuco, 108
animal remains, 68
Ankhtifi (nomarch), 143
Antiquities Coalition, 204
antiquities trafficking, 200–215, 229
    repatriation and, 208
Apulia, 120
Arab Spring, 152, 202–5
Arafy, Reda Esmat el-, 162
ArcGIS (software), 94–95
Archaeological Theory class, 47–48
archaeology and archaeologists. *See
    also* space archaeology; *and other
    subfields*
    academic research, access to, 188–89
    aerial photos become tool of, 29, 32–36
    "Aha" moment and, 31–32
    amateur, 15
    basic assumptions of, 47
    crowdsourcing and, 217–30
    diversity and, 187–88, 190, 193–94
    field-school opportunities and, 190
    figuring unknowns of, 104–5, 107–8
    funding and, 28, 172, 183, 191
    future of, 165–71

archaeology and archaeologists (*cont'd*)
  human story and, 198–99
  importance of small discoveries and, 45–48
  knowledge assembly and, 47–48
  low pay and, 68, 70
  museum curators and, 45
  path to career in, 2, 67–68, 70, 215
  perspective and, 195, 197
  project design and, 28, 38
  satellite imagery first used by, 35–43
  subfields of, 2
  technological advances in, 171–84
  unpublished records and, 189
  women and, 185–88
area unit supervisor, 68
ARGON, 35
Arnold, Dieter, 148
arrowheads, 9
Artaxerxes III, 16, 20, 20–25, 209
artificial intelligence, 5
Asaad, Khaled Al-, 10
"A-sitting on a Tell" (Christie), 186–87
Assyrians, 19
Aswan, 8, 186
Aswan Dam, 36, 133
Asyut, 143
Attirampakkam, 14
auger, 53–54
Aurelian, Emperor, 10
Austrian Academy of Sciences, 149
automatic wireless upload, 175
Aztecs, 108

Bader, Bettina, 149–50, 159
Baffin Island, 73
Bamha village, 148
Bayon, Temple of, 193
BBC TV, 51, 53, 57–59, 61, 71–77
Bedouin workers, 49
beer jar, 27–28
Bel, Temple of, 10
Belgium, 120
Belize, 28, 31–32, 108–9
Belize Valley Archaeological Reconnaissance Project, 109
Bell, Gertrude, 185
Beothuk culture, 74
Berger, Lee, 115
Bewley, Robert, 119
Biggings site, 61
Bing, 75
Bingham, Hiram, 111, 185
bioarchaeologists, 12–13, 48, 161
Birch, Thomas, 83
Birka site, 60

Blom, Ron, 41
Blue Nile, 24, 133
bog iron, 79–86, *80*
Bolender, Doug, 51, 53–55, 78, 82
bones, 11–13, 29, 47, 161, 174
Book of Settlements, The (*Landnámabók*), 51, 72
Boston Dynamics, 178
Brande, Scott, 82–83
Brazil, 6, 110–11, 194
Brissaud, Philippe, 96–97, *98*
Britain. *See* United Kingdom
British Ministry of Aircraft Production, 35
British Museum, 42, 71
British Royal Air Force, 35
British Royal Engineers' Balloon Section, 32
British Royal Flying Corps, 33
Bronze Age, collapse of, 47
Bunbury, Judith, 149, 150–51
Bush, George W., 204
Buto, 137
butternut tree, 74

Cairo, 196, 202
Cambodia, 41–42, 193
Camden, William, 34
Canada, 37, 71–86, 106
Canadian Geodetic Survey, 79
Canadian Hydrographic Service, 37
Canchari, *227,* 228
Caracol, 31–32, 42, 108
carnelian, 18, *60,* 91, 151
Carter, Howard, 46, 202
Castillo, Luis Jaime, 111, 226
Catherwood, Frederick, 185
cattle estates (Nile Delta), 126
cedarwood, 126
cell phones, 35, 176, 189, 223
Central African Republic, 116
Central America, 1, 108–11, 185
Chaco Canyon, 39–40, 174
Champollion, Jean-François, 185
Chancay culture, 111
charcoal, 80
Chase, Arlen, 31–32, 42, 108
Chase, Diane, 31–32, 42, 108
chemical signatures, 30, 39, 173–74, 178
Childs, Chase, 71, 75, 77–81, 155, 189
Chile, 112
Chimú culture, 111
China, 113, 191
Chinese Academy of Sciences, 113
Chinese Institute of Remote Sensing and Digital Earth, 41
Chirikure, Shadreck, 116

chlorophyll, 34
Christie, Agatha, 186–87
Christodoulou, Shakira, 159–60
civilizations, collapse of, 112–13, 135–45, 163–64, 197–98
Clarke, Arthur C., 181
Claudius, Emperor, 61
Cleopatra, 45, 193
climate change, 42, 72, 117–18, 135–44
Clinton, Bill, 35
Coben, Larry, 228
Codroy Valley, 81
Coffin Texts, 143
cognitive archaeology, 14
Cold War, 20, 35–37
color photography, 34
Columbia (space shuttle), 38
Coluzzi, Rosa, 119
Constantine, Emperor, 185
copper, 126, 128
coring, 17–19, 51, 149–51
CORONA satellite, 20–22, *21*, 25, 35–36, 41–42, 100, 113
Costa Rica, 40
Crawford, Osbert Guy Stanhope, 33
crop marks, 33–34, 42–43, 64, 100, 120

Dahlak Archipelago, 117
Dalga, 29
Darius III, Emperor, 42
Dashur, 137, 153, 192, 204
data sets, 40
    analysis of, 179
    cost of, 189
dating techniques, 39, 54, 74, 82–84, 112, 210
Death on the Nile (Christie), 186
Decker, George, 73
Defense Advanced Research Projects Agency (DARPA), 178
deflated sites, 38
deforestation, 108, 112–13
Deir el Medina, 11
Demotic writing, 19
Denisovans, 178, 192
Description de l'Égypte (Napoleonic report), 100
De Souza, Jonas Gregorio, 6
diet, ancient, 12–13, 47
differential GPS, 162
dig. *See* excavation; sites
dig artists, 48–49, 159
dig director, 48, 68–70
DigitalGlobe, 31, 64, *65*, *77*, 92, *204*, *221*, *225*
DigVentures, 190–91

disease, 13, 47
Djedet (Egyptian god), 28
Djedkare Isesi, King, 127
Djoser's Pyramid complex, 203
DNA analysis, 13, 47, 167, 178–79, 192, 194
Dorset culture, 74, 81, 85
Drake, Frank, 181
Drake, Martha, 76, 78, 83
Drake Equation, 181
drones, 29, 42–43, 107, 111, 121, 172–75, 179, 222, 226, *226*, 229

Earth Resources Technology Satellite 1 (ERTS-1; *later* Landsat-1), 36–37
East Africa, 113, 192
Easter, Brent, 209
Easter Island, 112–13
Eastern Mediterranean, 90
Eastern Settlement (Greenland), 72
eBay, 201–2
Edfu, 135, 141
Egypt, ancient, 1, 2, 14, 87. *See also* Egyptian Dynasties; Nile Delta; *and specific kings; periods; and sites*
    ancient Nubian sites in, 117
    ancient trade and, 16
    building traditions and, 162
    capital cities and kings of, 47
    civil war in, 90
    fall of civilizations in, 123–24
    hominids predating, 38
    information revealed in tombs and, 45–46
    Nile flood failures and, 136
    nomes and bureaucracy in, 126
    population of, 46
    span of pharaonic civilization in, 16–17, 45–46
    unification of, 45, 47
    unknowns remaining about, 47, 105
Egypt, modern
    antiquities restrictions and, 206
    looting and, 208–13
    permitting and, 96
    potters' methods and, 14
    weather and, 69–70
Egyptian Dynasties
    Fourth, 8, 126
    Fifth, 126
    Sixth, 127
    Eighth, 27, 135
    Ninth, 135
    Tenth, 135
    Eleventh, 158
    Twelfth, 146–47, 151, 154, 158
    Thirteenth, 150

Egyptian Dynasties (cont'd)
  Nineteenth, 88
  Twentieth, 89–90
  Twenty-first, 88–90
  Twenty-second, 89–90
  Twenty-fourth, 90
  Twenty-fifth, 19
  Twenty-sixth, 19
Egyptian Ministry of Antiquities, 152, 162, 191–92
Egyptian Museum. See Museum of Egyptian Antiquities
Egyptian National Authority for Remote Sensing & Space Sciences, 149
Egyptian Nuclear Materials Authority, 162
Egyptian provincial officials, 127
Egyptian sarcophagus, illegally acquired, 209–12
Egyptian Supreme Council of Antiquities, 17
Egyptologists, 14, 36, 46, 188
electromagnetic spectrum, 37
Elephantine Island, 133
elevation models, 114, 148
El Hibeh, 178
Emme, Eugene, 38
Endangered Archaeology in the Middle East and North Africa project (MEGA-Jordan), 119
Endeavor (space shuttle), 148
epigraphy, 68
Erik the Red, 72
Eritrea, 117
ER Mapper (software), 92, 148
Estrada-Belli, Francisco, 109–10
Ethiopian plateau, 133, 136
ethnoarchaeology, 14
Et-Till, 16
Europe, 1, 68, 107
  aerial photos of, 33, 35
  Easter Island and, 112–13
Evans, Damian, 42
Everglades, 107
excavation (digs), 6. See also sites; and specific excavations
  accommodations and food at, 69
  budget and, 69
  challenges of, 49
  context and, 49–50
  core staff and, 70
  deciding where to begin, 28–29
  first, at Mendes, 27–28
  following, online, 190–91
  management of, 48–50
  permitting and, 69
  record keeping at, 49, 189

specialists at, 48–49
students and field-schools at, 190
supply transportation, 69
surprises at, 50
test, 78–79
time limits on, 28
volunteering at, 68, 191
weather and, 69–70
work crews at, 69–70
experimental archaeology, 13–14
extraterrestrials, 182
Eyewire, 217, 220
Eyjolf the Foul, 72

Facebook, 224
facial recognition, 176
facts, truth vs., 46–47
Falcon Heavy, 182
"false color," 30
false door of Intef, 157–58, 158
Farasan Islands, 117
Farouk, Omer, 154, 162
Fawcett, Percy, 110
Feast of Wagy, 27
Feathers, James, 84
field boundaries, 53
fieldwalking, 29
First Intermediate Period (FIP), 130, 140–43, 145, 164
First Nations, 106
Flanders Heritage Agency, 120
Flannery, Kent, 68
Florida, 106–7
Ford, Harrison, 2, 4–5
forestry, 2–3, 30, 34
fossil-rich deposits, 115
4.2 ka BP event, 136–37, 140
France, 17, 34, 90–91, 96
Fundación OACUNAM, 109
furnace or hearth, 81–85, 81

GalaxyZoo, 217
Gale, Edwin "Hockey," 77, 79
Garamantes civilization, 118
gates (site type), 15
Gathings, Dave, 71, 75, 77–79
Gebel Barkal site, 117
gender archaeology, 187
Genographic Project, 178
geoarchaeologists, 17, 83
GeoEye-1 imagery, 64
GeoEye Foundation, 203
geoglyphs, 50, 110
georeferencing, 21
Georgia Department of Natural Resources, 106

geospatial analysis, 112
Germany, 33
    Nazi, 91, 198, 215
Gerstenblith, Patty, 207
Ghaggar-Hara channel, 114
Giza, 6, 8, 123–24, 183, 193, 203
GlobalXplorer (GX), 219–30, *221*, *225*
gold, 16, 19, 23, 45–46, 90–91, 126, 146,
    151, 200
gold falcon pectoral, 91
gold mining, 117
Google Earth, 2, 15, 32, 34, 53, 75, 94,
    110–11, 113, 115, 118–19, 121
Google Ngram Viewer, 177
GPS location data, 189
grave goods, 12, 161
Great Zimbabwe site, 116
Greece, 16, 18, 28
Green family, 206–7
Greenland, 72
grid system, 79
ground-based remote sensing, 51, 62, 65
ground-penetrating radar (GPR), 63, 65, 175
ground surveys, 114
    cost of, 95–96
ground-truthing, 5, 40, 96–97
Guatemala, 109
Gulf of Saint Lawrence, 73–75, 86
Guo Huadong, 41
Gupta, Sanjeev, 114

Haakon, Duke of Norway, 61
Haight, Molly, 155
Hall, Frank, 37
Hanson, Katharyn, 206
haptic technology, 180
Hathor (Egyptian goddess), 128
Heckenberger, Michael, 110
Helena, Saint, 185
Helluland, 73
Herakleopolis, 135, 143, 145
Herculaneum, 176
Herodotus, 20, 193
Hieroglyphics, 47, 91, 185
high-resolution imagery, 15, 30–31, 35,
    40–42, 63, 75, 92–93, 101–2, 111–12,
    115–19, 152, 203–5, *204*, 215
Hissarlik, 105
History Channel, 71
Hobby Lobby, 206–7
Hohokam canal system, 40
hollow ways, 36
Holmul, 109–10
Holt, Andy, 57
Holt-Brook, Sabina, 57
Homeland Security Department, 209

homo erectus, 38
Hop, 81
Horne, Tom, 59–60
Horus, temple of (Tanis), 92, 97–99
Hranf the Dueller, 72
Hu, N. K., 113
Huari culture, 111
human ancestors, 38, 115–16, 192, 197
Hummel, Rexine, 159, 190
Hunt, Terry, 112
hyperspectral imaging, 115, 166, 173–74

ice-core dating, 54
Iceland, 50–56, *52*, 72–74
Icelandic sagas, 51–52, 72, 74
IKONOS, 40
Iliad (Homer), 105
Immigration and Customs Enforcement
    (ICE), 208–10
India, 14, 113–14, 137, 191, 228
Indiana Jones films, 28, 46–47, 171
Indian Institute of Technology, 114
Indigenous cultures
    Amazonian, 110–11
    Easter Island, 112–13
    Mayan, 108–10
    North American, 74–75, 78, 81, 106–7, 208
Indonesia, 113
Indus Valley Civilization, 114, 228
infrared imagery, 30, 34, 37, 40, 64
Ingstad, Anne Stine, 73, 74
Ingstad, Helge, 73–74
Intef (military man), looted tomb of,
    157–64, *158*, *160*
Intef (son of Ankhtifi), 143
International Conference on Satellite
    Archaeology (Beijing, 2004), 41
International Space Station, 29, 230
Inuit, 81
Ipi (Intef's mother), 157–58, *160*, 160, 162,
    164
Iran, 113
Iraq, 36, 118, 137, 185, 203, 207, 212
Iraqi Kurdistan, 42–43
iron, 19, 73–74, 79–80, *80*
iron hydroxides, 136
Islamic Period Nilometers, 133, 136
Islamic State of Iraq and the Levant (ISIL),
    10, 212
Israel, 98, 118, 137
Italy, 34, 61–63, *62*, 119–20
Itj-Tawy, 145–52, 157–63. *See also* Lisht

Jericho, 186
Jet Propulsion Laboratory, 41
jewelry, 14, 45, 91, 151

Johns, Chris, 203
Johnson, Katharine, 107
Johnson, Lyndon B., 36
Jones, Doris May, 224–25
Jordan, 15, 119, 214
Jordanian Department of Antiquities, 119
Juyan Oasis, 113

Karima, 117
Karnak, 191
Keay, Simon, 62–65
Kennedy, David, 15, 119
Kennedy, John F., 36
Kenya, 115, 192
Kenyon, Kathleen, 186
Kersel, Morag, 214
Khartoum, 133
Khmer Empire, 42, 113
Khnum-Nakht mummy, 13
Khonsu (Egyptian god), 89
Khouli, Mousa "Morris," 209
Kinect technology, 180
kivas, 174

Labrador, 73
Lahun, 151
Lake Abhe, 136
Lake Huron, 121
Lake Manzala, 19
Lake Tana, 133, 136
Lake Turkana, 136
Lake Victoria, 133
Lake Zway-Shala, 136
Lancashire, England, 120
Landsat satellites, 36–40, 114, 148
    Landsat-1, 36
    Landsat-8, 121
Landsat Island, 37
landscape, 15–16, 19, 31, 39, 50, 62, 149
    scanning devices for, 174–75
L'Anse aux Meadows site, 73–75, 81, 82, 85
LANYARD, 35
lapis lazuli, 18–19, 91, 151, 161
large-scale satellites, 30
Lasaponara, Rosa, 111, 119
lasers, 175
Late Period, 19, 209, 210
Late Ptolemaic Period, 46
Late Roman Empire, 71
Late Roman Period, 64
Leakey, Louis, 115
Leakey, Louise, 115
Leakey, Maeve, 115
Leakey, Mary, 115
Leakey, Richard, 115
Lebanon, 33, 118, 126

Lee, Christine, 161
Lehr, Deborah, 204
letters, ancient, 14–15
Levantine Ceramics Project, 217–18
Lewis, Joseph, III, 209
LGBTQ+, 187
Li, X., 113
Libya, 19, 118, 212
Libyan tribes, 89–90
LIDAR (LIght Detection And Ranging),
    31–32, 42, 86, 106–11, 114, 120, 166, 173
    hyperspectral cameras and, 174
    3-D maps and, 42
light spectrum, 30, 40, 50, 64. See also
    electromagnetic spectrum; infrared
    imagery
limestone fragments, 29
linguistic exogamy, 194
Lipo, Carl, 112
Lisht, 146–64, 152, 172, 192
    cemeteries and pyramids at, 147, 153–54
    coring near, 149, 149–51
    excavation at looted tomb at, 152–62
    mapping tombs at, 162–63
    modern city of, 46, 146, 153
    record registration at, 189
    reuse of inscribed blocks at, 196
    search for Itj-Tawy at, 146–51
    SRTM 3-D models and, 148
lithic stone tools, 14
Little Ice Age (1450), 72
looting, 152, 199–215
    analysis of, in Egypt, 201, 205–6, 208–9
    causes of, 212
    crowdsourcing to detect, 221, 222, 229
    Itj-Tawy or Lisht and, 152–54, 152, 163
    Jordan and, 214
    mapping, from space, 203–5, 204, 210
    Peru and, 111
    preventing, 214–15
    tiny robots to explore, 178
Louis IX, King of France, 196
Lower Egypt, 126
Luxor (Thebes), 24, 98, 135, 143, 193,
    214–15
Lyminge project, 191

ma'at (divine balance), 137, 143
Mabila, 106
MacGinnis, John, 42
machine learning, 176–77
Machu Picchu, 111, 185, 193, 222, 226
magnetometry, 17–18, 63, 65, 71, 77–79,
    95–96, 175
Maine, 72
Mallowan, Max, 186

Man and His Past (Crawford), 33
Manchester Museum, 13
Mansoura, 18
Mansoura, Battle at, 196
manuscripts, ancient, 175–76
Mapela Hill, 116
Maritime Archaic culture, 74
Markland, 73
Mars, 198
mastaba (tomb), 27
Mattingly, David, 118
Maya, 31–32, 38–39, 108–11, 185, 199
Maya Biosphere Reserve, 109–10
McRae, Georgia, 106
Mediterranean, 47, 68, 136–37
Memphis, 20, 24, 91, 126, 135, 137, 151
Mendes, 17, 19–20, 27, 131, 140, 186
Mentuhotep II, 145–46
Meredith-Williams, Matthew, 116–17
Mertz, Barbara (Elizabeth Peters), 188
Meryt (Tell Ibrahim Awad woman), 124–26,
    128–35, 137–42, 144
Mesopotamia, 137, 185
metal production, 173
metal ring pin, 74
Metropolitan Museum of Art, 12, 47–48,
    148
Mexico, 39, 108
Microsoft, 180
Middle East, 1, 18, 33, 35, 113
Middle Kingdom, 13, 46, 140, 143, 145–64,
    209
    artistic explosion and, 147, 161–62
Middle Woodland culture, 107
mining sites, 175
Minnesota, 72
Mississippi Conference (1984), 39–40
mitochondrial DNA, 106
moai sculptures, 112–13
Mo'alla, 135
Mondo Robot, 220
monsoon rainfalls, 133, 136–37
Montet, Pierre, 90–91, 97
Monuments Men, 215
mortuary cults, 126–27
Mubarak, Hosni, 203
Mueller, Tom, 208, 209
multispectral imagery, 37, 75, 92–94
    merging with panchromatic, 93–94
Mumford, Gregory, 12, 17, 41–42, 68–69,
    71, 78–79, 82, 86, 94–95, 127–28, 154,
    160–61, 196, 200, 218, 219
mummies, 12–14, 161, 178
Museum of Egyptian Antiquities (Egyptian
    Museum), 12–13, 91, 149, 178, 202–3
Museum of the Bible, 207

Musk, Elon, 182
Mut (Egyptian goddess), 89
    temple of, at Tanis, 97

Nakht-Ankh mummy, 13
Napoleonic expedition, 90, 100, 193
NASA (National Aeronautics and Space
    Administration), 36–40, 121, 148–49, 182
    Space Archaeology program, 30
National Geographic Magazine, 87, 203, 208–9
National Geographic Society, 178, 203, 205,
    223
National Museum of Iraq, 185
National Science Foundation, 38
National Stolen Property Act (Egypt), 209
Nature, 6
Nazca lines, 50, 110, *226*, 226
Neanderthals, 105, 178, 192
Near East, 36, 39, 47, 136–37, 186
near infrared, 34
Nectanebo II, 20
neolithic sites, 32
New England, 107
Newfoundland, 73–86, *76*, 95
New Kingdom, 11, 19, 46, 89
New York Times, 38
Nile, 8–9
    ancient branches of, 24–25, 133–34, 141
    failure of, 133–41
    flooding of, 24–25, 101, 133
    Mendesian branch of, 17, 25, 88, 140
    relic courses of, 117
    Sebennytic branch of, 140
    shifting and silting of, 151
    Tanitic branch of, 88, 98–99
Nile Delta, 18–20, 24–25, 68, 117, 133–34,
    151. *See also* Lisht; Mendes; Tell Tebilla;
    Tanis; *and other specific sites*
    ancient rivers and, 25
    archaeological losses in, 25, 36, 100
    cattle estates in, 126
    first dig at Mendes in, 27
    flooding and drought in, 133–41
    Persian invasion of, 24–25
    settlement patterns in, 130–31
    workwomen in, 196
Nilometers, 133, 136
nomarchs, 126–27, 142, 155
North America, 71–72, 105–7, 121–22
North Carolina, 106
North House, Papa Stour, 57–61, *58*, *60*
Nubia, 6, 16, 19, 98, 117, 126–27, 146
nutrition, 13, 140, 161. *See also* diet

obsidian 192
ocean drones, 121

ocher, 192
Okasha, Adel, 192
Old Kingdom, 24, 27, 46, 126–28, 130
    collapse of, 135–45, 163–64
on-site specialists, 68
open-access imagery, 75
open-access journals, 189
OpenROV ocean drone, 121
Operation Mummy's Curse, 208–9
optically stimulated luminescence (OSL), 84
Osiris (Egyptian god), 23
osteoarchaeological analysis, 47. *See also*
    bones
Ostia, 61
Ouimet, William, 107
oxygen isotope analysis, 137
Oxyrhynchus, 14

Pachacamac, 226–27
PACUNAM LiDAR Initiative, 109
Pakistan, 114
paleobotanists, 48
Paleolithic period, 11, 39
Palestine, 99
Palmyra, 9–10
panchromatic data, 92–93
pansharpening, 93
Papa Stour, 56–61, *56, 58*
Pappu, Shanti, 14
Parcak, Aaron, 1
pareidolia, 63
Parks Canada, 74
Pärssinen, Martti, 110
Pavlish, Larry, 17, 18
Pepi I, 127
Pepi II, 127–28, 135
Per-Banebdjedet, 27
permitting, 76–77, 96, 172, 191–92
Persians, 19–20
Peru, 111, 193, *221,* 221–28, *225, 226*
Peruvian Ministry of Culture, 222
Peters, Elizabeth, 188
Petra Junior Rangers, 214
Petra National Trust, 214
Petrie, Cameron, 114
phase-contrast X-ray imaging, 176
Philae island, 8
Phoenix, Arizona, 40
photographs. *See also* aerial photographs; *and
    specific satellites; and types of satellite imagery*
    automatic uploading of, 189
    dig site, 49
physical anthropologists, 13
Pi-Ramesses, 88–91
Piramide Naranjada, 111
pixels, 30–31

planets, archaeology on other, 181–82
plantations, 107
plant remains, 48, 68, 83
platform mounds, 6
Poidebard, Father Antoine, 33
point cloud data, 32
Point Rosee, 75–86, *76, 77*
Polynesia, 112–13
Pompeii, 10, 45, 176
Portus, 61–65, *62, 65*
pottery, 13–14, 29, 49, 97, 149–51, 159, 173
processual archaeology, 39
Protect and Preserve International Cultural
    Property Act (2016), 206
Provincial Archaeology Office of
    Newfoundland and Labrador, 76
Psamtik, King, 19
Psusennes I, 90–91
Ptolemaic period, 45, 209, 210
Punt, 126, 146
Purépecha people, 108
Pyramid Age, 27, 127, 131
Pyramid Texts, 127, 143

Qakare Ibi, King, 135
Qalatga Darband, lost city of, 42–43
Queen of the Desert (film), 185
Qufti people, 154, 162, 190
QuickBird, 111

radar data, 38–39, 114
radiocarbon dating, 74, 82, 84, 112, 210
Raghava KK, 219
Raiders of the Lost Ark (film), 2, 4–5, 87, 94,
    208
Ramesses II, 92
Ramses VI, 218
Ramses XI, 89–90
Rapa Nui civilization, 112–13
recession of 2009, 205
recycling, 195–96
"red edge" bands, 64
Redford, Donald, 186
Red Pyramid at Dashur, 126
Red Sea
    Old Kingdom fortress on, 127–28
    shell-midden sites, 116–17
Re (Egyptian god), 137
Registan Desert, 119
Reilly, Tom, 4
remote excavations, 180
remote sensing, 7, 21, 74, 106, 107, 130. *See
    also* specific types
    drones and, 172–73
    first used in archaeology, 38–40
    revolution in, post-WWII, 34–35

remote-sensing specialists, 30–31
research design, 68, 74–75
resistivity, 175
Rhoda Island, 133
Riley, Melanie, 106
rivers and water sources, ancient, 4, 15,
    17–18, 36, 38, 114, 120, 148, 175
Robinson, Amy, 217, 220
robotics, 177–78, 180
Roman Period Egypt, 27–28, 46, 105, 168
Rome, ancient, 10, 71, 34, 61–64, *62*, 120
Ro-nefer, 16, 17, 23–25
Rosetta Stone, 185
rubber sheeting, 21

Saeed, Abdullah Al-, 15
Saga of Erik the Red, 72
Saga of the Greenlanders, 72
Sahara, 38, 117–18, 137
Sais, 19
San el Hagar, 88, 100
Saqqara, 125, 153
    looting in, 203–4, *204*, 211
sarcophagi, 29, 90–91, 209–12
Satellite Archaeology Hall of Fame, 41
satellite imagery. *See* space archaeology; *and
    specific satellites; and imagery types*
Saudi Arabia, 41, 117
Scalera, Mary Marguerite, 37
scarabs, 91
Schliemann, Heinrich, 105
Schwarz, Fred, 78, 79–81
Science, 38
Scotland, 56–61
Search for Extra-Terrestrial Intelligence
    (SETI), 181
seeds, 68
semiprecious stones, 151
Senwosret I, 147–48, 157–58
    pyramid of, 153–54, 157
settlement archaeology, 39, 91
Settlement Exhibition Reykjavík 871 +/-2,
    51–52
Sever, Tom, 39–41
shabti figurines, 142–43, 147, 211
Shakespeare scholarship, 177
Sharpe, Philip Henry, 32
Sheets, Payson, 40–41
Shesep-Amun-Tayes-Herit, Lady, 209–12
Sheshonq (biblical Shishak), 90
Shetland Islands, 56–61, *56*, *58*, *60*
shipwreck mappings, 121
Showalter, Pamela, 40
Shuttle Radar Topography Mission
    (SRTM), 148
Siem Reap, 42

signature databases, 173
Silk Road, 113–14
silver sarcophagus, 90–91
Sinai, 4, 49, 68, 126–28, 146
Singh, Ajit, 114
Siskiyou County, California, 106
sites. *See also* excavation; *and specific sites*
    categorization of, 229–30
    defined, 9–11
    destruction of, 25, 216 (*see also* looting)
    finding, 5, 28–29, 222–29, *225*
    record keeping and, 49, 189
    as time machines, 193
    time needed to map and excavate, 171–72
site survey, 5, 29
site supervisors, 48
Sithathoryunet, Princess, 151
Skagafjörður Church and Settlement
    Survey, 51–56, *52*
Sloan Digital Sky Survey, 217
Smendes, King, 90
Sneferu, King, 126–27
soapstone vessels, 59
Society of Antiquaries, 32
soil scientists, 83–84
solar radiation, 137
Sopdet (Sirius), 129, 131, 137, 139, 141
Soto, Hernando de, 105–6
South Africa, 115
South America, 1
Southwest, American, 39, 202
"Spacecraft Detects Sahara's Buried Past"
    (McHugh), 38
space archaeology. *See also* CORONA
    satellite; Landsat satellites; LIDAR;
    NASA; WorldView satellites; *and specific
    sites; technologies; and types of imagery*
    "Aha" moments, 31–32
    analyzing data with help of computer
        scientists, 104
    choice of career in, 2–4
    defined, 2–6, 29–31
    efficiency of, vs. ground surveys, 95–96
    finding new sites through, 104
    future of, 165–84
    grant proposals and, 102
    ground-truthing and, 96–97
    GX crowdsourcing and, 221–30, *221*, *225*
    history of, 33–43
    looting documented with, 203–8, *204*
    machine learning and, 176–77
    miniaturized tools for, 172–73
    named by NASA, 30
    perspective gained from, 230
    question of where to begin digging and,
        28–29

space archaeology (cont'd)
  satellite imagery and, 5–6, 15, 29–43, 50
  scope of, 5–7
  season and weather and, 101
  timing and, 33
  types of imagery and, 30–31
  what can't be determined through, 50
spectrometer, handheld, 173
Spindle whorl, Viking, 73
SPOT (Satellite Pour l'Observation de la
    Terre), 40
spy satellite data sets, 35–36
Star Wars films, 109, 171
State Department, 206
"St. Augustine's Cross," 34
stereoscope, 3
Sterry, Martin, 118
St Joseph, J. K., 35
Stone, Elizabeth, 203
Stonehenge, 32
Strutt, Kristian, 65
subsurface-sensing, 174–75
Sudan, 117
Sustainable Preservation Initiative (SPI),
    222, 226–28
Sutlej River, 114
Syria, 33, 36, 118, 137, 206, 212

Tale of Sinuhe, 147
Tampa Museum of Art, 211
Tanis (biblical Zoan), 87–103, 88, 89
  ancient watercourses and, 100
  big picture on, 101–2
  daily life at, 98–101
  ground-truthing at, 96–97
  high- vs. low-resolution data on, 92–93
  modern cities and, 102–3
  Napoleonic expeditions and, 90–91,
    100
  Nile flooding and, 101
  satellite mapping of, 93–96
  size of, 88–89, 92
  temple complex at, 88–90, 92, 98
  test excavation at, 96–97, 98
Tapajós Basin, 6
taxes, ancient Egypt and, 105, 126–27,
    133
TED, 4, 178
  Conference (Vancouver, 2016), 220
  Prize, 219
teeth, 11
  enamel hypoplasia, 140
  dental plaque, 179
Tell Akhdar, 131
Tell Ibrahim Awad, 124–44
Tell Sharufa, 131

Tell Tebilla, 12, 16–22, 88, 130, 131, 151,
    196, 209, 215
  CORONA imagery and, 20–22, 21
  excavating wall at, 21–24, 22
Temple Blair, 83
terrorism, 10, 212
Thailand, 113
Thebes, war vs. Herakleopolitans, 143, 145.
    See also Luxor
Thematic Mapper Simulator, 39
Theon (ancient letter writer), 14–15
thermal infrared imagery, 35, 166, 173–74
Thermal Infrared Multispectral Scanner,
    39
thermoluminescence (TL), 84
Third Intermediate Period, 19, 89, 99
Thomas, David, 118–19
Thoresson, Lord Thorvald, 60–61
3-D imagery, 35, 162, 166, 178
3-D reconstructions, 54–55, 101, 107, 114,
    117, 175, 177, 181
Tiber River, 62
Tiffany, Joseph, 106
Tikal, 109
TIROS (Television Infrared Observation
    Satellite), 36
Tombs of the Nobles (Luxor), 193
Toolesboro Mounds National Historic
    Landmark, 106–7
total station, 162
Trajan, Emperor, 61
tree-ring dating, 54
tree species, chemical signatures and, 30
triremes, 19
Troy, 105
Tulip Hill plantation, 107
Tunisia, 118
turf buildings, 52–56, 82–83, 85
Turkana Basin (Kenya), 115
Turkey, 118, 137
Turner, Val, 59
turquoise, 91, 126, 128, 146, 151, 161
Tuskaloosa, Chief, 106
Tutankhamun, 46, 91, 200–202

Ubar, lost city of, 41
Udall, Stewart, 36
ultrasonic waves, 175
Umayyad period, 168
underwater archaeology, 120–21
UNESCO, 212
  World Heritage sites, 116
United Arab Emirates, 209
United Kingdom, 33–35, 67, 120, 191
Upper Egypt, 126, 141, 143, 151, 161
Upper Xingu, 110

US Agency for International Development
(USAID), 17
US Army, 2–3
US Congress, 206
Uses of Air Photography, The (St Joseph), 35

Valley of the Kings, 11, 98, 174, 218
vegetation, 33–34, 136–37
Vesuvius, Mount, 176
Vietnam, 113
Vikings, 1, 50–61, *58, 60,* 71–86, *80, 81*
Vikings (History Channel show), 71
Vinland, 72–74, 86

Wales, 121
Wallace, Birgitta, 74, 85–86
Wallace, Rob, 85
Washington Post, 38
weather satellites, 30, 36
Weishampel, John, 31–32
West Africa, 116
Western Asia, 90
Western Desert (Egypt), 117
Western Isles (Scotland), 51

Western Settlement (Greenland), 72
White Nile, 24, 133, 136
wild olive trees, 115
Windsor Antiquities, 209
Wiseman, James, 39
WorldView satellites
    WorldView-1, 92, 93, 111
    WorldView-2, 64, *65, 77,* 92–93
    WorldView-3, 31, 101–2
    WorldView-4, 31, 102
World War I, 33, 185
World War II, 2, 35, 91, 196, 215
worldwide database of sites, 215
Wye Hall plantation, 107

Young, Harold, 2–4, 34, 35, 230
Youth Engagement Petra Program, 214

"Z," lost city of, 110
Zaghloul, Elsayed Abbas, 149, 150
Zaire, 3
Zenobia, Empress, 10
Zimbabwe, 116
Zooniverse, 217

About the Author

SARAH PARCAK is a professor of anthropology at the University of Alabama at Birmingham. She serves as the founder and president of GlobalXplorer, a nonprofit dedicated to using cutting-edge technologies to protect and preserve our shared cultural heritage. She is the co-director of the Joint Lisht Mission with Egypt's Ministry of Antiquities, focusing on the excavation and survey of Egypt's Middle Kingdom capital, and she has worked on archaeological projects across the globe. She wrote the first textbook on the field of satellite archaeology, *Satellite Remote Sensing for Archaeology*, and has published many peer-reviewed scientific papers. Her research has been featured in multiple BBC Discovery and PBS Nova documentaries, as well as in talks on TED.com. Sarah is a National Geographic Explorer, a fellow of the Society of Antiquaries, and the winner of the 2016 million-dollar TED Prize. She is a Young Global Leader, TED Senior Fellow, and recipient of the Smithsonian American Ingenuity Award and the Explorers Club Lowell Thomas Award. Sarah lives in Birmingham, Alabama, with her husband, Greg Mumford, her son, Gabriel, and her beloved cats.